The Socio-Cultural World of Women in Medieval Andhra

[From 11th to 13th Centuries A.D.]

The Socio-Cultural World of Women in Medieval Andhra

[From 11th to 13th Centuries A.D.]

A. Padma

Bharatiya Kala Prakashan
DELHI - INDIA

Published by **C.P. Gautam**
BHARATIYA KALA PRAKASHAN
3421-A, IInd Floor, Narang Colony, Tri Nagar,
Delhi-110035. Phone : Off. 7153083

First Published : 2001

ISBN : 81-86050-75-2

Laser Typesetting by :
SHRI BALAJI COMPUTERS
Phone : 7108270

Printed at :
SANTOSH OFFSET, DELHI

Dedicated

to

My Dear Husband

C.S. Murthy

"You share my dreams and bring a smile — to light the darkest day."

Contents

Foreword

The present book entitled, ***Women in Medieval Andhra, From 11th to 13th Century***, seeks to examine the place of women in the medieval Andhra region from a women's studies perspective. The main objective of this work has been to bring women to the center of the historical process in Andhra in medieval times by investigating into the various aspects of women's lives during this period. Most of the women's studies books in history concentrate on the European experience and there are very few books, which have attempted to look at women from women's perspective in the Indian context. The problem is more so with regional history, in the Deccan.

The feminist movement of the 1960's and the consequent developments of women's studies have drawn attention to the fact that, "though women like men have been actors and agents in history, their experiences and actions are not recorded." Traditional historiography has always focussed on areas of human activities in which the males are dominant, i.e. wars, diplomacy, politics or commerce, as worthy of studying and women's participation in agriculture, animal husbandry, family, rituals, folk art are regarded as unimportant and outside the realms of the study of history. Men's history has been presented as universally human. The framework, concepts and priorities of these universal histories reflect male interests, concerns and experiences. (Mathews, 1985) Traditional historiography has thus either ignored the positive role of women or portrayed it as insignificant. We often have a chapter in the end of; lets say; Vedic period, Later Vedic period, Vijaynagar period, entitled, "Women", and there is a discussion on dress, jewellery, festivals and pastimes. While this may be important, it in no way does justice to the role of women. In any case, the fundamental contribution of women to the socio-economic life has not been fully brought out.

The general principle of a patriarchal society is that men work in the public domain and women are to be restricted into the private domestic sphere. Since, it is the public domain, which is considered important, women become mere passive participants in the historical process. Hence, this is reflected in the lack of any substantial and substantive documentation about them. There cannot be any doubt that a social science, which ignored the role of women, is a social science, which can only give a distorted picture of society as a whole.

To many, women's history is not "intellectually interesting". A wide spread impression is that it is held in low esteem and the field itself lacks legitimacy. Many feel that the study of women must be the ultimate harbinger of scholarly chaos. Scholars suffering from this lingering, "victorianism" might well feel that women are too eternal or unwordly to have much to do with politics and economics (Johnson, 1976).

Historians who are working in the field of women's history find it necessary to develop an, "underlying conceptual framework", for their field primarily due to three inter related reasons. First, a low evaluation of past work in the field closely related to skepticism about its legitimacy within the discipline of historical study. Second, the unique character of the group which the field seeks to study and third, the existing tradition of theories attempting to explain the historical experiences of women (Carroll, 1976).

The reluctance to accept work in women's history for its own sake is a reflection of the low esteem and stereotypic image in which women are held. Women's history besides trying to set right the balance could also be for its own sake. One does not ask a Jew, Chinese, a black or an Indian to justify their interest in their own history.

Women as a category of history have always been distinct from men and their activities. Sexual divisions have been one of the most basic distinctions within the society encouraging one group to view its interests differently from another. Just as class, race and religion help formulate a man's or woman's view of him or herself, so sex has been used to create a separate identity for men and women. By studying the history of men and assuming that this would cover the women also, we cannot find out the realities of women's lives during any given period. Gender like any group, class or race has always been a powerful factor in history. It is therefore necessary to view the development of women's history from the feminist perspective of women as a distinct sociological group which experiences both overt and covert controls through legal, political and social restrictions (Pande, 1999).

Since, history has been taken away from women it is necessary to put them back into the picture and to document their role and work, a task which may take many years of painstaking work. However, this is not enough. The effort is not just to tackle on women's history to the existing framework but to work for a better understanding of the past, to understand the evolution of an ideology, social relations and institutions that led to the subordination of women. This perspective has proved extremely fruitful both in terms of theoretical insights, as well as in detailed empirical studies.

The starting point of women's history is that, although men and women are different, what is historically significant is that; women constitute a social as opposed to a biological group. Biological explanations are contradicted by the fact that behaviour prescribed for women and men vary enormously from one society to another. There are also large variations in gender roles from one time period to another in the same society. Social forces are crucial determinants of the opportunities and limitations available to individual women (Davidson, 1975).

However, now due to the contributions of feminist sociologists and anthropologists and people's historians, new paradigms have emerged. Women's studies approach to the study of women in different historical contexts have enabled us to have a better and fuller understanding of women, their status and relation with the rest of the society and their contribution to socio-economic development. A big lacuna is that most often works related to woman's studies in the historical background are based in European context, and there are very few works which have attempted to look at women with a women's perspective in the historical context, in the Indian situation. The problem is more so in the medieval period with its male biased elitist sources. In order to write a new history worthy of the name we will have to recognize that no single methodological and conceptual framework can fit the complexities of historical experiences of all women (Lerner, 1979).

Therefore, the present work becomes very important for it examines the socio-cultural role of women vis-a-vis the men in Medieval Andhra Society, from a wholistic perspective. This is a relatively unexplored area, and one has to rely on chronicles, literature and archival information and to read in between the lines and ask for each and every aspect, "What about the women?"

The period from 11th to 13th century is a very important transitory phase in Andhra history, for the feudal elements were gaining strength not only in state formation but in socio-economic aspects also. The period marked the rise to power of the Kakatiyas in the Telengana region, which ultimately facilitated political unification of Andhra. In this work an attempt has been made to see how various changes taking place in Andhra had affected women and the historical process.

The book starts with the various trends in women's historiography and then makes a literature survey of women's studies. Some of the trends related to biological reproduction, studies done by anthropologists, maternalists, people associated with women's history, the subaltern school are highlighted and touched upon briefly. The methodology used is making contextual readings of various source material, literatures, inscriptions, folk materials etc. The writer also uses archival sources through the context of "post modernism". Using historical source material, literature and folklore this work attempts to examine the 'total picture' of women, the institutions governing their place in society such as marriage and family and the impact of changes taking place during 11th to 13th centuries on women of these two groups and their inter-relationship. Besides using inscriptions, archival material, literary works and published sources, this work also uses information gathered from important temples, built, renovated and patronaged during this period.

A very interesting aspect of this work is that instead of just dividing women into family women, courtesans and prostitutes (Kulastree, Bhogastree and Vesya) as broad categories, as has been done traditionally by many scholars writing in this area, it divides women into elite and folk and then looks as the different tensions that developed within each group. The elite women were assumed to be women belonging to the landed aristocracy, feudal lords, merchants and other ruling classes while women belonging to small peasant and artisan communities and other lower orders of the society were considered as folk. Culturally the elite women represented the 'higher tradition', while the folk women belonged to the 'little or common tradition'. Using the historical source material, such as literature, inscriptions, folklore, the book examines the total picture of both these women, the institutions governing their place in society such as marriage and family, and the impact of the changes taking place on the group of the women of these two categories and their inter-relationship.

The author attempts to examine the geo-political milieu of the region. This region has three distict ecological zones, which can be identified. The wet zone of the coastal tract inhabited by people with feudal polity, the dry zone of Telengana with a peasant warrior culture and the arid forest zone, which involved semi-ideological control or ritual extension of sovereignty (Stein, 1984). Each region had its distinct influence on status of women. Women in medieval Andhra responded to the contextual demand in two ways, women belonging to the higher tradition of ruling classes such as Rudrama Devi and Nayakuralu Nagamma participated in the affairs of the state actively besides attending several social activities such as gift giving and land reclamation. Rudrama Devi received several titles and exemplified as a great military general and also as an efficient administrator. Nayakuralu Nagamma was a minister with wide knowledge of political diplomacy. Some women and wives of mandalika chiefs like Prolama, Chanama, Silama and Manchala had even participated in wars and were used as instruments of matrimony-based diplomacy. Thus, marriage and polity were intricately linked, demonstrating the role of women in state formation. Many a times women belonging to tribes actively participated by taking up certain jobs in military administration. For example to learn details about enemy's position, secret of their war strategies etc. The book gives various examples of women's involvement with politics both actively and passively. We have women as ministers, women carrying out administrative, religious and welfare activities of the state. The spread of good will in the state was also by the wives of the kings, various grants for construction of temples was an extension of this good will. The kings in medieval times adopted various titles, as an insult to enemy wives, for this was the greatest insult to the enemy. This highlights the attitude of the enemy towards the women of the conquered. Therefore, we have women both as active participants and passive participants in state polity.

We have also interesting insights into the economic role of women in different activities. While the women belonging to the common section of society participated in several economic activities, the state, temple and society. The occupation of the women can be divided into three heads, Kulastreelu (family women), Bhogastreelu (entertainment women) and Temple girls. We have the elite, folk variation under each category. Among the Kulastreelu we have women belonging to all castes and category, who appeared to be engaged in some or other form of economic activity. Women worked in palaces or in other caste-based occupations such as selling rice, selling bangles or working as domestic servants. Therefore, women contributed in either cash or kind to the family income. Among the Bhogastreelu we have the courtesans, concubines and prostitutes. It is interesting to note that these professions were recognized by the state and they were brought under the protection of law. The courtesans belonged to the elite class and they received special training and thus enjoyed a high status. Scholars and poets also patronized them. The children of courtesans had legal entitlement. The Vesyas or prostitutes were also given protection. There were separate courts to check the unfair practices by Vesyas in earning money. There were laws to punish customers of vesyas for not paying them and also for causing physical injuries.

Women were also employed in temples. The devastana (temple) maintained the same bureaucracy as that of rajasthana (the kings court). Women from the king's court were transferred to temple service and vice versa. Women were employed in both the categories of temple rituals – Angabhoga and Rangabhoga. Women earned lands, dhanya, gold and prasadams. They were provided with quarters. We also have instances of a professional guild of temple dancers. The guild provided services such as maintaining temple property, supervision of grants, mobilization of temple resources etc. They also determined rules and procedural aspects of temple girl's services. However, all these earnings of the temple girls did not mean economic independence for women, because the Dharmashastras say that the wages earned by women on her own exertion are not included in her property, but they become part of the joint property of the family. The Dharmashastras provide for certain rights of women on property, when they have acquired them as gifts on the occasion of their marriage.

Though women could get streedhana and property, there were certain restraints and limitations on their appropriations. The women did not have full rights of disposal over immovable property. Therefore, one can say that women were economically independent only to a limited extent.

We also find that the type and content of education provided to the girls varied with respect to their status, profession and needs in medieval Andhra. All formal and informal education was designed to preserve the family system and kinship relations, wherein men and women perform complementary roles. However, in the case of women from higher tradition, formal education was more important than in respect of women belonging to common sections of the society. Similarly, while education for livelihood is important for common folk, education for understanding affairs of the state was important for women of royal descent. These women appear to have received knowledge of statecraft since they had to take part in the polity. But it appears that the formal education for women was not favoured. There is really not much information available from our sources on the modes of learning and therefore, one can only generalize. The courtesans and concubines received training in music and dance of both marga and desi style and also some formal education. They also appear to have received knowledge of statecraft since they were used in political strategy sometimes. Temple girls and girls in the profession of fine arts followed a particular syllabi. For their training in fine arts the temple girls had to learn Telugu and Sanskrit scripts.

It is certain that women received some form of informal education. Women from the elite groups received informal education in statecraft, political diplomacy, and code of conduct etc. Whereas the common women received informal education in rangoli making, knowledge of day to day medicines, cosmetics etc., women belonging to crafts and other household occupations learnt the crafts at home. Learning was very much based upon the socio-economic differences.

Women from both the classes seem to have received the benefit of religious education. The various religious rituals women followed bears testimony to this. Women learnt and sang devotional songs. Observance of Vratas, making gifts, involving oneself in philanthropic activities and undertaking pilgrimages were part of the religious practices of the period. Every religious ritual also had a social counterpart of making gifts or donas of a redistributive nature in which both elite and common women participated. Women observed vratas and made gifts but their main role was to carry on the tradition. Both elite and women from the folk tradition observed various rituals though the socio-economic differences existed in the manner of observances and gifts. Marriage and family played an important role in the lives of most women. There was a complementarity in the roles of husband and wife for religious practices and rituals, though women had to seek the husbands' consent for making pilgrimages.

The attire and ornamentation styles as well as use of cosmetics by women belonging to the two classes reflected the socio-economic distinctions. But there was an element of commonality in the sense that there was compulsory ornamentation irrespective of class variations. Adornment was also functional. Ornaments for the Vesya was an important adornment. The king even as a punishment could not confiscate these. Attire was considered as a reflection of class to which the women belonged. The widows were not allowed to wear bangles, coloured sarees and other decorations. There are nearly fifty-six varieties of sarees. There were different textures, cloth and material that were used. Even in art form and amusement practices by the women of the two groups there was a certain element of assimilation of classical and native traditions which served as a cultural medium to bring people together. But it cannot be denied that dress and ornamentation reflected the environmental influences, occasions and professional demands and the impact of socio-economic status. Adornment was thus a medium of distinctions and hierarchy by which people and their hierarchies were recognized by mere sight.

The state in medieval Andhra also played the role of cultural integration through performing arts. The process of sanskritisation and brahmanisation enabled the medieval rulers to effectively incorporate the pastoral and forest dwelling communities and their deities into the main stream of society. The medieval bhakti sects, besides the classical art forms; as media for popularizing their faiths also adopted native or folk art forms. In the same way the literature of the period reflected the culmination of marga desi tradition, the art forms and amusements also had a combination of the two. Thus, during the Kakatiya period there is an attempt made at greater assimilation of elite as well as folk traditions.

The study of women in distant past, in general and studying their socio-economic and cultural status in particular presents, a difficult task especially in the face of inadequate published material. Using a women's studies perspective for this purpose, that to in the context of a region, is still more difficult, in view of the fact that the subject of women's studies is only few decades old. This book is very important because it has collected substantial material from inscriptions, archival sources, and literary works subjecting the material to very meticulous analysis. This has been supplemented by secondary sources as well as data gathered from field visits to important Kakatiya temples as well as to various archaeological centers and museums. The information collected has been subjected to very meaningful analysis. Analysis is presented in the form of tables.

Our interest in women's studies stems from the various problems faced by women in our society today. We find that in several aspects the status of women today particularly in rural areas does not seem to have changed much from the study period. The status of widows, the negative attitude to women's formal education, the importance of marriage and family in women's lives, gender games played by girls is a case in point. What sets the study period apart is the better position of concubines, courtesans, prostitutes enjoyed in that period when compared to today. In today's society also women are victimized by war and such victimization existed in the study period also. Thus, this book is successful in studying how women experienced changes in the medieval period in Andhra and how these in turn affected the historical process. In doing so this work is an earnest attempt to return "history to women". This book is an important addition to the area of women's studies and would be of immense use to academicians and scholars interested in regional history and women's studies.

REFERENCES

Bernice A. Carroll, "Introduction", in Bernice A Carroll (Ed.) *Liberating Women's History,* Chicago, 1976.

Laura Davidson and Laura Kramer Gordon, *The Sociology of Gender.*

Sheila Ryan Johansson, "Her Story as History : A new field or another fad", in Bernice A Carroll (Ed.) *Liberating Women's History,* Chicago, 1976.

Jill Mathews, *Good and Mad Women : The Historical Construction of Femininity in 20th Century Australia,* 1985.

Rekha Pande, "Bringing in the invisible women back into history", in *Adhyayan*, Vol.IX, No.1 & 2, 1999.

Stein, Burton, "South India : Some General Considerations of the region and its early history", in Tapan Ray Choudhry and Irfan Habib (ed) *Cambridge Economic History,* Vol.I, Cambridge University Press, New Delhi, 1984.

Gerda Lerner, *The majority finds its past,* O.U.P. New York, 1979.

25th April, 2001
Hyderabad

Rekha Pande
Department of History
School of Social Sciences
University of Hyderabad
P.O. Central University
Hyderabad-500046
Andhra Pradesh
India

Preface

The present monograph is based on my Ph.D. Thesis titled **Women in Medieval Andhra (From 11th to 13th Centuries A.D.)** completed under the guidance of Dr. Rekha Pande, Department of History, University of Hyderabad, and was awarded in the year, 1997.

The gift of knowledge is the most precious one to receive. It is with this deep sense of gratitude, I thank my teachers Dr. Rekha Pande and Dr. P.S. Kanaka Durga (Dept. of Folk-Culture Studies) for their co-operation and constructive suggestions which immensely helped in widening my knowledge on the subject. The invaluable and lengthy discussions we had, during the course of my research have contributed greatly in giving ultimate shape to this book. Specially I thank Dr. Rekha Pande, who has immediately given her consent to write the Foreword.

I am greatly indebted to my examiners Prof. K.A. Parvathy and Prof. Rameshwari Varma who encouraged me for the publication of the thesis. Their suggestions have been incorporated and that greatly helped in refining the original version. I express my sincere thanks to them.

I owe a great deal to all my teachers, Department of History, University of Hyderabad for extending their full co-operation to me in all aspects. I remain thankful to all those who have willingly shared their knowledge with me. Particularly Dr. Nagi Reddy for his immediate help in preparing the maps, plates and figures wherever necessary.

My thanks are due to Sri C.P. Gautam M/s. Bharatiya Kala Prakashan, Delhi, who has kindly agreed to publish the dissertation and for bringing the book in an attractive cover within the shortest time possible.

I may fail in my duty if I do not express my deep sense of gratitude to my husband Sri C.S. Murthy and children Swetha and Varun who have constantly encouraged me to pursue my goals and giving a patient hearing to me every time.

I shall remain greatly rewarded if this book comes of use to the research scholars, students and readers interested in understanding the past from a gender perspective.

26th Jan., 2001 **Dr. A. Padma**
Hyderabad

Transliteration Chart

Vowels				**Consonants**			
a	अ	k	क्	t	त्	sh	ष्
ā	आ	kh	ख्	th	थ्	s	स्
i	ई	g	ग्	d	द्	h	ह्
u	उ	gh	घ्	dh	ध्	aḷ	ळ्
ṛ	ऋ	i	इ	n	न्	ksh	क्ष्
e	ए	ch	च्	p	प्		
ē	ऐ	chh	छ्	ph	फ्		
ai	ऐ	j	ज्	b	ब्		
o	ओ	jh	झ्	bh	भ्		
au	औ	ñ	ञ्	m	म्		
aṁ	अं	ṭ	ट्	y	य्		
aḥ	अ:	ṭh	ठ्	r	र्		
		ḍ	ड्	l	ल्		
		ḍh	ढ्	u	व्		
		ṇ	ण्	ś	श्		

Note : Diacritical marks have been used for non-English words. However, for names of places and persons accepted in the general English, they have not been used. Place names denoting ancient cities are shown with the marks.

Abbreviations

AR	Annual Report on Indian Epigraphy and South Indian Epigraphy.
CSSH	Comparative Studies in Society and History.
CWDS	Centre for Women's Development Studies.
EI	Epigraphica Indica.
HAS	Hyderabad Archaeological Series.
IAP : CD	Inscriptions of Andhra Pradesh : Cuddapah District.
IAP : KD	Inscriptions of Andhra Pradesh : Kurnool District.
IAP : WD	Inscriptions of Andhra Pradesh : Warangal District.,
IESHR	Indian Economic and Social History Review.
IHR	Indian Historical Review.
JAHRS	Journal of Andhra Historical Research Society.
JEHR	Journal of Economic History Review.
JESHO	Journal of Economic and Social History of the Orient.
MAS	Modern Asian Studies.
NDI	Nellore District Inscriptions.
PAPHC	Proceedings of Andhra Pradesh History Congress.
PIHC	Proceedings of Indian History Congress.
SII	South Indian Inscriptions.
TIAP	Temple Inscriptions of Andhra Pradesh.

List of Maps and Charts

List of Plates and Figures

FIGURE

FIGURE

CHAPTER I

Introduction

Women's studies can be defined as 'studying women with a woman's perspective'[1] or 'Looking at women from a woman's point of view'.[2] Women's studies is fast expanding in the recent years into interdisciplinary approaches with distinct methodological and conceptual frame works. This has given rise to some interesting insights and perspectives.

Trends in Women's Historiography

The early reflections on this subject came from feminist sociologists and anthropologists. Their studies proved that women played a major role in shaping the society from ancient times. They have argued that there was no activity that can be termed either male or female, nor was there any categorisation between the sexes.[3] The sociological concept of gender differentiates it from the concept of sex. According to sociologists sex is a biological factor and gender, a social role. Masculine and feminine characters of work are thus socially imposed and gender roles are to be seen as social products.[4]

Another approach viewed women as a social group and tried to understand the complexity of women's situation in terms of oppression.[5] According to the proponents of this theory, women as a social group has a certain entity that it has experienced both overt and covert controls through political, legal and social restrictions. While oppression has taken various forms in the society for different social groups, the position of men and women is different within the same social group. Such concerns led to theoretical discussions on the issue as those postulated by Engels in his *Origin of the Family, Private Property and State* (1983) linking women's oppression to changes in economic and political realm.[6] Thus, this approach assumed women's oppression to be a historical feature rather than universal and eternal.

Few studies linked female subordination to women's capacity for biological reproduction and connected functions of child bearing.[7] This has brought issues like child bearing and rearing, domestic work and motherhood to the centre of explanation for social hierarchy and social analysis.

The concept of patriarchy as the ever present element from primitive times and the theory of man the hunter kind of syndrome are debated by anthropologists through their recent researches focusing on primitive societies. They argued that in the early societies, the tasks performed by both the sexes were indispensable to group survival and were equal.[8] In fact, both the sexes were complimentary to each other. Elise Boulding has shown the myth that man as hunterer and its perpetuation are socio-cultural creations which saw the interest of maintaining male supremacy and hegemony.[9] Maternalists like J.J. Bachofen while describing the various stages in the evolution of society from barbarism to modern patriarchy, argued that there was a stage of matriarchy which led the society out of barbarism.[10] Thus, they traced the evolution of patriarchy to the triumph of superior religious and political thought.

Further, each of these postulations, theories and perspectives are questioned, debated and refined during the recent years thus making the potentials of the field of women's studies immense. However, all these studies are limited by their methodological frameworks and influenced by the cultural or religious ideology. Their main concern is the nature of relationship between men and women or male-female interaction and they have framed important observations regarding the evolution and categorisation of societies.

In the wake of women's movement, historians have also attempted to study women as agents of history questioning the existing notions of history. Their argument is that, women like men have also been actors and agents in history but their experiences and actions are not recorded and are neglected or ignored in interpretation.[11]

The contents of traditional historiography are court history, geneology, political history or history of the elite where women, except a few, had no role to play.[12] Even the few like Razia, Rudramadevi, Nurjahan, or Jhansi Laxmibai are mentioned because they were rulers and performed supposed male roles.

The recent trends like Peoples history,[13] Socio-economic histories[14] and Subaltern studies[15] succeeded in correcting the elite and political biases in history by bringing to light the subordinate groups like peasants, slaves, proletariats central to the historical process. They highlighted issues concerning class struggles for political representations and lives of lower orders of the societies. They brought about clearly the gulf between common men and ruling elite and produced meaningful generalisations about social change.[16]

But women are short listed even in these, as their activities were considered purely domestic, stereotypic and unchanging for ever. They were made silent spectators of social change. Historical scholarship viewed them as marginal to the making of civilisation and considered them as unessential to those pursuits defined as having historical significance. The possible reason for this is the nature of historical process itself.

Literature Survey

History is a matter of selection of facts recorded by someone at a given point of time and for some purpose. It could be here that women are neglected. In daily life women exist and relate to the other male members of the family through specific roles as daughter, wife, mother and so on. Through these roles they react in diverse ways to the varying problems in different circumstances and at different times. The nature of this social change cannot be understood unless the study of women becomes a part of any attempt of studying history of a given period. Women need to know what the flow of time meant for them. As A.S. Altekar points out, "To understand any given civilisation in its fullest sense and to realise its limitations and excellencies, it is essential to study the position of women and their status in it."[17]

Therefore, it is necessary to put women back into the picture to document their role and work. The effort is not to trace women's history on the existing framework but for a better understanding of the past, the evolution of an ideology, social relations and institutions that led to the subordination of women.[18]

Thus, the main concern of feminist historians is inclusion of women in the historical writings. They questioned the subordination of women, social inequalities between men and women, oppression and patriarchy as natural factors. They argued for placing women back in history and giving them their lost place and identity. Thus, if a struggle is to be waged against all structures of oppression and gender inequalities and attempts are to be made to construct a more human and humane society, it is necessary not only to return women to history but even more important is to return history to women.[19]

Considerable work has already been done in this field. Initially efforts were made to put women's issues at par with those of men. The Orientalists and Evangelical scholars formed the base of writing on women's issues in India.[20]

While the former attempted the collection of the data of laws, rituals and other traditions,[21] the latter argued that the Hindu religion itself was the cause of backwardness of Indian women.[22] These arguments were put on the common platform of social reform movements in India. A.S. Altekar's *The Position of Women in Hindu Civilisation (from pre-historic to modern times)* (1962) is a nationalistic construction which served as a major break through in the studies on women in India by attempting at a broad survey of the position and the status of Indian women from Vedic age to modern times. Soon, there were accounts of Indian women through the ages, with a positive analysis.[23] They tend to glamourise women by giving various instances from the past. Similar works were taken up by scholars with respect to different regions and different periods of history evaluating the position and status of women.[24] The socio-economic historians included women in their discussions on the societies in the context of their position and status in the society.[25] The subaltern historians too have incorporated gender inequality with class inequality.[26]

Subsequently there were contributory histories talking about the contribution of women in different movements.[27] General theoretical framework for women's history in India was also prepared by the feminist historians[28] giving a clear understanding of the need for women's studies in India and the necessary methodology for such a study.

These attempts in historical writings prove to be quite useful for building a new comprehensive history in which women could share their positions with men. But they could not be made an integral part of the traditional history.[29] The influence of women as a group in the socio-economic changes of a particular period or the changing patterns of their lives in accordance with the changes in the polity, society and religion are not sufficiently examined. The socio-economic historians included in their discussions women in a chapter or two and tried to arrive at their status without examining the influence of women as a group in the socio-economic changes of the given period of history. The studies about women in various movements could not clearly bring out the role of women as the central emphasis was the movement and they examined the place of women as peripheral in the movement which was shaped by men. The argument of subaltern historians is a fight against oppression considering men as a dominant group. They claimed women to be passive victims of the atrocities of dominant gender. Feminist theory concentrated its efforts mainly on exposing the patriarchal urgencies that underwrite the representations of women. According to them patriarchy is the sole cause for oppression of women.

To put this simplistically, women's history is not viewed as a part of the totality of history but was treated with isolation. These writings clearly reflected the male perspective and women's actual space in history has not been defined. Women were viewed as a subservient gender and not as complimentary to the other gender.

Women's position in relation to historical formation was not highlighted. In addition, these studies are shaped by the Western ideologies based on changing productive relations and production as the determinants of gender differences. The Indian context has not been identified clearly.

Contrary to the Western situation, in India, the tradition and socio-cultural base determines the gender roles- men to participate in the public and women, the private. The Dharmasastras too, keeping in line with the complimentarity of men and women in the family structure, stressed the importance of interdependence of both these domains.

Thus, the new task for women's historians is to develop a clear concept towards balancing these two groups and giving emphasis to both public and private world in building the civilisation or culture of any given period.[30] In the past also there have been attempts to show the clear link between the world of the home and state within the patriarchal society.[31]

In the light of above discussion, for the study of history from a wholistic perspective, emphasis on the participation of women in culture is essential. There exists a need to examine the position of women dialectically in historical studies. Moreover, much of the work done in this regard is mostly confined to modern period evaluating the status of women, nature of working conditions, education offered to them, various movements in which they participated and the struggles undertaken by them or even led by them for emanicipation of their class, etc.[32] This was possible because of the availability of source material which includes biographies, letters, diaries, personal interviews, oral traditions, etc. In addition to these, the survey and statistical reports are also of much help. Medieval period remained unexplored owing to the difficulty of sources wherein one has to rely on chronicles, literature or archival material which mainly highlighted political or religious aspects.

Among the attempts to project women of medieval India, Rekha Misra's *Women in Moghul India* (1967) becomes the first of its kind. Published in the late sixties of this century, the book covers a complete study of women during the Mughal rule. It highlights the political participation of women. In addition, it also depicts the position of women chiefly of the class of aristocracy, where women lived in isolation. The social, religious and cultural aspects of their lives are also dealt with in detail.

Saroj Gulati, in her *Women and Society in Northern India* (1985) presents a detailed analysis of the position and status of women during eleventh and twelfth centuries with reference to various rituals including marriage and their legal status as per Dharmasastras.

A similar attempt is also made by Kamala Gupta in *Social Status of Hindu Women in Northern India (A.D. 1206-1707)* (1987). She observes that during the rule of Delhi Sultanate and the Mughals, the Hindu women of North India could not remain aloof from the impact of social customs of the Muslim women.

These and such other works[33] prove to be of great help in evaluating the position of women in medieval India and to reconstruct the history of women. However, their scope is limited to northern region alone. No serious attempt has so far been made to perceive the issues concerning women of south. The paucity is much more with reference to women of Andhra.

Alladi Vaidehi's published work in Telugu, *Āndhradēśamu-Streelu* (Women in Andhra) (1975) discussed about the position and status of women classified into distinct groups from Satavahana period to modern times. This is the earliest among the efforts to bring to light the women of Andhra. The social and economic historians of medieval Andhra, however, discussed women's issues as a separate chapter in their works relating them to discussions on social classes, economic conditions and religious life with emphasis on religious observances and temple rituals.

Suravaram Pratapa Reddy's *Āndhrula Saṁghika Charitra* (A Social History of The People of Andhra) (Reprint, 1982) is a comprehensive account of the society of Andhra. This book is divided into various chapters based on the political history of Andhra and gives a detailed account of the social life of each period. Interesting details about women like the dress and ornamentation patterns, recreations of girls and women, marriage celebrations, religious observances, social customs are discussed in this work. He mentions a specific practice of divorce among the class of soldiers in medieval Andhra taking evidence from the contemporary literary sources.[34]

Nanduri Venkata Satya Rama Rao presents a socio-cultural history of Andhra through his *Āndhrula Sahityamu Saṁghika Jīvana Pratiphalanamu* (Literature of Andhras, Reflections of Social Life) (1979). Taking evidences from the contemporary literary sources, he talks about such issues of women as her role in the family, the various social institutions, in addition to a detailed account on types of food and dress as mentioned in literary works of the period.

Vaidehi Krishnamoorthy in her *Socio-economic Conditions in Eastern Deccan (A.D. 1000-1250)* (1978) analyses the position of women in Andhra in detail. In the chapter on women, she classifies them into three different categories namely *Kulastreelu* (family women) *Bhōgastreelu* (pleasure women), and *Vēśyalu* (prostitutes).[35] She discusses the position and status of each class of women. In addition, she also describes the duties and functions of temple girls and important professions of women. A description of tribal women is also given in the same chapter.

Ootukuri Laxmikanthamma through her *Āndhradēśamu Kavayitrulu* (The Poetesses of Āndhradeēśa) (1980) gives a narrative account of the poetesses of Andhra like Prolama, Chanama, Tallapaka Timmakka, Molla, Gangadevi, etc.

K. Laxmiranjanam and K. Balendusekharam in their work, *Āndhrula Charitra-Saṁskṛti* (History and Culture of Andhras) (1985) highlight the political participation of women in addition to the general discussion on women.

K. Satyanarayana talks about the institution of temple girls and the changing economic status of women corresponding to the religious liberalism through his *A Study of the History and Culture of Andhras* (1975, 1983) published in two volumes. Quoting extensively from the medieval legal text, *Vijnāneśvaramu* of Ketana, he argues that women's right to property was recognised for the first time after Manu.[36] He also points out the evils of prostitution, widely prevalent in the society of medieval Andhra.

Though women do find mention in all these works, due emphasis is not given to the issues concerning women making them as the central point of discussion. Their observations only marginalised the role of Andhra women. Moreover, much attention was paid to women who were directly involved in politics, for example, Rudramadevi, the Kakatiya queen, Nāyakuralu Nagama, the woman behind the war of Paland or Ganapamba, the Kota queen. The religious involvement of women was explained in terms of their giving grants to various temples or observing religious rituals like nōmu, vṛta etc. Among the professions, that of temple service, concubinage and prostitution were highlighted uniformly.

Even the classification of women into *Kulastree, Bhōgastree,* and *Vēśya* is debatable as it does not include in itself women in temple service, women dedicated to temple, common women and forest dwelling women. Moreover, issues like women involvement in state formation, their role in agriculture and other professions like dairy farming, weaving, are not touched upon.

Taking these aspects into consideration, an attempt is being made in this book to study about women vis-a-vis the society in Āndhra during the eleventh, twelfth and thirteenth centuries, A.D.

The region of the present study is confined to Āndhradēśa as defined by K. Sundaram in his *Studies in the Social and Economic Conditions of Medieval Āndhradēśa (A.D. 1000-1500)* (1968). According to him, the area extending from Mahendragiri in the north to Kalahasti in the south and from Bay of Bengal in the, east to Srisailam in the west constituted Āndhradēśa. Kakatiyas, the major ruling power during the period however extended their frontiers to neighbouring areas up to Bidar, Kolar in the west and Kanchi in the south. Hanumakoṇda and Ōṛugallu were their capitals and Āndhra became the core region for their political activity (Map I).

Methodology and the Sources for the Study

The period from 11th to 13th centuries in the history of Āndhra is important because it is a transition stage between the early medieval and late medieval periods. Feudal elements were becoming strong in the state formation and their influence pervaded all spheres of society and economy. The rise of Kakatiyas to power with their base in Telaṅgāṇa is another important development of the period. They brought political unification of Āndhra and made Āndhra central to the state formation. Further, they achieved perfect synthesis between the native and classical traditions by introducing several cultural variations.

Therefore, through the present work, *Women in Medieval Andhra (from eleventh to thirteenth centuries A.D.)* a modest attempt is made to study hcw various changes of the period in Āndhra were experienced by women and in turn affected the main stream of historical process.

The analysis is being done by classifying women into two broad categories the 'elite' and the 'folk' and effort is made to study the different tensions that were developed within these two groups. As the aim of Kakatiyas was *Mārga, Dēśi* synthesis,[37] it is inevitable to study the socio-cultural and religious processes which served as a bridge linking the two groups in the society.

The basic criteria adopted for this division of women into elite and folk is the economic factor. The ruling landed aristocracy, different grades of feudal chiefs, wealthy merchants, etc., comprise the class of elite enjoying a higher socio-economic status in the society.[38] The word folk is used to denote a particular group of women who were different from the upper sections of the society and those who have a

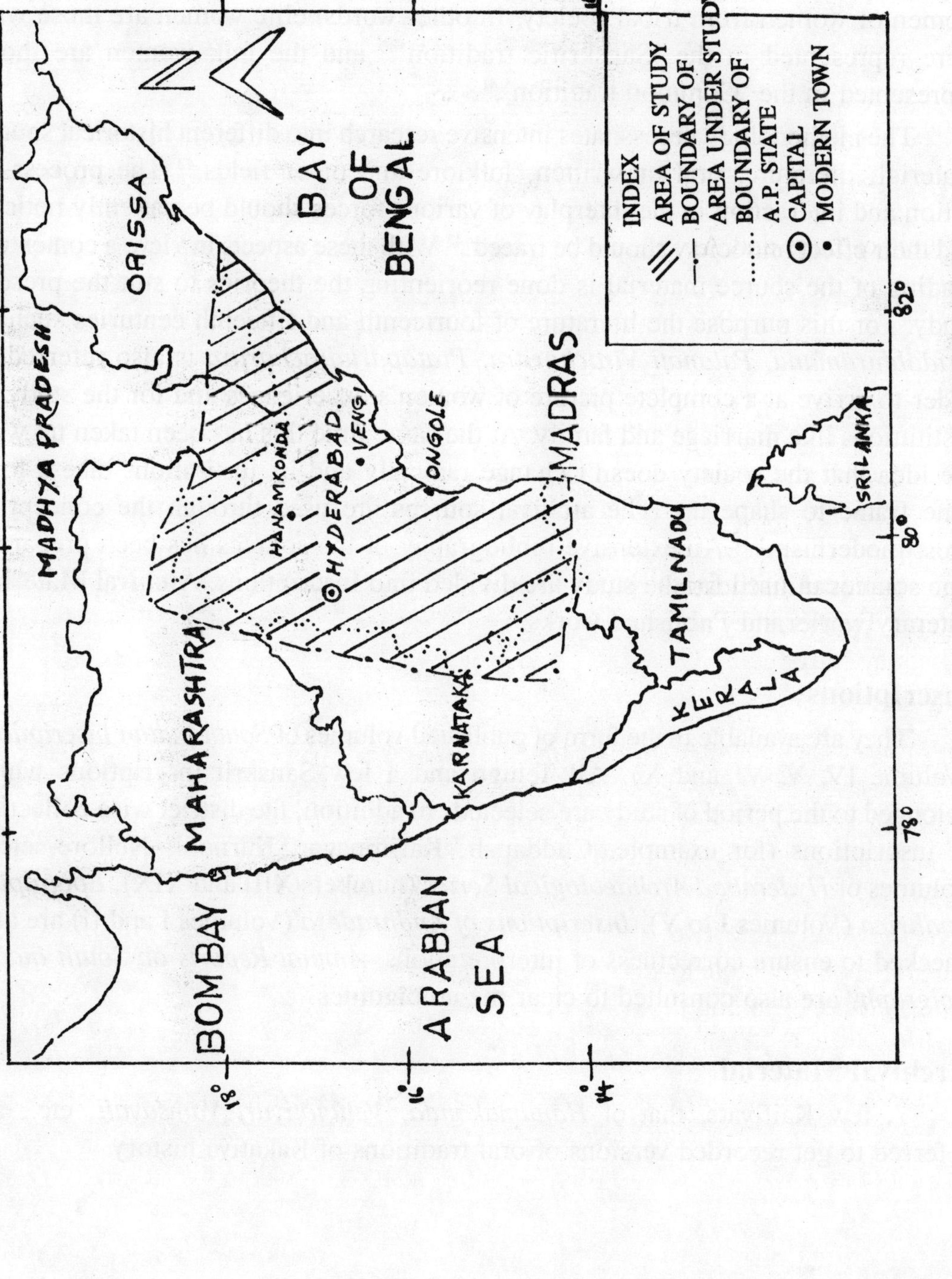

Map I AREA OF STUDY : ANDHRADESA

common element to share with, for example their weak economic status. Women belonging to the groups of petty peasants, artisan communities and other lower orders of the society including the forest dwelling women can be placed under this category.[39] The meaning of the word is not restricted only to a section of rural women or women from tribal society. In other words, elite women are those who were represented in the 'Sanskritic tradition'[40] and the folk women are those represented in the 'Common tradition'.[41]

The methodology necessitates intensive research into different historical source material, literature, oral or written, folklore and other fields.[42] The process of action and interaction in the interplay of various forces should be patiently noticed and their effect on society should be traced.[43] With these aspects in view, a contextual reading of the source material is done reorienting the theories to suit the present study. For this purpose the literature of fourteenth and fifteenth centuries such as *Kriḍābhirāmanu, Palanaṭi Vīracharitra, Pratāparudracharitra* is also referred in order to arrive at a complete picture of women's experiences and for the study of institutions like marriage and family. At the same time this has been taken up with the idea that the society doesn't change radically and its institutions take a long time frame to shape up. The archival sources are used through the concept of 'Post-modernism'.[44] An extensive bibliography of the sources has been prepared. The sources utilised for the study are divided into Inscriptions, Archival Material, Literary works and Published works.

Inscriptions

They are available in the form of published volumes of *South Indian Inscriptions* (Volume IV, V, VI and X). All Telugu and a few Sanskrit inscriptions which belonged to the period of study are selected. In addition, the district wise collection of inscriptions (for example, Cuddapah, Karimnagar, Kurnool, Nellore, etc.), Volumes of *Hyderabad Archaeological Series* (numbers XIII and XIX), *Epigraphia Andhrica* (Volumes I to V), *Inscriptions of Andhradesa* (Volumes I and II) are also checked to ensure correctness of interpretations. *Annual Reports on South Indian Epigraphy* are also consulted to clear the ambiguities.

Archival Material

A few Kaifiyats, that of *Hanumakonḍa, Velugōṭivāri Vaṁśāvali*, etc., are referred to get recorded versions of oral traditions of Kakatiya history.

Literary Works

Several literary works of the period are available to us in the printed form. Important of those include,

Andhra Mahabharatamu : Telugu rendering of the Sanskrit epic Mahabharata undertaken by Nannaya and Tikkana is an important source for the present study. The work besides giving a picture of socio-political life particularly of elite women, also indicates attempts of the rulers to bring religious integration.

Kumarasaṁbhavamu : A translatory work by Nannechoḍa, a Telugu Choḍa chief of Konidena region. But for the theme, the picturisation and depiction of life are reflective of the social life of Āndhradēśa during the period of composition of the work. The institution of prostitution and the life of women following the practice are described in detail. The poet provides information also about the pattern of education rendered to the girls and their pastime activities. A particular reference to the life pattern of forest dwelling women is given by the poet in this work.

Keyūrabāhucharitramu : Written by Manchana, based on the story of *Vidhasalabhanjika* of Rajasekhara. It provides insights into the life of women and prostitution as a profession.

Mānasollasa (Abhilashitārdhachintāmaṇi) : Somēśvaradēva, the Western Chalukyan emperor is the composer of this great piece of literature. Written in Sanskrit, it contains plethora of information about the life of ruling elite, their dress and adornment patterns, food, attendants, recreations and such other matters.

Sivatatvasāramu : Written by Mallikarjuna Paṇḍitārādhya, the book contains the philosophy of Virasaivism and the liberties sanctioned by the religion to women.

Sri Paṇḍitārādhyacharitra : Written by Pālkuriki Sōmanātha, a poet of later half of thirteenth century, the work is about the life of Mallikarjuna Paṇḍitarādhya, the propounder of Aradhya sect in Andhra. Further, the poet gives information about the religious rivalry of the period, life and conditions of prostitutes, women going for pilgrimages along with their husbands and also about the social life and folk medicine.

Basavapurāṇamu : A hagiography of the Virasaiva saint Basavēśvara composed by Pālkuriki Sōmanātha. Besides giving the details of the philosophy of Virasaivism, this book is a reflection of the contemporary social life. It gives an idea of the religious participation of common women through religious assemblies.

Vijnāneśvaramu : Written by Ketana, a thirteenth century poet and a desciple of Tikkana. This is a Telugu translation of *Mitākshara* of Vijnāneśvara, court poet of Western Chalukyan emperor Vikramaditya. This book serves the purpose of a comprehensive legal digest of medieval period. A good source to learn about the property rights of women and protection given by the state to the institutions of concubinage and prostitution. In brief, through this book, we can understand the legal domain of medieval Andhra women.

Dasakumaracharitramu : Also by the same author, this book, is a translation of the work of Dandi. Syllabi of education for the children of royal families, details of the institution of prostitution, the feelings of *Vēśyamātha* (mother of the *Vēśyas*) are described in this work.

Ranganātha Rāmāyaṇamu : Gona Buddhareddy and his sons Kacha and Viṭṭala are the authors of this book. It contains certain oral traditions which were in practice in Andhra during that period. The practice of Sati, celebration of marriage and such other details can be known through this book.

Pratāparudra Yaśōbhūshaṇamu : Vidyānātha, a court poet of Prataparudra-II composed this *Alaṅkāra* work in Sanskrit. It gives us an idea about the general attitude towards women in a feudal political setup. Its Telugu translation by Chelamacharla Rangacharyulu is taken as the source.

Kriḍābhirāmamu : A street play the author ship of which is attributed to Vinukonḍa Vallabharāya as well as Srinatha. It is a valuable piece of information about urban life in the city of Warangal during the Kakatiya period. Information about different professions of women, the religious observances practised by them and about the legal sanctions for prostitution can be gathered from this work.

Palanaṭi Vīracharitra : Written by Srinatha, a fifteenth century poet. The story is a recorded version of the war of Palanāḍu, held during the last quarter of twelfth century. We also learn about the nature of feudal polity and other political traditions wherein women were involved to a great extent.

Simhāsandavātṛṁśika : Koravi Goparāju composed this work. It provides information about the various aspects of political life of the period and women's role in political matters.

Pratāparudra Charitra : Written by Ekāmranātha, a chronicler of Kakatiyas, who belonged to the fourteenth century. A good source of information about Kakatiya polity. It gives us details of Rudramadevi's administrative policies and about the syllabi of education for children of the royal families besides throwing light on the general conditions of the Kakatiya rule.

Śri Siddhēśvara Charitramu : Composed by Kase Sarvappa, also a chronicler of Kakatiyas. It is a valuable source for Kakatiya history. Much information regarding the administrative policies of Kakatiya rulers can be gathered from this book.

Sakalanītisammatamu : A compilation of verses of moral instinct by Maḍiki Singana. Though he belonged to the later period he collected verses which were popular in Andhra by his time and included them in his work. They concern political diplomacy, importance of education among royal class and the qualities to be developed by king.

Published Works

In addition most of the published works on the history of Kakatiyas are analysed to ensure totality of the picture. The collection of P.V. Kane's *History of Dharmasastras* (Volume I to V), *Buhlar*'s *Collected works on Manu* from the *Sacred Books of the East* series edited by F. Maxmuller are also consulted to get a clear picture of the legal status of women in India.

Field Work

Field work is undertaken to supplement the observations. Important Kakatiya temples (Ramappa temple, Thousand pillar temple) are visited to document women depicted in various sculptures. Field work is also taken up at Warangal to get information about the historicity of *Sammakka-Sāralamma jātaṛa* which was said to have been instituted by Prataparudra-II. In addition copies of photographs of women in temple sculptures have been collected from the albums available in the Department of Archaeology and Museums, Govt. of A.P., Hyderabad, to know more about the dress, ornamentation styles, activities in which women were involved and such other information.

Chapterisation

All the available data is analysed and observations are divided into different chapters based on the subject matter of discussion.

The first chapter, *Introduction* includes discussions on the need and significance of women's history, historiographical sketch of women's studies in general and history in particular. Further the aim, methodology, sources and gist of the contents of the remaining chapters are outlined.

The second chapter titled, *Geo-political Milieu* is an attempt to understand the geo-ecological features of Andhra region, resulting in the formation of different cultural zones and their influence on the socio-political formation of the contemporary times. This study is essential to have a clear view of women's involvement in political formation. In addition, the different schools of state formation and the varying kingship relations are also discussed here.

The third chapter, *Women and Polity* discusses the legal rights of women for political succession and the need for women's participation in matters of state. The involvement of women both elite and folk communities in political affairs of Āndhradēśa is discussed under active or direct and passive or indirect role. Further, the views of the contemporary society towards women's place in polity, nature of political marriages, expressing feudal loyalties in terms of family relations are also described.

The fourth chapter, *Professions and Property Rights* gives details of the occupational activities of women. While elite women were known for their political participation, women generally of the weak economic groups of the society took to various professions. These ranged from direct occupations like royal service, temple service, concubinage to prostitution. They were also taking up petty business activities like running inns, or street vending. While this was the direct role, the indirect contribution of women belonging to artisan class in their respective craft occupations was however almost continuous though not a paid job. Our study of the professions of prostitution and concubinage are aimed at understanding the limitations of these women and the control of the state. At the end the chapter also attempts to link the economic independence of women achieved through their economic activities with the property rights allowed to them by the tradition.

The fifth chapter, *Women and Education* deals with the two modes of learning, the formal and informal with respect to women. It also describes the influence of political conditions and professional requirements on the syllabi of education for various classes of women. The role of bhakti movement and the liberal religious outlook of the period in bringing religious education closer to women specially of lower strata of the society is also outlined.

The contents of the sixth chapter, *Religious and Social Observances* include, the various rituals and observances both sacred and secular practised by women and the impact of radical religious sects like Virasaivism in liberalising the rules.

The seventh chapter, *Dress and Ornaments* discusses the reflections of environmental influences, occasion and professional demands and the socio-economic status on the dress and ornamentation patterns adopted by women. The preference given to use of cosmetics by elite women, mode of preparation of cosmetics using domestic products are also described.

The eighth chapter, *Performing Arts and Recreations* discusses the attempts of the rulers (Kakatiyas) to bring cultural integration through performing arts and recreations. The aim of Kakatiyas, as cited earlier was *Mārga-Dēśi* syncretism and therefore there appears to be a great assimilation of elite as well as folk traditions in every aspect of Kakatiya history, polity and religion. The same trend was also witnessed in the pastime activities and performing arts that were developed during the period. The native dance styles and tunes of music were incorporated into the classical tradition by the temple girls. Similarly, most of the recreations of the children of the street made their way into royal palaces and houses of the elite. These issues are discussed in the chapter in relation to women.

In the last chapter, broad *Conclusions* are drawn from the study. Typography of ornaments and description of bridal decoration in various literary texts are outlined in the appendices. The appendix also includes figure and plates which support the text.

REFERENCES

1. Maithreyi, Krishna Raj, 'Why Women's Studies' in Maithreyi Krishna Raj, (ed.), *Women's Studies in India, Some Perspectives*, (Bombay, 1986), p. 34.
2. *Ibid*.
3. Kartina Honeyman and Jordan Goodman, 'Women's work, Gender (Conflict and Labour Markets in Europe' in *JEHR*, Vol. XLIV, No.4, (Oxford, November, 1991), pp. 608-628.
4. E. Friedl, *Women and Men : An Anthropologist's View,* (New York, 1975).
5. J. Gadol Kelly, 'The Social Relation of the Sexes : Methodological Implications of Women's History' in *Signs*, Vol. I, (Chicago, 1976), pp. 809-24. For further discussion on the idea of forms of oppression, kindly see Kumkum Roy 'The Challenge of Women's History', Mimeographed version of a paper presented at the *Workshop on Women's Studies, Methodology*, Mother Theresa Women's University, Kodaikanal.
6. Gerda lerner, *The Creation of Patriarchy*, (London, 1980), pp. 21-23 contains a review of Engel's hypothesis.
7. Dubois, Gail Laradisekelly, Elizabeth Lapovsky Kennedy, Carolyn Korsmeyer and Lillian S. Robinson, *Feminist Scholarship* (University of Illinios press, 1985), p. 97.
8. German Greer, *The Female Eunuch,* (Toronto Bantam Books, 1972).
9. Elise Boulding, *Women in the Twentieth Century World* (New York, 1979), Also, Elise Boulding, (ed.), *Handbook of International Data on Women*, (New York, 1976).
10. J.J. Bachofen, *The Mother's Right*, as quoted in Engel '*The Origin of Family, Private Property and the State*, (Moscow, 1983).

11. Gerda Lerner, *Op. cit.*, 1986, p. 4.
12. For instance, any popular Indian History text book prescribed for school and college students contains reference to these women.
13. For example, we have such works as A.L. Marton, *People's History of England,* (London, 1948), T.W. Holdernen, *Peoples and Problems of India*, (Delhi, 1985), Raphael Samuel, (ed.), *People's History and Socialistic Theory*, (London, 1981), Howard Zinn, *People's History of the United States*, (London, 1980), etc. For further discussion on People's history kindly see, Irfan Habib, 'People's History in *PAPHC*, (Nagaram, 1987), pp. 221-240.
14. S.C. Ray Choudhary, *Social, Cultural and Economic History of India* (From *Earliest Times to Modern Times*), (Delhi, 1984), Mohammed Yasin, *Social History of Islamic India*, (1605-1748), (Delhi, 1974), Deitmar Rothermund, *Economic History of India from Pre-Colonial Times to 1986*, (Delhi, 1988).
15. Ranajit Guha, (ed.), *Subaltern Studies, Volume I-V,* (London).
16. Works like R.S. Sharma, *Social Changes in Early Medieval India, (A.D. 500-1200),* (Delhi, 1969), Romila Thapar, *Ancient Indian Social History, Some Interpretations,* (Delhi, 1978), etc.
17. A.S. Altekar, *Position of Women in Hindu Civilisation* (*From Prehistoric to Modern Times*), (Delhi, 1962), p. 3.
18. Olwen Hufton and others, 'What is Women's History,' in *History Today*, Vol. 35, (London, June, 1995), pp. 38-48.
19. P. Sudhir, 'Reconstructing Women's History : Problems and Paradigms', Lecture at the *Workshop on Women's Studies, Methodology,* Mother Theresa Women's University, Kodaikanal, p. 2.
20. A detailed discussion on the subject is attempted by Uma Chakravarti, 'Whatever Happened to the Vedic Dasi? Orientalism, Nationalism and a script for the past' in Kumkum Sangari and Sudesh Vaid, (Ed.), *Recasting Women : Essays in Colonial History*, (Delhi, 1989), pp. 44-45. Also see, Susie Tharu and K. Lalitha, (Ed.), *Women Writing in India (From 600 B.C. to present)*, (New York, 1991), pp. 41-51.
21. For Example, F. Maxmüller, *Sacred Books of the East Series*, (Delhi).
22. Marcus Fuller *The Wrongs of Indian Womanhood,* (Delhi, 1984).
23. Works like, S.K. Ghosh, *Indian Women through Ages,* (Delhi, 1989), Swami Madhavananda, R.C. Majumdar, (Ed.), *The Great Women of India,* (Mayavati, 1982), Tara Ali Baig, *Women in India,* (Delhi, 1958), P. Thomas, *Indian Women through Ages,* (Bombay, 1964), Tikoo Prithvinath, *Indian Women, A Brief Socio-Cultural Survey*, (Delhi, 1985), etc.
24. Such as, Indra Devaki, *Status of Women in Ancient India, (Survey of social, religious, political and legal position in ancient India)*, (Banaras, 1955), Awadh Kishore Prasad, *Devadasi System in Ancient India*, (Delhi, 1991). Neera Desai and Maithreyi Krishnaraj, *Women and Society in India,* (Ajanta, 1990), etc.

25. Kalikinkar Datta, *A Social History of India*, (Delhi, 1975), S.C. Ray Choudhary, *Social, Cultural and Economic History of India*, (Delhi, 1984), etc.
26. Gayatri Chakravorty Spivak, 'Subaltern Studies, Deconstructing Historiography in Ranajit Guha, (Ed.), *Subaltern Studies,* Vol. IV, (London, 1987), pp. 330-363.
27. For example, Renu Chakravarthy, *Communists in Indian Women's Movement*, (New Delhi, 1980), P. Sundarayya's chapter on women in *History of Telangana People's Struggle,* (Calcutta, 1972) can be regarded as contributory histories, where women are not seen making History, but only as having shaped the movement. For a detailed discussion on contributory histories, see K. Lalitha, *We were Making History, (Life stories of women in Telangana people's struggle*), (Delhi, 1989), pp. 19-32.
28. Maithreyi Krishnaraj, (Ed.), *Evolving New Methodologies in Research on Women's Studies,* (Bombay, 1988), Maithreyi Krishnaraj (Ed.), *Women's Studies in India, Some Perspectives,* (Bombay, 1986), etc.
29. Mani Kamerkar, 'History Where Are Women?' in Maithreyi Krishnaraj (Ed.), *Op. cit.,* 1986, pp. 86-94.
30. Dair Dre Beddoe, *Discovering Women's History : A Practical Manual*, (Pandora press, 1983), p. 8.
31. Adolf Hitler, Speech to the National Socialist Women's Organisation, 8th September, 1934, quoted from T. Mason, 'Women in Germany 1925-1940' *History Workshop,* Vol. I, (1976), "If we say the world of the man is the state, the world of the man is his commitment, his struggle on behalf of the community, we could then perhaps say that the world of the woman is a smaller world. For her world is her husband, her family, her children and her home. But where would the big world be if no-one wanted to look after the small world? How could the big world continue to exist, if there was no-one to make the task of caring for the small world at the centre of their lives? No, the big world rests upon the small world! The big world cannot survive if the small world is not secure".
32. Works like K. Lalitha, *Op. cit.*, 1989, C.A. Hate, *Changing Status of Women in Post-Independence India,* (Bombay, 1969), Manmohan Kaur, *Role of Women in Freedom Movement (1857-1947)*, (Jullunder, 1958), S. Shridevi, *Gandhi and Emanicipation of Women in India,* (Hyderabad, 1969), etc.
33. For example, we have such works as, Lokesh Chandra Nand, *Women in Delhi Sultanate,* (Allahabad, 1989), Frances Mary, *Women of India, A study of Medieval Period,* (Delhi, 1974), etc.
34. Suravaram Pratapa Reddy, *Āndhrula Saṁghika Charitra*, (Hyderabad, 1962), p. 6.
35. Vaidehi Krishnamoorthy, *Socio-Economic Conditions in Eastern Deccan, (A.D. 1000-1250)*, (Hyderabad, 1970).
36. K. Satyanarayana, *A Study of History and Culture of Andhras*, Vol. II, (Delhi, 1983), p. 62.
37. P.S. Kanakadurga, *Kākatīyulanaṭi Samājika Jīvanamu*, (Vijayawada, 1992), p. 1.

Mārga can be defined as the tradition recorded in the Sanskrit texts. *Dēsi* is the tradition which belonged to the native people of Andhra region.

38. The concept of elite is used to describe certain fundamental features of organised social life. All societies whether single or complex, agricultural or industrial need authorities within. Elites are those minorities which are set apart from the rest of the society by their pre-eminence in one or more of these various distributions, such as the ruling caste, aristocracy, strategic white or the ruling class, etc. R. David Sills, *International Encyclopaedia of Social Sciences,* Vol. V, (New York, 1972), pp.26-29. Also B.N.S. Yadava, 'Problems of the Interaction between Socio-economic classes in the Early medieval context', in D.N. Jha, (ed.), *Feudal Social Formation in Early India*, (Delhi, 1987), pp. 198-219.
39. Folk society is a homogeneous society with a strong sense of group solidarity. The ways of living are conventionalised into that coherent system which is called a culture. Behaviour is traditional, spontaneous, uncritical, personal with no legislature or habit of experiment. Familial group is the unit of action. The sacred prevails over the secular. Certain common features can be found among folk peoples such as their lower economic status. David R.Sills, *Op.cit.,* Vol. III, p. 177. Also, B.N.S.Yadava, *Op.cit.*, pp. 198-219.
40. 'Sanskritic tradition' is the recorded version which is preserved in the literature of any period. This can be utilised as a source for the study of the practices, beliefs of upper classes of the society.
41. 'Native Traditon' is not recorded in the form of texts, but is preserved through 'Oral tradition' (songs, ballads, folklore, etc.) Sometimes it comes through the practices referred to by the poets in their works, which are included under Sanskritic tradition. In other words, *Mārga* is the Sanskritic tradition and *Dēsi* the Native tradition and that which was generally practised by the people of common strata of the society. Further it is a localised tradition.
42. M.A. Ansari, 'Problems of Writing Medieval Social History' in *Problems of Historical Writing in India*, Proceedings of Seminar, India International Centre, (Delhi, 21st to 25th January, 1963), pp. 30-34.
43. *Ibid.*
44. 'Post-modernism' is a powerful configuration of new sentiments and thoughts. Connected with post-structuralism, Post-industrialism, it had advocated new parameters on social, cultural, political and intellectual criticism. Originated around early 1970's, this new thinking had entered into several debates. David Harvey in his, *The Condition of Postmodernity,* (U.K., 1990), presents the features of modernism and post-modernism as contrasting each other. Not going into those debates, in its supposed opposition to all forms of metanarratives including Marxism, freudianism and others and its close attention to other worlds and 'other voices' that have for too long been silence (such as those of women, blacks, colonised peoples with their own

histories), the idea of post-modernism is linked with women's studies or feminist arguments for a women's history. The post-modernists' style is simply to view any work as a 'text' with its own particulars rhetoric and idiolect but which can in principle be compared with any other text of no matter what sort. It is in this connection, inscriptions and archival material is analysed taking into consideration their subjectivity.

CHAPTER 2

Geo-Political Milieu

The period from eleventh to thirteenth centuries in Āndhradēśa, is characterised by several political developments. The most prominent of which was the shift in political activity from coastal region to interior Āndhra. Earlier, Āndhra region, specially the deltaic strip formed the peripheral part of the empires either in Karnataka, as in the case of western Chalukyas or Tamilnadu as in the case of Chalukya - Cholas. The upland region was seldom incorporated as it was sparsely settled. The rise of Kakatiyas to power with their base at Telaṅgāṇa region brought prominent political changes. With the imperial control now at the heart of Āndhra a significant change was witnessed in the status of Āndhra. Moreover, the period marks a transition stage between the early medieval and the late medieval periods in the political picture of Āndhra. Feudal elements were becoming strongly based in the state formation and their influence can be noticed in all spheres of society and economy.

To understand these changes in detail and to examine the part played by women at various levels in the polity, it becomes necessary to look at the geography of Āndhradēśa and the nature of the state that existed during early medieval period in this region. There must be a tendency to explain cultural development in terms of environment or of resources, because, the history of a given region is very much determined by the geo-ecological and environmental factors of that region.[1] Similarly, physical features like location, climate, hilly areas, rivers, forests, all these shape the cultural, socio-economic and political history.[2] Recent studies made on medieval south India by scholars like, Brain J. Murton, David Washbrook, C.J. Becker and Burton Stein stressed the importance of the study of geo-ecological factors to understand the nature of historical formation.[3] In the light of the above discussion, an attempt is made to understand the geography of Āndhra region to begin with and study the political development in relation to it. The region of present study corresponds to Āndhra region as cited earlier, extended from Bay of Bengal in the east to Srisailam in the west, Mahendragiri and Kalahasti comprising the north and south boundaries.[4] Kakatiyas (A.D. 1150-1323) extended the empire to the whole of Āndhradēśa from the south of Godavari to the north of Kaveri.[5] Further, their authority was spread to Bay of Bengal in the east, Bidar in the north-east, Raichur in the west and Kolar in the south-west.[6] Geographically, it is a peneplained country forming a part of the Deccan peninsula and chiefly composed of a basement of the pre-Cambrian gneisses.[7] Forming the lower basin of Krishna and Godavari rivers,[8] the country stretched far back to the Deccan plateau, thus causing to it a great physical dichotomy, which was reflected in its political history.[9]

Within Āndhradēśa, three distinct ecological zones can be identified, the Godavari-Krishna deltaic region which was a bone of contention between various political powers, the Telaṅgāṇa and the region comprising modern Rāyalaseema which were a long belt of peneplains and undulated plain surface intersected by almost completely graded river valleys.[10] The semi-arid region stretching across the Telaṅgāṇa and Rāyalaseema was inhabited by pastoral communities and supported dry farming.[11]

Hills

Stretching along the eastern line of Āndhradēśa, there lie a series of broken chains of elongated hills forming a large crescent belt coinciding with the outcrops of Cuddapah and lower Vindhyan systems.[12] This hill range is widely referred to as Eastern ghats.[13] To the south of river Krishna these hills are grouped as *Nallamalai, Velikoṇḍa, Eṛṛamalai, Śēshāchalam* and *Pālakoṇḍa* ranges. They bear a thin forest cover owing to scanty rainfall and porous nature of rocks. These hills were generally inhabited by the tribal settlements like *kōya, śabara, chenchu,* etc.

Rivers and Rainfall

The whole of Āndhra region is drained by three principal river systems. They are the Godavari, the Krishna and the Pennar. Godavari takes its birth in the Vindhya ranges and enters Telaṅgāṇa. After collecting waters from its tributaries the river takes a south-easternly direction and enters the Bay of Bengal. Originating from the Western ghats and flowing through the north-easternly direction, river Krishna enters into the Eastern sea. Along the valleys formed by the flow of these two rivers, through the eastern hill ranges, lay fertile regions suitable for rich rice cultivation.[14] River Pennar along with its tributaries flows in the northern direction but takes a right angular bend in the Nandyal basin. There it takes an eastern course again. The streams of this river carved a number of wide valleys in the southern Āndhra region.[15]

The amount of total annual rainfall gradually decreases from north-east to south-west monsoon.[16] Coastal region received the highest range of rainfall. Telaṅgāṇa remained dry almost throughout the year with deficit rainfall. This is due to its location at a high altitude and due to long range of hills throughout the region. Rāyalaseema too is a rain shadowed area for both the monsoons because of its location between the two uplands, the Karnataka plateau in the west and the Āndhra ghats in the East.[17] As such the region remained semi-arid to some extent.

Forests

Āndhradēśa particularly Telaṅgāṇa region was inhabited by a dense forest, during the medieval period, as suggested by inscriptional and literary evidences. The region surrounding Hanumakoṇḍa and Warrangal was covered by dense forests with many trees.[18] Similarly, the *Papikonḍa* region was also thickly forested and was referred to as *Malaya* region.[19] The areas along the foot hills of Eastern ghats too were enveloped by woodland forests and thickets. However, much of the forest region was cut down by the Kakatiya monarchs as well as their feudatories in the process of extending habitable and cultivable areas. Inscriptional evidences abound, of several villages established by the ruling chiefs after clearing waste lands and forests.[20] At the same time, recourse had been taken to maintain the ecological balance through raising groves and gardens.[21]

Soils and Vegetation

There is a regional variation in the soil pattern of Āndhradēśa. We find four different types of soils as the red soil, black cotton soil, laterite and the alluvial soil. Red soil is spread along the eastern Āndhra, Rāyalaseema and parts of Nellore and Guntur districts.[22] It is fairly cultivated. In major parts of Telaṅgāṇa the red sandy loam prevails which is subject to heavy erosion and has poor monsoon retention capacity.[23] Therefore, new improved techniques of farming were introduced by rulers to make the region productive. Black cotton soils are found as narrow strips or at few places as wider patches mostly in north Telaṅgāṇa and in Kurnool, Cuddapah and Mahaboobnagar areas.[24] In these soils, the fertility content though good is very much influenced by the local topographical features. The laterite soil is found in the Hyderabad region and is very poor in its fertility.[25] One sees the alluvial soils only along the course of Godavari and Krishna rivers.[26] These are the most fertile lands.

The differences in the amount of rainfall, forest coverage and other geographical factors determine the population density, size and spacing of settlements in addition to influencing the cropping patterns. The agricultural lands of Āndhra region can thus be divided into three categories : The wetlands spread along the Krishna-Godavari deltaic region of coastal Āndhra where the settlements were small with linear arrangement (linear clusters),[27] The dry lands of Telaṅgāṇa where irrigational facilities were provided through rain fed tanks or reservoirs. Groups of 6 to 7 villages developed surrounding these water resources, each dependent on the other for their social and economic necessities. These settlements are referred to as nucleated settlements.[28] To the third category belonged the semi-arid lands of Telaṅgāṇa-Rāyalaseema transition zone which bore a thick forest coverage. The settlements here were in an isolated pattern and mostly inhabited by pastoral and tribal communities.[29]

Contemporary epigraphs refer to the wet and dry lands as the principal agricultural lands. Wet lands are further mentioned as *Varipolamu*,[30] *Māgāṇi Kshētramu*,[31] *Nīru Nēla,*[32] *Jalakshētramu*.[33] Similarly, the dry lands were otherwise referred to as *Velipolamu*.[34] *Meṭṭapolamu*,[35] *Garavu Bhūmi*,[36] etc. In addition to these, we also find other types of lands as *Kuṁṭa*, (a square measure of land where cattle graze),[37] *Toṁṭa Bhūmulu* or *Pushpavaṭika* (the garden lands where flower and fruit trees are grown).[38] Few records refer to *Chilka Bhūmi* which could probably be a shallow land newly brought under cultivation.[39]

Corresponding to the geo-ecological features, distinct cultural zones can be identified.[40] Generally in the wet land, agricultural practices were almost regular. Being areas of advanced rice agriculture under prestigious cultivating brahman groups, they gave rise to peasant culture. The land holdings were usually small and agriculture was practised on labour intensive method in these lands. As such, there was scope for labour and boundary disputes. Inscriptions of the period refer to several such disputes in the coastal region.[41] The produce on land being high, several varieties of land taxes were collected. The population density too was high making it difficult for the kings to exercise complete coercive control in these regions. For this reason, imperial rulers depended on feudatories who were assigned with rulership rights over these political fragments.[42]

On the other hand nucleated settlements of dry zone necessitated rise of peasant-warrior culture with more or less shallow caste hierarchies. The land holdings were big because of non-availability of water, less fertile soil and other climatic fluctuations. Under these circumstances, it becomes difficult for the peasants to pay the taxes, as also for the government to collect. Therefore, revenue powers were delegated by the kings to local potentates who later emerged as peasant warrior groups. Their important function apart from cultivation was to protect the lands from the incursions of the tribal and pastoral people from outside. In the long run, these peasant-warrior groups gained prominence in their locality and kings began giving them more rights and powers which enabled them to rise to the supra-local level. At this level, they acted as buffer groups between the king and the local peasant-warrior groups and enhanced their status to that of *māṇḍalika* (a local chieftain with administration/revenue rights, power to assume titles, owing nominal allegiance to the king).[43] The stability of the kingdom depended upon the relationship between these *māṇḍalikas* with the central power. Based on the controlling power of the central authority, they changed their allegiances. If the central power was feeble, they immediately emerged as independent chiefs.[44]

The isolated settlements comprised tribal areas of dry agriculture and herding in which social distinctions paved way to small scattered politics under petty chiefs. One such instance can be that of the Kōya chiefs of Polavasa region forming independent political unit.[45] Thus, while the wet zone economy was responsible for the rise of a feudal political structure, the dry zone economy led to the rise of rural landed aristocracy.[46] Effective control on the forest zones was, however, manipulated inducting dharmic ideologies and 'Brahmanisation' processes involving the brahman priests, sectarian leaders and temples to integrate the tribal and pastoral communities.[47]

It thus appears that variations in geo-ecological factors relate to the various developments of state formation. Different structural models were proposed by different historians during their study of medieval political structures and state formation, which ranged from unitary, feudal or segmentary and pyramidal power structures.[48] In relation to these different models of state varies the nature of kingship too that prevailed in India till late medieval times. They are heroic, dharmic and ritual kingships, based on the pyramidal power structure survived on brahman-kshatriya alliances.[49]

By nineth century gift giving had replaced Vedic sacrifices and was considered as the most valued means to obtain religious merit, thus becoming the constitutive ritual of royal authority itself.[50] By gifts to temples, brahmans, men of authority (ruling chiefs) established their virtue and ensured prosperity of their kingdom, creating at the same time, a moral basis of authority. This system of gift exchange kept goods and people in circulation in a particular pattern and also acted as a means of maintaining political relationships.[51] The ritualised tribute payments made local leaders as members of royal alliance net work. Further, they received the titles from the royal authority and gained superiority over local rivals. These two authorities, the kings and the local leaders depended upon one another for their positions. The kings were in need of ambitious and resourceful chiefs to stabilise their royal powers and to carry out gifts on their part. The chiefs in their turn needed kings to legitimise their shares in tributes received from the subjects. In other words, the power structure in such a state operates through a dual sovereignty, the coercive and the ritual.[52] This phenomenon is specifically observed in Āndhradēśa during eleventh to thirteenth centuries.

Earlier to Kakatiyas, Āndhradēśa for most of the time was not under one unified political authority, though the region was supposedly extended from Bay of Bengal in the east to Srisailam in the west and in the north upto Mahendragiri, south upto Kalahasti.[53] Āndhra formed peripheral part of the empires of Chalukya-Cholas, Western Chalukyas and Eastern Gangas of Kalinga who ruled their respective portions in Āndhra through their feudatory chiefs (Map II).

During the later years of Eastern Chalukya rule, there were political upheavals due to frequent Western Chalukya intrusions into Vēṅgi. This resulted in their establishment of marriage alliances with the imperial Cholas (Tanjore) and the foundation of a new Chalukya-Chola line of kings beginning with Kulottunga Chola. The empire of Kulottunga Chola extended from Kanchi in the south to Godavari valley in the north along the coastal tract of Āndhradēśa.[54] Their seat of power was Kanchi and they ruled their portions of Āndhra through viceroys settled in Āndhra. These royal representatives sought political allegiances from the local feudatories such as the Cholas of Velanadu, the Kolanu chiefs, Kondapadumatis, the Kota chiefs and the Chagis. Western Chalukyas who replaced Rashtrakutas by A.D. 973 emerged into a great imperial power with the extension of their borders from Karnataka into Telaṅgāṇa. Their seat of power was Kalyani and they too followed the policy of ruling parts of Āndhra region conquered by them through local power groups giving them feudatory status. Important among them were, the Chalukya chiefs of Mudigonda, the Paramaras, the Bottu chiefs of Koravi, the Natavadis and the Kakatiyas.

The political history of Āndhra during this period is thus characterised by internecine wars among the feudatories of these two major political powers for supremacy over the another and their frequent shifting of political boundaries as well as their feudal allegiances. This internecine war-fare is most marked in the war of Palanadu (A.D. 1176-1182) fought between the brothers of Haihaya dynasty but in which almost all the *māṇḍalika* chiefs participated on one side or the other.[55] The resultant effect was the end of *māṇḍalika* era and the rise of Kakatiyas as an imperial power.

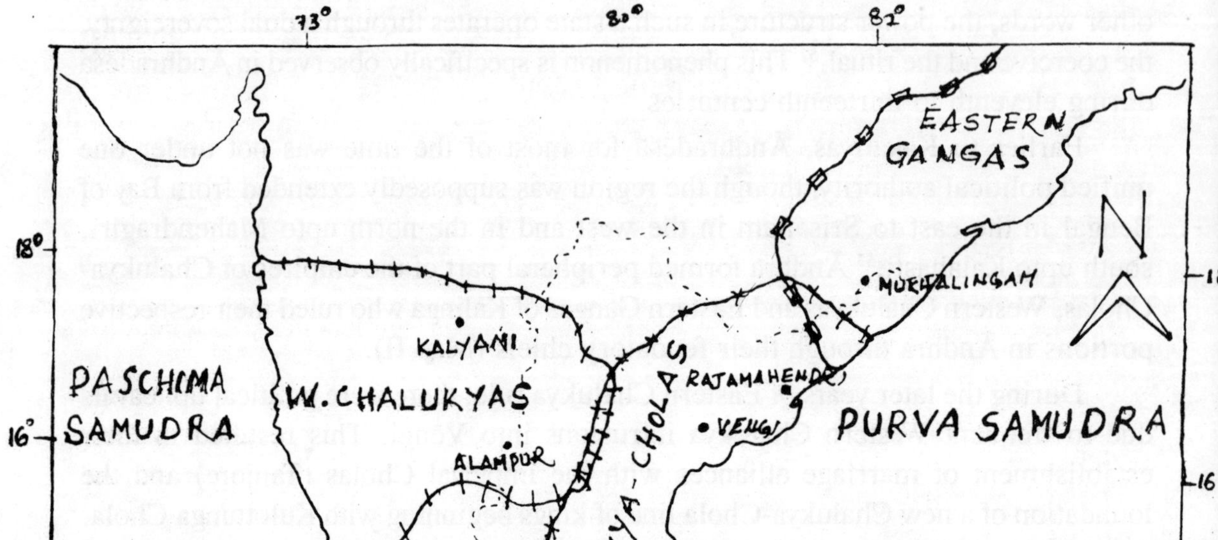

MAP II
POLITICAL BOUNDARIES OF THE PRE-KAKATIYA DYNASTIES

Kakatiyas were earlier feudatories under Rashtrakutas and later to the Western Chalukyas. They declared themselves as sovereigns of Āndhra during the period of Rudradeva - I by (A.D. 1158-1163-1195) and began extending their control into the Eastern ghats and deltaic coastal Āndhra.[56] By the time of Ganapatideva (A.D. 1199-1261), Kakatiyas emerged as the dominant power over whole of Andhradesa. In the process of expansion of territories (frontiers), they had to struggle hard with the rival contenders for power namely the Eastern gangas of Kalinga in the north coast, the Pandyas of Madurai in the south coast as also the Yadavas of the west. The control of Kakatiyas at its peak extended to entire Āndhra with their seat of power at Ōṛugallu (Warangal). It also included parts of northern Kaveri region and parts of Raichur and Kolar districts (Map III).

Like their predecessors Kakatiyas controlled their frontiers through feudatories and dominant peasant-warrior groups. Their attempts to bring in political integration are most prominent from the period of Ganapatideva, who created a post of *Bāhattara Niyogādhipati* (head of 72 units) as part of his policy of stabilising the empire.[57] The subjugated nobles were given feudatory status and their relations with the centre were further strengthened through the policy of marriage alliances. During the later part of Kakatiya rule, Rudramadevi (A.D. 1262-1289) continuing her father's policies, instituted the *Nāyaṅkara* system of revenue authority based on military fiscal control. Through this system an attempt was made to incorporate people of peasant-warrior class into the political net work and to check the defection of subordinate nobles from becoming independent.[58] This system was further developed by her successor and the last ruler Pratapa Rudra II (A.D. 1290-1323).[59]

Due to the effective political control brought about by Kakatiyas, the structure of political economy by and large remained unaltered. Trade was extensively developed with royal patronage and rise of temple as an important economic institution. Both foreign and inland trade prospered greatly through mercantile guilds and associations which became very powerful and wielded unlimited powers. They enjoyed full autonomy in the internal management of their affairs. There was a clear appropriation of surplus produce from agriculture and forest products through instituting boarding houses attached to temples and monasteries. With the rise of Kakatiya state, there was a shift in the nuclear areas from plain fertile regions to high and thickly forested regions.[60] Various factors are responsible for this, such as, the development of technology, growth of population resulting in colonisation in the high lands, growing importance to trade and industrial development, developing agrarian potentials by various methods like deforestation and afforestation, provision of irrigation methods through tanks and wells, etc. Moreover, Talaṅgāṇa offered a

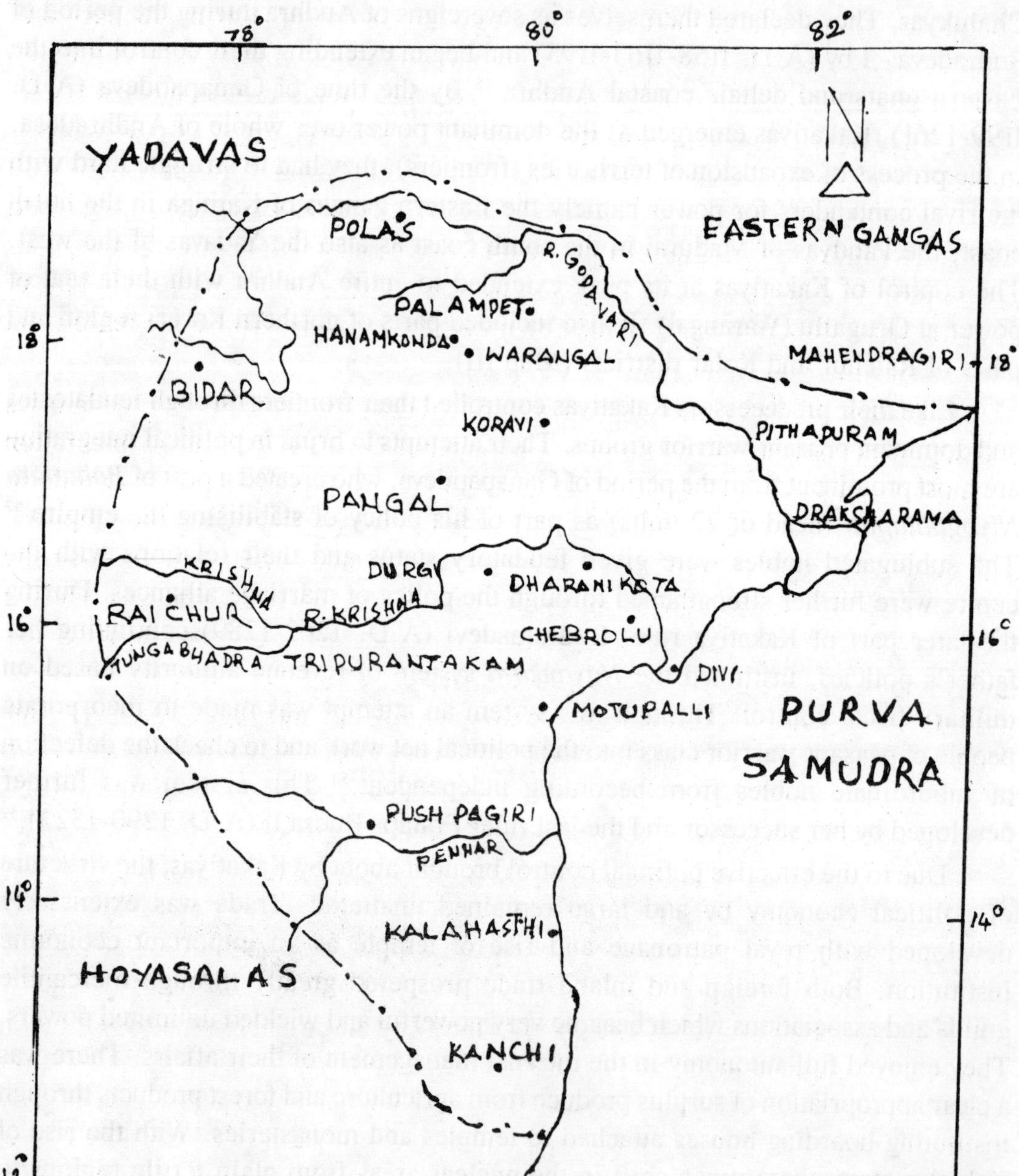

MAP III

POLITICAL BOUNDARIES OF THE KAKATIYAS

safe location for the Kakatiyas being located at a distance, from the powerful empires of the Eastern Gangas, Hoyasalas, Pandyas and Yadavas who were known for their almost continuous instrusions into Āndhra.[61] They continued their conquest of east and extension of empire in the north eastern region which was more fertile to ensure a sufficient resource base for the Kakatiya state to become a welfare state.[62]

Kakatiya kings organised administrative divisions of their kingdom in such a way as to maintain stable and well balanced relationships with the local chieftains and feudatories through extension of coercive, ritual and dharmic control. Middle Telaṅgāṇa region formed the core zone from where they controlled their dominions in entire Āndhra with their seat of power initially at Hanumakonda and later at Warangal. Within this core region, the king ruled directly through his ministers, maintained many of his political supporters and royal relatives through land grants and recruited bulk of officials from the local peasant-warrior groups.[63]

Next to the core region lay the zone of provinces, the authority of which was placed under revenue and administrative chiefs with titles like *Mahāsāmantha, Mahāmaḍalēśvara*.[64] Farther from the zone of provinces was the zone of tributaries in the eastern and southern Āndhra where the royal authority faded away into a mere ritual hegemony.[65]

Thus the king's control at the centre was coercive but on the peripheral zones was ritual, where he depended on feudatories for the settlement of the frontiers of the state. Further control on eastern Āndhra was brought through establishing marriage alliances with powerful ruling chiefs of the region as the Kotas and Chalukyas of Nidadavolu. Effective check on peripheral forest zones was brought about by Kakatiyas through the process of land reclamation and dharmic ideology. It was in these attempts by the royal authorities of maintaining a ritual relationship between the various power loci of the state such as the peasant-warrior groups, the non-brahmanical sectarian leaders, heads of mercantile guilds and indigenous forest peoples that women played a greater role. Significantly women from royal families actively engaged in welfare activities like construction of tanks, making endowments to temples or religious institutions and sectarian leaders thus enforcing ritual authority on the regions of their domain. Moreover, as the kings were, for most of the time away from the kingdom participating in the ensuing wars of feudal obligations, their women had to exercise authority over the administrative functions. At times, they were directly handling the issues of political concern in the capacity of co-regents or as guardians for minor chiefs. Instances are also many where they were made instrumental in linking various ruling powers through political marriages.

These arguments help u sto frame an idea that the nature of state and polity in Āndhradēśa necessitated involvement of women both of the elite and common categories to a greater extent in the political affairs of the state, the nature of which is discussed in the succeeding chapter.

REFERENCES

1. Norman, J.G. Pounds, *An Historical Geography of Europe (1800-1914)*, Vol. III, (Cambridge University Press, 1985), p. XIX.
2. Kunduri Iswaradutt, *A Historical Geography of Andhradesa,* (Hyderabad, 1962), p.5.
3. For details, David Ludden, *Peasant History in South India*, (Delhi, 1989), Burton Stein, *Peasant State and Society in Medieval India* (Delhi, 1980), etc.
4. K. Sundaram, *Studies in the Social and Economic Conditions of Medieval Andhradesa (A.D. 1000-1500),* (Machilipatnam, 1985), p. 1.
5. M.L.K. Murthy, Presidential Address, 'Environment, Royal Policy and Social Formation in the Eastern Ghats, South India (A.D. 1000-1500), in *INC*, 53rd Session, (Warangal 13-15th February, 1993), pp. 614-631.
6. P.S. Kanakdurga, *Kākatīyulanāṭi Sāmājika Jīvanamu,* (Vijayawada, 1992), p. 5.
7. M.L.K. Murthy, *Op. cit.,* p. 616.
8. B.Subba Rao, *Personality of India*, (Baroda, 1958), p. 16.
9. O.H.K. Spate, A.T.A.Learmonth and B.H. Farmer, *India Pakistan and Ceylon; The Regions,* (Bombay, 1972), p. 683 and p. 715.
10. R.L. Singh, *Op. cit.*, 1989, p.825.
11. M.L.K. Murthy, *Op. cit.*, p. 616.
12. R.L. Singh, *Op. cit.*, 1989, p. 824.
13. O.H.K. Spate, *Op. cit.*, 1972, p. 24.
14. The contemporary Inscriptional and literary sources, talk about the rich fertility content of the lands on either side of the river Godavari and the Godavari-Krishna deltaic region. Rice of *Kappurapu Bhōgi* variety, Sugarcane, Cereal crops, fruit and coconut trees were chiefly grown in these lands.
15. R.L. Singh, *Op. cit.*, 1989, p. 825.
16. *Ibid.*, p. 827.
17. *Ibid.*
18. Hanumakonda Kaifiat, *Meckenzie Manuscripts,* Vol. XXVI, p. 117.
19. M. Venkata Rangayya, (ed.), *Telugu Vijnāna Sarvasvamu, Telugu Saṁskṛti*, Vol. III, (Hyderabad, 1962), p. 213.
20. For ex. *IPA : WD*, Inscription Nos. 48, 50 and 64, *Epigraphia Andhrica*, Vol. I, No. 7, *S.I.I.*, Vol. X, Nos. 340, 448, 521, etc. and local records refer to the details of such villages founded by Kakatiyas and their sub-ordinates by clearing the forests.

Generally these villages are linked to cult centers and efforts were made by them to bring the forest peoples under the control of central power.

21. This idea is linked to the *Saptasantāna* concept of Dharmic ideology wherein raising a grove, excavation of tank, etc. is considered highly meritorious. Most of the kings and queens of medieval Āndhra claimed to have performed the *Saptasantāna* deeds as stated in their records, *SII*, Vol. IV, No. 1180, *HAS*, Vol. XIX, No. Wg 5, Inugurti, pp.131-134.
22. R.L. Singh, *Op. cit.,* 1989, p. 827.
23. *Ibid.*
24. *Ibid.*
25. *Ibid.*
26. *Ibid.* These lands are the principal rice fields of Āndhradēśa.
27. Santibhushan Nandi and D.S. Tyagi, 'Forms of Villages' in A.R. Desai, (ed.), *Rural Sociology in India*, (Bombay, 1984), pp. 206-217.
28. P.S. Kanakadurga, *Op. cit.*, 1992, p. 13.
29. *Ibid.* This theory of land settlements is discussed in detail by Tukkani Manmatha Reddy, *Sāmanta System in Medieval Polity, A Case Study of Kanduru Cholas (A.D. 1040-1250),* Unpub. M. Phil thesis, Telugu University, (Srisailam, 1991).
30. *SII*, Vol. VI, No. 123.
31. *Ibid*. Vol. VI, No. 904, Vol. IV, Nos. 705, 773. Also *EI*, XXI, 41-A.
32. AR, 116 of 1893.
33. AR, 273-C of 1899, *SII*, Vol. VI, Nos. 730, 772, 943.
34. AR, No. 213 of 1892.
35. *NDI*, Part, I, Atmakur (25). Also *HAS*, Vol. XIX, Pammi, Km 16.
36. *SII*, Vol. V, No. 80.
37. *HAS*, Vol. XIX, Pammi, Km 16 and Ramakrishnapuram, Km. 17.
38. *SII,* Vol. VI, Nos. 938, 943, 989.
39. *Ibid.*, Vol. V. No.80.
40. Burton Stein, 'Idiom and Ideology in Early Nineteenth Century South India', in Robb Peter, (ed.), *Rural India : Land, Power and Society Under British Rule*, (London, 1983), pp. 23-58.
41. N. Ramesan, 'Mallavaram Plates of Parankata Chola', in N. Ramesan, (ed.), *Studies in Medieval Deccan History*, (Hyderabad, 1972), pp. 79-121.
42. P.S. Kanakadurga, *Op. cit.*, 1992, p. 12.
43. *Ibid.*, pp. 13-15.
44. Thus we find constant shifting of alliances of local powers together with internal and external boundaries fluctuating constantly.
45. P.V. Parabrahma Sastry, *The Kakatiyas of Warangal*, (Hyderabad, 1978), pp. 58-64.
46. According to Burton Stein, the agricultural strategies differ according to the ecological factors and these variations tend to effect the social, economic as well as political formations of the region. Burton Stein, *Peasant State and Society*, pp. 27-28.

47. The kings and feudatories found it politically expedient to promote these groups (Brahmans, monastic organisations, temples) to bring in religious subordination of masses through the processes of Dharmic ideologies and Brahmanisation. This helped the rulers in perpetuating their political authority over these regions.
48. The idea of state in medieval India has been considered in different circles and from different angles over years. Three models are proposed in this connection, which are the Unitary State (centralised bureaucracy), Feudal state (division of power) and Segmentary state (separation of power at various levels). Each theory has numerous proponents. For details on this concept, Herman Kulke, 'Fragmentation and Segmentation versus Integration? Reflections on the concept of Indian Feudalism and Segmentary state in the Indian History', *Studies in History,* Vol. IV, No. 2., (1982), pp. 237-254. Arjun Appadurai, however, proposes that the medieval south Indian state can be desçribed more or less as a multifaceted, pyramidal power structure with power operating at different levels in relation to each other. Arjun Appadurai, 'Kings, Sects and Temples in south India (1357-1700 A.D.)', in *IESHR*, Vol. XIV, No. 1, (1982), pp. 49-73.
49. For details, Burton Stein, 'Perspectives on Kingship in Medieval South India' in Burton Stein, (ed.), *All the Kings Manu : Papers on Medieval South Indian History,* (Madras, 1984), pp. 1-67. Heroic kings are depicted as sacred extensions of tribal societies, ruled by virtue of their military prowess. Moral kingship is related to kingly authority expressed in moral or ethical terms while ritual kingship has a shared sovereignty among the powerful locally based persons through ritual exchange of honours, gifts, etc.
50. David Ludden, *Peasant History in South India*, (Delhi, 1989), p. 27.
51. *Ibid.*
52. *Ibid.*
53. K. Sundaram, *Op. cit.*, 1965, p. 1.
54. For details on Kulottunga Chola's rule and administrative policies kindly see, K.A. Nilakantha Sastry, *The Cholas*, (Madras, 1975) and *Telugu Vijnāna Sarvasvamu, Telugu Saṁskṛti*, Vol. III, pp. 191-202.
55. B.S.L. Hanumantha Rao, *Āndhrula Charitra*, (Guntur, 1983), pp. 223-224.
56. P.V. Parabrahma Sastry, *Op. Cit.,* 1978, pp. 97-98.
57. *Ibid*. P. 117 and 192.
58. *Nāyaṅkara* can be defined as a land grant given by the emperor to a local chief with all administrative and judiciary rights based on the agreement that he should provide military assistance to the emperor in times of need. Chiefs from various castes were recruited into the post by the queen.
59. Prataparuda made an elaborate arrangement for political control to ensure that disputes may not arise. He appointed *Padmanayaka* chiefs to the post. Ekamranatha, *Pratāparudra charitra*, (ed.), C.V. Ramachandra Rao, (Hyderabad, 1984), p. 39-40.

60. B.Thomas Reddy, *The Nature of Kakatiya State (A.D. 1158-1326)*, unpubished M. Phil thesis, Hyderabad Central University, (Hyderabad, 1992), p. 3. Also for more details on the nature of the state and the policies of control adopted by Kakatiyas, kindly see Cynthia Talbot, 'Political Intermediaries in Kakatiya Andhra, 1175-1325', *IESHR*, Vol. XXXI, No. 3, (Delhi, March, 1994), pp. 262-289.
61. P.S. Kanakadurga, *Op. cit.,* 1992, p. 6.
62. M.L.K. Murthy, *Op. cit.*, p. 617.
63. For more details on the administrative divisions and zonal distribution of political power during Kakatiya rule, see P.V. Parabrahma Sastry, *Op.cit.,* 1978, pp. 172-196.
64. *Ibid*. Also K. Satyanarayana, *A Study of History and Culture of Andhras*, Vol. II, (Delhi, 1982), p. 12.
65. It is essentially to exercise effective control in these regions, Kakatiyas adopted policies of establishing marriage alliances and other aspects of feudal relations.

CHAPTER 3

Women and Polity

In India, for many centuries, women did not assume the role of sovereigns, though there has been no written law which made them ineligible for political succession. This might be due to the general dependent position of women. Moreover, warfares and internal security were considered as male oriented activities and women were not fit to assume these roles.

The issue of political rights of a woman is not uniformly agreed upon by the legal text writers. Śāntiparva of *Mahābhārata* mentions that it is the duty of the conqueror to place on the throne of the conquered country, the brother, son or grandson of the vanquished ruler and if no prince is available, even the daughter of the deceased.[1] Thus, *Mahābhārata* accepts women as political heirs only in the absence of male heirs. Kauṭilya too, in his *Arthaśāstra* declares that in the event of a king dying without leaving behind a male issue, the minister should invest with authority, a princess or widow of the late ruler, to ensure continuity of rule in the same dynasty.[2] However, he made it clear that the princess was evidently not to succeed in her own right just as the widow was to wield the authority, till a son was begotten and was duly crowned.

On the contrary, Manu did not invest women with political rights. According to him, succession in monarchy is determined by the law of primogeniture and women do not come under this law.[3] A similar argument is put forward by another text *Nītivākyamitṛa*. According to this text, the order of succession to the throne is, the king, his son, full brother, half-brother, uncle, male of the same family, daughter's son, or even a stranger who is elected by the people or one who takes up the charge of the kingdom.[4] No reference is made either to the widow of the deceased or the daughter.

Despite the fact that law giving authorities are not unanimous about women's political participation, substantial references can be found in the records pertaining to ancient and medieval periods regarding women governors.[5] Such instances are more common in early medieval south India during the period of Rashtrakutas and Western Chalukyas.[6] Even in Āndhradeśa, early epigraphs indicate participation of women in politics eversince the period of Satavahanas.[7] This became a regular feature by the time of Kakatiyas. This development can be explained in terms of the political changes of medieval period. Several petty clans were ruling over portions of Āndhradeśa almost independently owing nominal allegiance to the emperors. The continuity of existence of each state depended upon the power of control exercised by the ruler. Thus, there were continuous wars between the feudatory chiefs. Further their feudal allegiances were not permanent and were frequently shifting from one imperial power to the other, according to the changing situation of political supremacy. Under these circumstances, the feudatory chiefs were, for most of the time away from their kingdoms either by participating in the wars for extension of their area of control or helping their emperors in the campaigns. For administration of their domains, they depended mostly on their ministers and officials. Under such circumstances, perhaps, their wives began interfering in the administrative affairs of their kingdoms. Sometimes, they had to assume the role of sovereigns in the absence of a male successor or as a guardian of the minor son in the event of sudden death of the king and to ensure continuity of political control. In addition constant wars might have damaged the peaceful life of the country, plundering the cities or razing forests. This was alleviated greatly by the acts of rebuilding taken up by the queens along with the kings, ministers and other officials of the kingdom.

Thus, it appears that women's involvement in the affairs of the state was almost continuous which was not highlighted so far. This could be due to the fact that the traditional society was not readily accepting the authority of women in politics. According to *Keyūrabāhucharitṛamu,* the king of Lāṭa country had no male issue. Fearing insult from the fellow kings, he decided to bring his daughter up in the attire of a boy and named her *Mṛgāṅkavarma* as against her true name *Mṛgāṅkāvaḷi*.[8] Similar is the case with the Kakatiya empress Rudramadevi who had to appear in the court in a male attire and had to take the name *Mahāmaṇḍaleśvara Rudradeva mahārājugaru*.[9] The various invasions of neighbouring rulers into Kakatiya kingdom soon after her succession too speak a lot about the view of the contemporary society towards the issue of women's political participation.

Nevertheless, these ridicules of the society and that of the great tradition did not hamper the process of women's involvement in the state craft particularly of

Āndhra region. This can be discussed under two heads, Active participation and Passive participation. Active participation can be defined as direct involvement in political affairs of a state like possessing the right- to issue orders, to make grants in the royal capacity, to take policy decisions with regard to administration and state craft, to participate in the wars and to involve in all matters of the polity of a state wherein physical presence of the ruler is required. On the other hand, passive role can be seen as involvement in the policy of a state from behind the curtain or making indirect contribution. In other words, acting as king-makers, counsellors or advisers to the king and serving as a source of inspiration to him.

Active Participation

Contemporary literature and epigraphs reflect the direct contribution of women in state craft. Interestingly the very base of Kakatiya state was formed by the diplomacy of a woman, Kāmasāni.[10] Guṅḍarāju of Kakatiya clan was ruling Koṛavi as a feudatory of Rashtrakutas at the time when Western Chalukyas rose to power at Kaḷyāṇi under Tailapa, replacing the Rashtrakuta rule. Tailapa in his attempts to stabilse his kingdom began appointing generals loyal to him as feudatory chiefs in place of those submissive to Rashtrakutas. Thus Boṭṭu Beta of Mudigoṅḍa family was appointed to rule Koṛavi in place of Guṅḍyana. Viṛiyāla Eṛṛabhūpati, a loyal general of Tailapa played a major role in defeating Guṅḍyana. However, his wife, Viṛiyāla Kāmasāni, who happened to be the paternal aunt of Gaṛuḍa Beta, son of slain Kakaṛtya Guṅḍyana, provided shelter to him. Further, she persuaded her husband and was successful in begetting Hanumakonda *vishaya* for the minor king from the Chalukyan emperor.[11] Thus, she saved the Kakatiya power in its infant stages by her act of shrewdness and diplomacy. The Buthpur inscription, praises her as a lady having established the Kakatiya power, the merit of which act of hers is worth crores of wealth.[12] Further Kakatiya empire is unique in having two women rulers, Rudramba and Gaṇapāmba. As daughters of the emperor, Ganapatideva, both received sufficient military and administrative training from their childhood. While Gaṇapāmba was married to Kōṭa Beta, son of Kōṭa Rudra, Rudramba was married to Virabhadra, a prince of the family of Chalukyas of Nidadavolu.[13]

Kōṭas were a powerful feudatory family ruling parts of Guntur region with capitals at Dharaṇikōṭa, Enamadala, and Tāḍikoṅḍa. The kings were prominent for their war strategies as well as their matrimonial relations with other powerful ruling chiefs of Āndhradeśa. A practice of joint rulership is also noticed in this family.[14] Generally it is seen that father and son or brothers becoming joint rulers. However, Kōṭa Beta and Ganapamba ruled their kingdom jointly as they had no children. Their joint rule continued for the period from A.D. 1241 to 1250. Owing nominal allegiance to the Kakatiya emperor Ganapatideva, they ruled almost independently. Records issued after A.D. 1251 mention Ganapamadevi, as *Mahāmaṅḍaleśvara* indicating her individual reign. Probably her husband might have died in the same year while fighting in the southern campaign of Ganapatideva at Kancheepuram.[15] The Īpūṛu record dated A.D. 1257 mentions her as *Mahāmaṅḍaleśvara Gaṇapamadēva ammaṅgāru*.[16] She assumed entire Kōṭa *praśasti* and imperialistic titles and ruled for a period of thirteen years, upto A.D. 1264.[17] The Enamadala inscription refers to Gaṇapāmba as the lady who was devoted to pious works after the death of her husband.[18] As Ganapamba assumed charge of the government at Enamadala much earlier than her sister, she showed loyalty to her father, the Kakatiya emperor. Besides the imperial power, she also maintained good relations with the other Kota chiefs at Dharanikota (Ganapati and Bhima), and with the neighbouring ruling powers throughout her regime.

Durgi rccord of Kāyastha chief Namaya Karaṇamu dated A.D. 1269 refers Rudramadevi as the *Paṭṭōddhati* (queen designator)[19] and Putṛika[20] which indicates that being the daughter of Ganapatideva she was made the legal successor of her father. Nevertheless, the prejudice against the rule of a woman was so strong in the contemporary political circles that she had to adopt a male name and attire herself in male garments whilst holding the court. She underwent a thorough training in the techniques of warfare like sword-handling, archery, horse riding, military science in addition to her father's able guidance in administration and state craft. As a co-regent during her father's rule (A.D. 1260-69) she gained practical knowledge in administering the empire.

As soon as she was coronated in the year A.D. 1269, she had to overcome many problems important of which include the Yadava, Pandya invasions accompanied by internal revolts in southern Āndhra under the leadership of Kāyastha chief Aṁbadeva. Kakatiyas had lost their authority in the regions south of river Krishna. According to traditional sources, there was a revolt of Hariharadeva and Murārideva, two sons of Ganapatideva by another wife whom she subdued very cleverly and diplomatically.[21]

Deluded into the belief that a woman's rule would be weak, the Yadava king Mahadeva led an expedition into the Kakatiya territories of the north-west and laid siege to the capital.[22] Due to a cleverly organised fight back of Rudrama, he had to retreat without capturing the fort. Rudrama personally led the battle and the Kakatiya army drove the Yadava forces accompanied by their king to the banks of the river Godavari, which was looked upon to be the border of Āndhra country. Bidar was occupied and a heavy tribute of about one crore *Nishkas* was collected from the Yadava king which was distributed as war booty to the soldiers.[23] Further, she constructed a Śivakeśava temple on the banks of river Chikili at Adilabad in memory of her victory over Yadavas.[24] The Bidar record of Sindhaṅvaya Bhairava indicates that after this victory, the queen assumed the title *Dāyagaja Kesari*.[25] Hemadri, unwilling to accept the truth of his master's defeat in the hands of a woman records that the Yadava king left Rudrama free because of his reluctance to kill a woman.[26]

Not only the Yadava king, but other frontier kings too tried to take advantage of the supposed weakness of a woman's rule. Prominent among them include Vira Rājendrachoḍa, a feudatory of Pandyas in Nellore, Vaidumbas of Cuddapah in the south and Kalinga and Oddadi chiefs in the east.[27] Rudrama, ably supported by her loyal military commanders, Jannigadeva, Tripurārideva and Gona Ganna Reḍḍy thwarted their attempts and thus brought back stability to the Kakatiya empire.[28] In order to prevent further damages to Oṛugallu fort, Rudrama strengthened the same by having dug a deep moat around the fort and posting sentries at the watch towers.[29]

Rudrama Devi was also famous for her administrative strategies and policies of state craft. Marcopolo praises her as a wise ruler.[30] She reviewed the feudal set up of the empire and reconstituted various administrative structures. She instituted *Nayankara* system based on military and fiscal control.[31] Additional powers were bestowed on the local chiefs and many posts of *Bahattara Niyogadhipathi* (head of 72 *Niyogas* or administrative units) were created.[32] In continuation of her father's policy of achieving political stability through marriage alliances, the queen gave her second daughter, Ruyyama in marriage to Annayamantri of Induluri brahman family. Her third daughter Rudrama was married to one Yadava prince Ellanadeva.[33] The son of her eldest daughter, Prataparudra was adopted by her and was nominated as her successor.

Much details are not known about the personal life of Rudramadevi. She was married to prince Virabhadra, belonging to the ruling feudatory family of Chalukyas of Nidadavolu.[34] However, he appeared to have died much before her accession, as two records register grants for his *punyaloka* by his mother Pina Odaya Mahadevi at Palakolanu.[35] The name of the queen is not figuring in both these records for reasons unknown. The reasons for his death are also not known.

Besides her military achievements, Rudrama was also a great administrator. She was a staunch follower of Saivism, but encouraged all other religious movements of the period. It appears that Harihara cult and Vaishnavism began to gain momentum in Āndhradēśa during her reign as temples were built for Gods Gopinatha and

Śivakeśava.[36] The cause of education was greatly promoted by her as is clear from her grants to scholars and sectarian leaders (Saivite teachers).[37] All measures were taken by her to promote the resource base of the empire by following dharmic ideological concepts. To bring in cultural integration among her subjects, she instituted festivals and *Tiṛunāḷḷu* (fairs) in the temples of newly constructed villages.[38] She also caused clearance of forests surrounding Hanamkonda and Warangal regions and constructed two villages Rudrēśvaram and Gaṇapēśvaram.[39] Irrigation facilities were provided to these villages through tanks, built for the purpose.

A sculpture from Warangal fort, showing a woman with a sword, a shield in her hands and mounted on a lion is believed to be of Rudramadevi.[40] Though she could emerge victorious out of the attempts by the various political circles which vehemently opposed her rule, she ultimately fell prey to the same. Ambadeva, a Kāyastha chief of Tripurantakam, revolted against her. She died in the battle along with her personal attendant, Mallikārjuna Nāyaka probably in the year, A.D. 1289 according to the Chandupaṭla epigraph.[41] Her death is an indication of the strong feeling of the great tradition that a woman was not eligible for political succession. It is an example of the oppression faced by a woman, even though she belonged to a prestigious ruling family.

Among the other women governors of the period, mention may be made of Paṁdāṁbika, belonging to Kōṭa family at Tāḍikoṇḍa. She ascended the throne after the death of her husband Maṅmapōta. She might have been contemporary to Ganapatideva and was known for generous behaviour and pious nature. Her Tāḍikoṇḍa inscription furnishes us with the details of her benevolent activities.[42]

Mailama wife of Malyala chief, Chauṅḍa Sēnāni also controlled the affairs of the state after her husband's death.[43] The Pammi inscription, refers Viṛiyāla Nāgasānamma as *Mahāsāmantha* indicating that she inherited feudatoryship after her husband. She visited the temple of Prasanna Vallabha at Pammi along with Malrāju and Mummaḍirāju of the same family and gave directions to the priests and the village assembly regarding arrangements for various endowments to the temple.[44]

Kuppāṁbika, in her Buthpur inscription was praised greatly as a woman who performed many religious observances and took up acts of charity for the welfare of the kingdom. After the death of her husband, Malyala Guṁḍa she might have ruled Varḍhamānapura region on behalf of her sons.[45] Muppaladevi of Chāgi ruling family too might have controlled the affairs of the state for some time as indicated by her title *Śrimanṅmahāmaṇḍaleśvara*. (SII Vol. X No. 305)

Nāyakurālu Nāgamma, the woman minister of the Haihaya kingdom of Palnadu is another example of women's participation in administration. She is known for her diplomatic policies which were supposed to be the chief cause for the war of Paland fought in the last quarter of twelfth century.[46] The historical significance of the war cannot be ignored as it involved all the *māṅḍalika* chiefs of Āndhradeśa. The war saw the rise of Kakatiyas under Rudradeva-I putting an end to the *māṅḍalika* era in Āndhradēśa.[47] Hailing from a peasant family of Palnadu region, she was the daughter of Virajaggāreḍḍy and was married into another Reddy family belonging to Guṛajāla.[48] But for these no other details are available from the text, *Palnāṭivīracharitra* of Srinatha regarding her personal life.[49]

Nagamma met the Haihaya king Anuguraju who was on his hunting expedition and obtained favours from him by providing comforts for him and his party at the village Gāmālapāḍu. Anuguraju permitted her to become the minister of Haihayas for a period of 7 *Gaḍiyas*.[50] From then she regularly visited the court of Anuguraju and after his death, his son Nalagama Raju's court. Her influence in the state affairs of Palnadu was not liked by the minister Brahmanayudu and there developed an enemity between the two as soon as she assumed the role of the minister of Nalagamaraju. Ultimately this led to a war of succession among the sons of Anuguraju. Nagama supported Nalagamaraju till the end and her acts of counselling are remarkable during the cock-fight,[51] peace agreement[52] and finally in the war fought at Karempuḍi.[53] Questioning Brahmanayudu's reluctance to a woman's participation in war, she fought in the warfield. Though she was defeated, Nalagama was declared victorious in the war.[54] The reasons for her enemity with Brahmanayudu are interpreted as religious rivalry.[55] However, according to local traditions, Brahmanayudu and his father were known to have ill treated the people of Guṛajāla. Therefore, Nagamma decided to oppose them. Moreover, she also opposed the desire of Brahmanayudu to divide the kingdom of Mācheṛla (Palnadu) between the brothers. She stood for the unity of Māchēṛla and received bitter experiences from Brahmanayudu and his associates.[56] The episode of Nagamma is another indication of the attitude of men towards a woman's political involvement.

In addition, there were many women who were actively involved in carrying out administrative, religious and welfare activities of the state. Dual sovereignty was exercised for the stability of the medieval state. Here the political sovereignty was in the hands of the king and ritual with the queens and the officers of the state (like the minister, commanders, generals, etc.) at the instance of the king. They extended their patronage to the temples, brahmans and to scholars and poets thus promoting literary activities. They tried to increase the resource base of the state by causing for extension of cultivable fields through deforestation, founding new villages and providing for irrigation systems. They tried to regulate the local governing systems by regular checks through visits to the villages and summoning the village assemblies. They also tried to regulate the tax structure and allocation of revenue to various power circles. All this goes on to prove the queen's role as a political integrator or maintaining ritual control on the state. However, this remained as hidden, uninterpreted talent so far.

Mailama and Kundama, sisters of Kakatiya Ganapatideva, were married to Natavāḍi Rudra. Both of them appear to be influential on the politics of their kingdom. Mailama had a title *Dharmakīrti* for her meritorious services which include construction of a great tank at Bayyāram (Khammam district), one of the biggest tanks of the Telangana region. Its engineering skill lies in the selection of the place where one or two streams pass between hillocks and giving irrigation benefits to as many as seven villages nearby.[57] She built three new villages near the tank in the name of her father (Mahadevapuram), mother (Bayyāram) and herself (Dharmapuram after her title). She observed many good deeds of Dharma to make the kingdom a glorious one. She also observed many *vratas* for the welfare of the kingdom and constructed many temples for Siva.[58] Her Tripurāntakam inscription registers grant of a village Dittālu to the temple at Tripurāntakam after consecrating the idol Mailambikeśvara is remarkable and suggestive of her authority and influence on the political affairs of the state.[59] Her sister Kundamamba constructed a village, a tank and a temple at Kundavaram in Jangaon Taluq and also a similar grant at Chennūṛu in Adilabad district.[60] Her inscriptions, praise her as the one whose acts of counselling were remarkable and to whose feet bow, almost everyday, wives of the other *māṅḍalika* chiefs.[61]

Sometimes, grants by the queens at places of religious importance suggest extension of king's authority over the area. Towards the last quarter of 11th century, eastern Āndhra region was governed by various feudatory dynasties and a part of it was also under the control of Western Chalukyan king, Vikramaditya VI. The grant by Mailambika, wife of Kandūri (Eṛuva) Toṅḍayachoḷa dated A.D. 1084-86 at Drākshārāma for the welfare of the kingdom of Western Chalukyan king Vikramaditya VI suggests the conquest of eastern Āndhra region by the king with the help of local chiefs of Telaṅgāṇa who were loyal to him.[62] By A.D. 1128, Drākshārāma region might have passed into the hands of the Eastern Gangas as suggested by a series of inscriptions registering grants of perpetual lamps by the wives of Anaṅtavarma Choḍagaṅga, namely, Sriyādevi, Laxmidevi, Kaliṅga Mahādevi, etc.[63] The land grant by the daughter of Lokaṁbika namely Somaṁbika to Madhukeśvara at Mukhalingam for the victory of the arms of Choḍagaṅgadeva is also of the same nature.[64] Rudradeva's wife Dannamadevi's grant for a perpetual lamp in the temple of Drākshārāma suggests Rudradeva's attempts to conquer eastern Āndhra.[65]

The series of inscriptions of Alaṁpuram in Mahaboobnagar district registering grants by Mannādevi wife of Chalukya Vikramaditya VI, also referred to as *Abhinava Saraswati* too indicate the political authority of Western Chalukyas over parts of north western Telaṅgāṇa.[66] She was the chief queen of Chalukya Vikramaditya VI who was famous for his conquests in Āndhradeśa. He ruled the conquered places of Āndhradeśa though his feudatories. Her title *Abhinava Saraswati* is suggestive of the scholarly nature of the queen and her patronage to the scholars and poets. She gave several villages (almost every year on the occasion of *Vishṇu Saṁkrānti*) as grants to the temple at Alaṁpuram. She also caused to have made the local chiefs to register grants to the temple priests at her instance.[67]

Recherla family was one of the important feudatories of Kakatiyas. Recherla Betireddi's wife Eṛakasāni was known for her righteousness, good virtues and pious behaviour. She constructed several temples at Pillalamaṛṛi and gave away lands for their maintenance. Further, she constructed canals, choultries for travellers, made arrangements for food to students in the hostels attached to the monasteries, established chalivēndras and performed many such meritorious deeds.[68] Women belonging to this family other than Eṛakasāni like Kāchāṁbika, wife of Kātachamūpati[69] and Itama,[70] wife of Nāmireḍḍy[76] are described as generous and helping the poor and needy. All of them patronised Saivite teachers and promoted education in their areas of control.

Women rulers exercised their control on the collection, donation of revenues in their respective dominions. Dhennamahādevi, the chief queen of Kandūri Nalla Bhimadeva Choḍa granted *siddāyamu* (a tax) to the temple of Rameśvaradeva at Gaṭṭutummena (Mahaboobnagar dist.) along with other monetary arrangements made annually.[71] It is also mentioned that the gift was made out of her free will indicating the right of the queens to spend royal income received through taxes.

Among the other prominent women, Guṇḍamadevi, wife of Velanāti Goṅka ıs praised as the one who treated her subjects as her children,[72] Pina Oḍayamahādevi, wife of Chalukya Indusekhara, is also known for her religious promotion.[73] Siṅgulādevi, niece of Prataparudra is known for her acts of reclamation of land by clearing forests and establishing new villages.[74]

Passive Participation

In addition to the above category of women who actively participated in the state affairs, there is another category of elite women who indirectly or passively assisted their husbands in administration in many ways. Inscriptions and the contemporary literature provide ample data in this regard. The work of Srinatha, *Palanāṭi Vīracharitra* which is an account of the war of Palanadu has many references to the acts of counselling by women.

Silama, mother of Brahmanayudu, had adequate knowledge in war-fare techniques and the rules of war. She is described as giving ample guidance to her son regarding these issues. She directs him to declare the war before proceeding against enemies and advises him not to kill brahmans, women or cows, as it is against the code of war.[75] She also asks him to protect the artisans and the poor.[76] Her expertise in the science of war-fare is suggested in her recognition of the spies who were in disguise.[77] She gives instructions to her son to cut the heads of soldiers like plants. She advises him to kill the horses and elephants of the enemy's side to drive them away.[78]

Itama, mother of Balachandra is also known for her act of counselling.[79] Manchala, the bride of Balachandra is depicted by the poet as a memorable character. Though assigned by her mother-in-law to prevent Balachandra from going to the battle-field, she prefers his participation in the war.[80] Further, she gives him weapons and asks him to stop his brahman friend Anapōtu from accompanying him, as it would be a great sin if a brahman is killed in the battle-ground.[81]

Kāṭamarāju Kathalu is a traditional account of the fightings due to cattle raids during the reign of the Telugu Choḍa chief Nallasiddhi. His commander Khadgatikkana participated in the war but fled from the battle field on being defeated. Enraged with this, his wife and mother tried to raise his valour. He returned to the warfield with a new inspiration and brought victory to the king. But he met with death in the course of the war.[82] This episode suggests the attitude of women belonging to royal families and wives of military commanders who preferred heroic death of their husbands in the war front rather than defeat. *Raṅganātha Rāmāyaṇamu* of Gona Buddha Reddy is another literary source which speaks a lot about the attitude of royal women. Through the characters of Mandodari,[83] Sulochana,[84] the author suggests that they prefer death to submission before the enemies.

Talking in terms of their wealthy position and higher status in the society, the participation of women belonging to elite group in the polity of the state can be easily explained. But at the same time, it appears based on the evidences that even common women were involved in administrative matters. They were aware of the various changes in the political conditions of the period and were reacting to those changes. Two records at Mukhalingam temple register grants by Viṅjama, daughter of Gōkanāyaka and another woman, the daughter of Rājamānikaseṭṭi for the victory of the Eastern Gaṅga king in his battles.[85] Various references in the contemporary literature too support the involvement of common women in political matters of the state.[86]

Even women belonging to forest dwelling communities like *Eṛuka*, *Cheṅchu* families are employed in various political strategies of the kings and ministers, to learn details of the enemy's position and other secrets of their war strategies. *Cheṅchu* women were described as holding bows and arrows.[87] Brahmanayudu is said to have understood the war strategy of Nagamma through an *Eṛukala-Sāni*.[88] Though sufficient evidences are not available to prove the influence of these women within their communities, it can be presumed that they preferred their husbands to be brave and fight back.

According to a tradition, Sammakka and Sāralamma are two tribal women belonging to the *Kōya* tribe. They participated in the war of Kōyas with Kakatiyas (during the rule of Pratapa Rudra) and sacrificed their lives.[89] They both are deified and a *Jātaṛa* (fair) in their name is instituted which is being celebrated now in Telaṅgāṇa region once in two years. It is considered to be the biggest gathering. However, there is no historical evidence for the conflict of *Kōyas* with Kakatiyas.

Marriage, being an important and sacred ritual of the sixteen *saṁskāras*, is aimed at providing the four *purushāṛthās (Dharma, Artha, Kāma and Mōksha)* to the individual.[90] Dharmasastras mention eight different types of marriages, which are listed the contemporary legal text *Vijñāneśvaramu* of Ketana.[91] While giving the necessary caste rules and procedural aspects of these eight marriages, the author also discusses about *Anulōma* and *Pratilōma* marriages with a view of their prevalence specially among the royal circles.[92]

A woman, through marriage becomes a binding medium in uniting two different families. On the same ground, a royal princess was often offered as a medium of peace between two warring kings.[93] According to *Sakalanītisammatamu*, marriage relations between powerful political rivals is an important aspect of diplomatic *Rājanīti* (moral of polity).[94] There was no bar of caste or creed in such marriages. What mattered was only a political contract for which a girl was used as a medium of contract. In the middle ages, particularly in Āndhra with various empires in the battle fray for supremacy, this became a regular feature.

The matrimonial alliances for about 3 continuous generations between Eastern Chalukyas of Veṅgi and the Imperial Choḷas of Tanjore are shown in Chart-I. They yielded far reaching results of establishing a new line of kings, the Chalukya-Cholas and the shift of political activity from Veṅgi to Tanjore. These relations between Eastern Chalukyas and Cholas were initially planned by the Chola emperor Rajaraja in order to have a control on Vengi which would become a fertile base for the extension of their authority in the north and to check the rising power of Western Chalukyas and their intrusions into Āndhra.[95]

CHART I

MARRIAGE ALLIANCES BETWEEN CHOLAS AND EASTERN CHALUKYAS

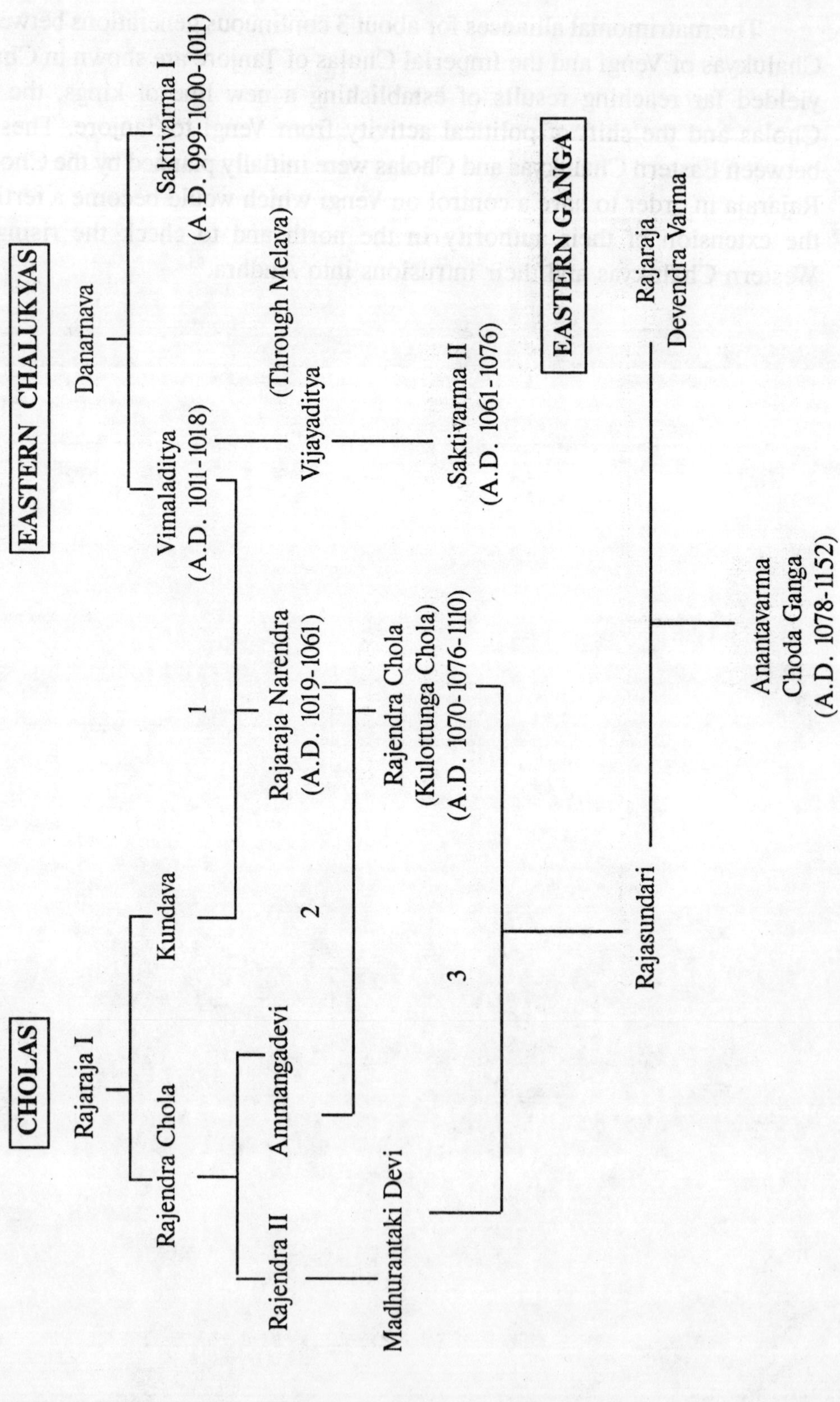

In the later period, Kakatiyas achieved the best of this policy of political marriages (Chart-II). With the aim of establishing their control almost all over Āndhradeśa, the rulers of this dynasty established diplomatic marriage relations with the contemporary powerful ruling chiefs.

Every ruling family of Āndhradeśa was connected with one or the other neighbouring ruling family through marriage (Chart-III). Similar is the case with the Eastern Gaṅgas of Kaliṅga who ruled northern parts of Āndhradeśa. Sometimes, the victorious kings regarded it as prestigious to demand the daughter of the vanquished, or ladies of his harem. The defeated king had no other alternative but to accept, failing which he would not be pardoned. The various epigraphical and literary references support this theory. Rudradeva demanded the daughter of Meḍarāja of Polavāsadeśa.[96] Refusal of the demand resulted in plunder and destruction of the kingdom of Meḍarāja. Similar is the case with Kandūri Bhimachoḍa who had to give his sister Padmavati in marriage to Rudradeva in order to save his kingdom.[97] The Jalālpuram inscription mentions that Rudradeva defeated one Gaṅḍanārāyaṇa and Udayana the father of Kanduri Bhima Choda and then made friendship with Udayana by marrying his daughter.[98]

CHART II

MARRIAGE RELATIONS OF KAKATIYAS WITH CONTEMPORARY RULING CHIEFS

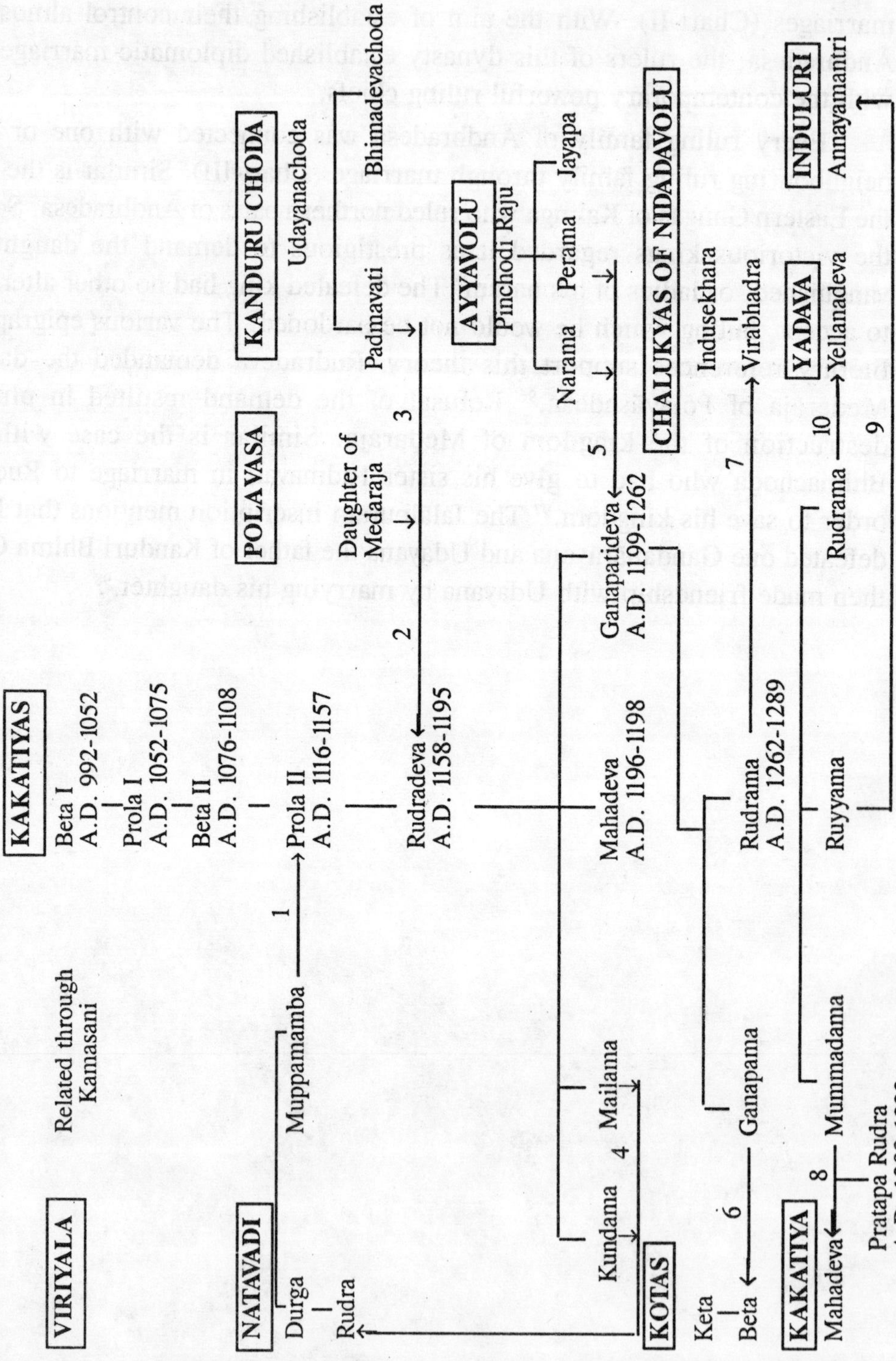

CHART III
MARRIAGE ALLIANCES BETWEEN VARIOUS POLITICAL POWERS OF ĀNDHRA DEŚA

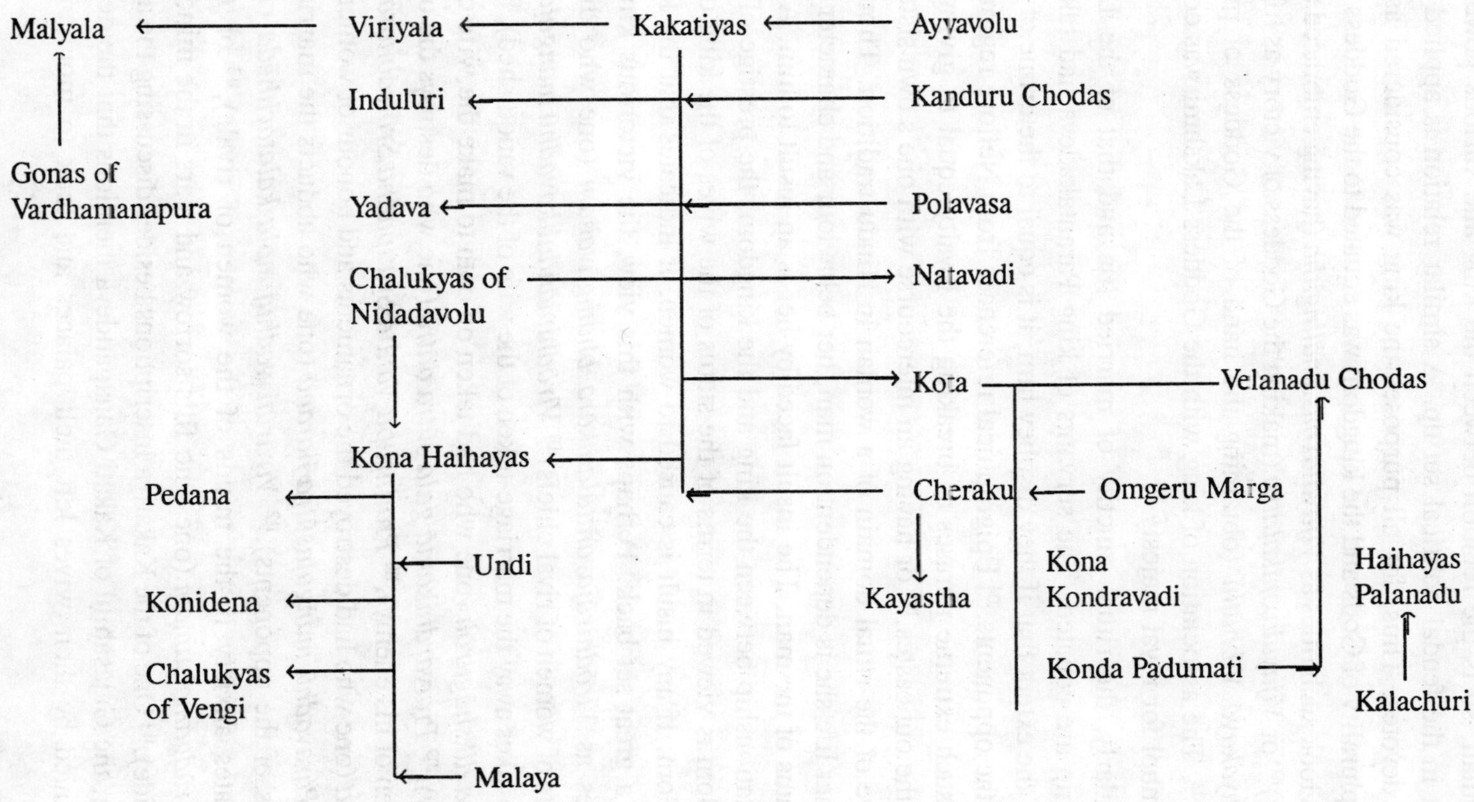

Note : The head of the arrow indicates the political power into which the girl is entering in lieu of marriage.

Just as the continuity and stability of married life is necessary to bind a man and a woman, so is the relation between the king and various power structures important in the feudal political set up. A similar relation is applied even to the God and devotee. Thus, for all purposes the king was considered as an earthly image of plurality of Gods and the kingdom was equated to the Goddess of victory.[99] The kings took such titles as *Vijayalaxmīsamāliṅgitha* (having embraced the Goddess of victory)[100] or *Vijayalaxmīkaḷatṛa* (making the Goddess of victory as life-partner)[101] *Vijayakanyakayā Vibhāthi* (obtaining the hand of the Goddess of prosperity in marrige)[102]. The association of king with the Goddess Lakshmi was considered as a real symbol for royal majesty.[103]

Similarly, the ritual sanctity of married life and that of the Lord-servant relationship are equated. The servants of king Parantakadeva had taken oaths of loyalty of the extent that if they disobey him, it is equal to the crime of giving their wives to the opponents.[104] Epigraphical references from Nellore region too record oaths of such extreme phrases as breaking the loyalty equal to giving away their wives to the out castes,[105] or having an intercourse with one's own sister.[106] This is suggestive of the ritual domain of a woman in Hindu tradition. Though at every stage of her life she is dependent on man, her behaviour and character indicate the social status of the man. The insult faced by her is an insult to him. Applying this to the relationship between the king and the kingdom, the prestige of the king or the kingdom is viewed in terms of the status of the wives of the king or women of the kingdom. If any insult is caused to women, it indicates that the king's status received a great set back. Perhaps with this view, the victorious kings assumed such titles as *Virōdhirājavanitālaṁkāra bhaṁgāvaham* (one who disturbed the ornaments of women of rival chiefs)[107] *Virōdhimāṅḍalikavadhū maṅgaḷasūtṛadātṛa*, (one who takes away the marriage-token of the wife of the vanquished),[108] *Paravadhū vaidhavya dikshāgurōh* (one who had taken on oath to make the wife of the enemy as widow),[109] *Pratyaṛdhikantā gala sūtra dātra* (one who destroys the ornaments of the women of his enemy),[110] *Pratinṛupa Vanitā Śṛutipadha Śrōtṛābharaṇa Gaurava Vaiphalya* (one who had destroyed the ornaments and honour of women of the rival king),[111] *Paravadhū maṅgaḷasūtṛa haraṇa* (one who abducts the maṛriage token of the wives of the opponents),[112] *Virārāti vadhūjanāla kalatāchhēda chhidoh* (one who creates anxiety in the minds of the women of rivals),[113] or *Ripustrīṇāṁ santāpāsrūdgamaisamam* (one who fills sorrow and tears in the minds of woman of rival side).[114] One of the Kakatiya inscriptions besides discussing the achievements of Jayapa, the Gajasāhiṇi of Kakati Ganapatideva mentions that the defeated kings accompanied by their wives left their palaces and took to mountainous paths.

During their journey, women were asked by their husbands to cover their faces with veils.[115] Similar references are found in *Pratāparudra Yaśōbhushaṇamu* of Vidyanatha.[116] The forcible abduction of women belonging to the vanquished kingdom also reflects this idea.[117] These evidences link the marriage and polity in an unseparable way.

To summarize the arguments, woman's right to political succession is recognised by law atleast on certain occasions. In line with this one can notice a great involvement of women in the political affairs of the medieval Āndhradeśa. The state of affairs demanded their active or passive participation. In addition, one can also find that the institution of marriage, the relationship between husband and wife and the ritual domain of wife with in the family are all related to historical relationships in feudal polity. Inscriptional evidences show clear similarities between lord-servant, deity-devotee and husband and wife relationships. The idea of submissiveness and loyalty are clearly enforced in all these and an attempt was made to raise the ritual position of the king, which was very much essential for the stability of the kingdom when viewed with reference to the multifaceted power structure of the state.

REFERENCES

1. तेषां पुराणि राष्ट्राणि गात्वा राजन् सुहृद्कृत:।
   भ्रातन् पुत्रांत्व पौत्रांश्रव स्वे स्वे राज्येभिषेचय:।
   कुमारो नास्ति येषां च कन्यास्तत्राभिषेचय।
   Mahābhārata, Śāntipaṛva, 33-43-46 refered to by P.V. Kane, in his *History of Dharmaśāstras*, Vol. III, (Pune, 1974), p. 40.
2. R.P. Kangle, *The Kautilya's Arthaśāstra, A Study,* Part III, (Delhi, 1986), p. 116.
3. G. Buhler, *The laws of Manu*, F Max Muller, (ed.), *Sacred Books of the East* (Translation by Oriental Scholars), Vol. XXV, (Delhi, 1975), IX, 134.
4. P.V. Kane, *Op. cit.*, 1974, p. 43.
5. *Ibid.*, p. 40. The author gives examples from *Rājataraṅgini* of Kalhana and *Raghuvaṁsa* of Kalidasa.
6. To quote a few –
   1. Revakammāḍi, daughter of Amōghavarsha (Rashtrakuta) was the governor of Eḍatōre region during the first half of 9th century A.D.
   2. Mailala Devi, wife of Chāḷukya Someśvara held the charge of Banavāsi region in A.D. 1053.
   3. Kētala devi, another wife of Chāḷukya Someśvara was incharge of Ponnavaḍ agrahara.

4. Akkadevi, sister of Western Chalukyan monarch Jayasiṁhavallabha is described as a great warrior and governor of Koṅkan region during her brother's reign.
5. Daṇḍimahādevi, queen of Gaṅjām region had typical Chalukyan titles, *Paramabhaṭṭārika, Mahārājādhirāja Parameśvara* indicating her political status.
6. A record from Savikeṛi mentions Srimadevi, wife of Rājāditya of Banavāsi as the governor of Samkaṛige-12.

7. There are evidences to prove that Nāganika, wife of Satavahana king Satakarni I assumed power for a short period. Wives of the nobles took titles as *Mahārathni, Mahābhojini* indicating their participation in the polity. Mahadevi, queen of Vishṇukuṇḍin Govindavarma was also a remarkable personality known for her interest in administration and promotion of state religion. For details, B.N. Sastry, *Āndhradeśa Charitra, Saṁskṛti*, Vol. I, (Hyderabad, 1992).
8. Manchana, *Kēyūrabāhucharitramu*, (ed.), Vedam Venkatarayasastri and Brothers, (Madras, 1970), p.1 4, verse 74.
9. Md. Abdul Waheed Khan, *A Monograph on Yēleśvaram Excavations,* (Hyderabad, 1963), Nos. 14, 30.
10. *HAS*, Vol. XIII, Gudur inscription of Viriyala Kamasani, No. 23, pp. 78-79.
11. *Ibid*. According to a tradition, Kuṅtalidevi, the paternal aunt of Eṛukadevarāju ruled Hanumakonda Vishaya on behalf of the minor boy for a period of 9 (19) years. She was said to have collected heavy tributes from neighbouring Gujarat and Yadava Kingdoms. Though the historicity of Kuntalidevi with Kamasani could not be established, we can presume so, as Eṛukadevarāju was identified with Beta I. The traditional account is recorded in Ekamranatha's, *Pratāparudra Charitra*, Kase Sarvappa's, *Siddheśvaracharitra* and also in *Mackenzie Manuscripts,* Vol. XXVI, (Hanumakonda kaifiyat).
12. *Has*, Vol. XIII, Buthpur Inscription.
13. These marriages are part of the political diplomacy of Ganapatideva to conciliate his authority in eastern Andhra region.
14. Y. Yasodadevi, 'A History of Andhra countrry, Subsidiary Dynasties' in *JAHRS*, Vol. XIX, (Rajahmundry, July 1948-April 1949), pp. 1-84. (KOTAS, pp. 60-81).
15. M. Venkata Rangayya, *Saṁgrahāndhra, Vijñana Kosamu*, Vol. III, (Hyderabad, 1962), pp. 95-96.
16. *ARE* No. 535 of 1913.
17. N. Ramesan, 'Mogalutla grant of Kota Ganapamba' in *Epigraphia Andhrica*, Vol. IV, (Hyderabad, 1975), pp. 93-102.
18. *EI*, Vol. III, p. 94.
19. B.N.Sastri, *Kāyastha Rājulu*, (Hyderabad, 1991) Ins. No. 13.
20. Arudra, 'Putṛika Elaṅti Kūturu', in Arudra, (ed.), *Vyāasapitham*, (Vijayawada, 1985), pp. 54-59. *Putṛika* is an appointed daughter and becomes the natural successor to

the father who has no male issue (Manu, IX, 137). It appears that Ganapatideva's decision to nominate Rudramadevi as his political heir falls under this perception.

21. *Hanumakonda Kaifiyat*, p. 58. Also, K. Balendusekharam, *Andhras Through Ages* (Hyderabad, 1973), pp. 20-24.
22. G. Yazdani, *The Early History of Deccan*, Vol. II, parts VII-XI, (Delhi, 1982), p. 626, Also, K. Balendusekharam, *Op. cit.*, 1973, p. 24.
23. B.N. Sastri, *Op. cit.*, 1992, p. 724.
24. *Ibid.*
25. *Ibid.*
26. Hemadri, 'Vṛata Khāṇḍa', Rāya Prasasti, I, *Bombay Gazeteer,* Vol. II, (i) p. 273, quoted from G. Yazdani, (ed.), *Op. cit.*, 1982., p. 625. *Kākatīya Saṁchika*, Appendix, 'Rāja Prasasti', Govt. of Andhra Pradesh, (Hyderabad Reprint, 1991), p. 341.
27. K. Satyanarayana, *A History and Culture of Andhras*, Vol. II, (Delhi, 1982), p. 3.
28. *Ibid.*
29. Kase Sarvappa, *Sri Siddheśvaracharitra*, (ed.), K. Laxmiranjanam, (Hyderabad, 1960), pp. 129-130. Also, *Hanumakanda Kaifiyat*, p. 57.
30. K.A. Nilakantha Sastry, (ed.), *Foreign Notices on South India from Megasthenes to Mahavro*, (University of Madras, 1938), p. 174. The quotation runs thus, "She was a lover of justice, of equality, and of peace, she was more beloved by those of her kingdom than ever was a lady or lord of theirs before".
31. *Epigraphia Andhrica,* Vol. IV, (Hyderabad, 1975), p. 128.
32. *Ibid.*, These steps were taken by her probably in the light of changing political situation in Āndhra which necessitated more of warrior control than of feudal loyalties.
33. P.V.Parabrahmasastry, *The Kākatīyas of Warangal*, Hyderabad, 1978, p. 121. Also, *A.P. Government report on Epigraphy*, (Hyderabad, 1968), No. 14.
34. *SII*, Vol. X, No. 360.
35. *SII*, Vol.V, Nos. 121 and 122.
36. B.N. Sastry, *Op.cit.*, 1992, p. 747.
37. *SII*, Vol. X, No. 395, pp. 205-209, and Abdul Waheed Khan, *Op. cit.*, No. 30, pp. 62-63.
38. Kallakuri Narayana Rao, *Pratāpa Rudramadevi*, (Vijayawada, 1961), p. 33.
39. *Ibid.*, Also, *Siddheśvara Charitra*, p.134.
40. P.V.Parabrahmasastry, *Op. cit.*, 1978, p. 122.Another sculpture available at Ramappa temple depicting a woman with a sword and shield, riding on an elephant and accompanied by woman guards is also believed to be of the same queen.
41. B.N. Sastry, *Cheṛaku Vaṁsacharitra : Sāsanamulu*, (Hyderabad, 1989), (*Studies in Indian Epigraphy*, I, No.9), registering grants by her general Puvvala Mummadi for the religious merit of the queen and her attendent supports this.
42. *Epigraphia Andhrica*, Vol. V, 'Tāḍikoṇḍa Inscription of Paṁdāṁbika', pp. 89-94.

43. B.N. Sastry, *Mahabubnagara Jilla Sarvasavamu*, (Hyderabad, 1993), p. 256.
44. *HAS*, Vol. XIX, Pammi Record (Km. 16), pp. 31-35.
45. *Ibid.*, Vol. XIII, Buthpur Inscription, pp. 140-142. Also, B.N. Sastry, *Op.cit.*, 1993,p. 242.
46. Vinukonda Vallabharaya, *Kriḍābhirāmanu* (ed.), Veturi Prabhakara Sastry, (Hyderabad, 1960), verse 119.
47. B.S.L.Hanumantha Rao, *Andhrula Charitra*, (Guntur, 1983), p. 224.
48. Srinatha, *Palnāṭi Vīracharitra*, (ed.), Pingali Laxmikantham, (Vijayawada, 1961), p. 34.
49. She is described in *Kriḍābhirāmamu*, as 'Araveli Nagama'. She was supposedly involved in the profession of money-lending (Sewell, R., *Antiquities* I App. A. p.5 quoted from V. Yasodadevi, 'A History of Andhra Country' in *JAHRS*, Vol. XXIII, Rajahmundry, p. 23).
50. *Palnāṭi Vīracharitra*, p. 35. A *Gaḍiya* was a Hindu hour which consists of 24 minutes. Thus, 7 *'gaḍiyalu'* refer to 168 minutes.
51. *Ibid.*, pp. 108-129.
52. *Ibid.*, pp. 228-233.
53. *Ibid.*, pp. 281, 286-290, 361-62, 422-425, 435-36.
54. *Ibid.*, pp. 449-450.
55. K. Balendusekharam, *Op. cit.*, 1973, p. 22.
56. B.S.L. Hanumantha Rao, *Op. cit.*, 1983, pp. 223-224.
57. Epigraphia Andhrica, Vol. I, 'Bayyaram Tank Inscription of Kakati Mailama', pp. 71-94.
58. *HAS*, Vol. XIX, No.59, Inugurti, pp. 179-182.
59. *SII*, Vol. X, No. 254.
60. P.V. Parabrahmasastry, *Kākatīya Sāsana Sāhityamu*, (Hyderabad, 1974), p. 45.
61. *IAP : WD*, (Hyderabad, 1974), No. 57, (Nidigonda) and 58 (Kundavaram).
62. *Drākshaārāma Sāsanālu*, (Hyderabad, 1982), No. 10, pp. 10-11.
63. *Ibid.*, Nos. 136, 137, 138 .....
64. B.N. Sastry, *Mukhaliṅga Devālaya Charitra, Sāsanamulu*, (Hyderabad, 1985), No. 31. Initially the eastern Andhra region was under the administrative jurisdiction of the Eastern Chalukyas of Vengi and then passed into the hands of Chalukya Cholas, Velanadu Chodas and various other feudatory dynasties before being brought under the control of the Kakatiyas.
65. *SII*, Vol. IV, No. 1094 [A.R. 244 of 1983].
66. *Telaṅgāṇa Sāṣanamulu*, Vol. II, Laxmanaraya Parisodhaka Mandali, (Hyderabad, 1935), Nos. 19 and 20.
67. B.N. Sastry, *Op.cit.*, Alampuram inscriptions of Bikkarasu, No. 47, pp. 965-966.
68. B.N. Sastry, *Recherla Reḍḍi Vaṁsa Charitra, Sāsanamulu*, (Hyderabad, 1989), Nos. 5 and 6.

69. *Ibid.*, p. 14.
70. *Ibid.*, p. 22.
71. *Has*, Vol.XIX, Mahabubnagar, No. 10, *IAP : KD*, (Hyderabad, 1974), No. 37 records gift of taxes by the queen of Rudra to the temple of Ramanathadeva. *SII*, Vol. X, No. 381, *A.R. on South Indian Epigraphy*, No. 303, (1932-33) too are of the same nature.
72. *SII*, Vol. IV No. 1137. In the text of the inscription, it is stated: यत्कारुण्यमेशेष भूजनरतेऽमतृित्वमानन्ददम्।
73. Her various grants registered at the temple of Ksheerārāmeśvara at Palakolanu and Narasaraopet indicate her greatness. *SII*, Vol. V, Nos. 121 to 127.
74. K. Satyanarayana, *Op. cit.*, 1982, Vol. II, p. 24.
75. *Palanāṭi Vīracharitra*, p. 191.
76. *Ibid.*, pp. 191-193.
77. *Ibid.*, pp. 174-175.
78. *Ibid.*, p. 31.
79. *Ibid.*, pp. 329-330.
80. *Ibid.*, p. 357.
81. *Ibid.*, pp. 356-357.
82. Ootukuri Laxmikanthamma, *Andhra Kavayitrulu,* (Bapatla, 1980), pp. 4, 5, 6. Chanama, wife of military general Khadga Tikkana, arranged for the bath of her husband in the manner of a lady taking bath. When questioned, she replied, "If you come showing your back to the enemies, don't brave men laugh at you? Now, we are three in the family. So don't feel bad for this type of arrangement".
 Similarly his mother Prolama serving him with split curds, replied thus "Just as you returned from the battle field defeated, the cattle too came home back running in a timid fashion only to give split milk."
83. Gona Buddhareddy, Kacha and Vittala, *Raṅganātha Rāmāyaṇamu*, (ed.), Pingali Laxmikantham, (Hyderabad, 1989), pp. 333-334.
84. *Ibid.*, pp. 411-415.
85. *TIAP*, Vol. I, Srikakulam District, (Hyderabad, 1980), Nos. 173 and 166.
86. For instance, *Palanāṭi Vīracharitra*, p. 315. While Balachandra was playing in the streets, the ball hit a woman walking in the street, Hurt by the same, she criticised the playful mind of Balachandra while men of the whole community were engaged in the war.
87. The sculptures available from temples belonging to the period bear ample testimony to this.
88. Ambati Subbarayachetti, 'Kākatīyulanāṭi Saṁghika Jīvanamu' in Maremanda Rama Rao, (ed.), *Kākatīya Saṁchika,* pp. 141-149.
89. Local Records at Endowments department, Warangal available in the form of *Sthalapurāṇamu* of Medāram region refer to the storv of these two women. An

attempt to link the story with Kakatiyas and to prove its historicity was made by Sri Dendukuri Somesvara Rao, through his article, 'Samakka-Saralakka Jātaṛa' published in *Ōṛugallu* (Hanamkonda, 7th March, 1986). However he tries to prove that the incident relates to Rudradeva I and he asserts that the deification of the two women and institution of fair in their name was done by Prataparudra.

90. P.S. Kanakadurga, *Kakatiyulanāṭi Sāmājika Jivanamu*, (Vijayawada, 1992), p. 195.
91. Ketana, *Vijñaneśvaramu,* (ed.), C.V. Ramachandra Rao, (Nellore, 1977), Acharakaṁdamu, verses 95-101.
92. *Ibid.*, Acharakaṁdamu, verses 134-141.
93. P.V. Parabrahma Sastry, 'Contribution of Women to the growth of Ancient Indian Culture', in L.K. Tripathi, (ed.), *Position and Status of Women in Ancient India*, (Varanasi, 1988), pp. 119-129.
94. Madiki Singana, *Sakalanītisammatamu,* verse, 646.
95. P.V. Parabrahmasastry, *Op. cit.*, 1988, p. 123.
96. *IAP : WD*, p. 122.
97. B.N. Sastry, *Kandūrichoḍula Sāsanamulu Charitra*, (Hyderabad, 1991), p. 23 Also *HAS*, Vol. XIII, No. 3, pp. 8-21.
98. B.N. Sastry, *Cherṛaku Vaṁsa Charitra, Sāsanamulu,* Jalalpuram inscription, pp. 41-49. The grant reasserts the information contained in the above cited inscription, Bhimadeva (Kanduri Bhimachoda, whose sister is married to Rudradeva) being the eldest son of Udayana.
99. We find this concept in the epithets assumed by the kings, for example : *Epigraphia Andhrica*, Vol. IV, 'Ollala Inscription of Kanduri Mallikarjuna Choḍa', No. 8, pp. 55-65.
100. B.N. Sastri, *Op. cit.*, 1993, pp. 928-929.
101. *SII*, Vol. IV, No. 928-663.
102. *Ibid.*, Vol. X No. 97, 177, Vol. IV, No. 1041.
103. J.G. De Casparis, 'Inscriptions and South Asian Dynastic Traditoins' in R.J. Moore, (ed.), *Tradition and Politics in South Asia*, (New Delhi, 1979), pp. 103-127.
104. *SII*, Vol. IV, Nos. 1274, 1275-A, 1270, 1271, 1272, 1273.
105. *NDI*, (New Delhi, 1990), Part II, Ongole, Kandukur, Nellore records, Part III, Raipur.
106. *Ibid.*, No. Ongole, 7.
107. *SII*, Vol. VI, No. 124.
108. *AR*, 721 of 1920.
109. *SII*, Vol. V, No. 105.
110. *Ibid.*, Vol. X, No. 74.
111. *Ibid.*, Vol. VI No. 594.
112. *Ibid.*, Vol. VI, No. 249.
113. *SII*, Vol.IV, No. 662.

114. *Epigraphia Andhrica*, Vol. IV, pp. 55-65.
115. P.V. Parabrahmasastry, *Op. cit.*, 1974, pp. 27-28.
116. Vidyanatha, *Pratāparudra Yaśōbhūshaṇamu*, Telugu Translation by Dr. Chelamacherla Rangacharyulu, (Hyderabad, 1972), *Dōshapṛakaraṇamu* is full of the problems faced by wives of defeated kings in the forests.
117. B.S.L. Hanumantha Rao, *Op. cit.*, 1983, (Hoṭṭur inscription mentions that in order to divert the Western Chalukyan king Satyasraya who was compaigning Veṅgi, the Choḷa emperor Rajendra I sent his son to occupy Raṭṭavāḍi region, which was probably destroyed and many women of the city were abducted by him).

CHAPTER 4

Professions and Property Rights

Indian tradition determines the space of men and women in public and private domains respectively. However, interchangeability of gender roles is observed at times. Even in the classical tradition though a man is deemed to succeed to the throne, in the absence of a male heir/co-regent, his wife becomes the ruler to ensure continuity of rule. Women belonging to the weak sections of the society take up economic activities along with men to supplement the family income. Thus, it appears that there is no clearcut demarcation between the gender roles and they are very much influenced by the demands of the situation.

The law givers too provided ample space for women making them political heirs under certain circumstances. They enabled women to enter into valid contracts or pledge their husband's property for the purpose. Not only these, they have also allotted certain rights on property to women whether inherited or acquired by them. This largely explains the economic participation of women in the medieval times. This can be discussed under two heads, Professions and Property rights.

Professions

In the primitive societies, no division of labour is found between the two sexes. Anthropological studies project women of ancient societies as food gatherers and food processors.[1] In due course, agriculture and crafts which necessitated a heavy muscular power and labour were taken by men and the works which involved patience, skill and forbearance were practiced by women.

Certain leisure time activities of women, like spinning, weaving, stitching clothes, etc. contributed for the family economy. The dharmic literature also provided space for different occupations to be held by different categories of women. For example, entertainment maids in the royal courts.[2] The duty of attending to the personal works of a king and his family members was also assigned to women. Similarly, the profession of dance in the courts became exclusive of women, with the result that a new class of courtesans came into existence. Some of the wealthy and learned courtesans were patronised by kings as their concubines. Concubinage became an established and respectable profession in the medieval times. By about the same time, the temple too emerged as an important feudal institution creating provisions for temple dancing girls and women attendants for carrying out various ritual services to the temple deities, thereby widening the scope for their participation in almost all spheres of socio-economic, politico-cultural lives.

The occupations held by different categories of women can broadly be discussed under 3 heads; Occupations of *Kulastṛeelu* (family women), Women as *Bhōgastreelu* (entertainment maids) and the temple girls. Under each category folk-elite variation and integration are discussed.

Occupations of *Kulastṛeelu* (family women)

Occupations taken up by women belonging to both elite and common sections of the society whose marital status (maiden, married or widow) is specific are included in this category.

Generally women of elite group did not take up any profession. The exception being women of ruling elite who entered into administrative jobs. This can be viewed more as hereditary right to that of profession, as discussed in the earlier chapter. However, women of the common sections of the society had to take up various economic activities to supplement the income of their husbands and to help them in the smooth running of the family. These include :

(a) Service in Royal Palace

A king's household is a big affair. Royal palace served as the biggest employer with several attendants for each type of work. Women are employed in the inner circles of the palace. *Manu* holds that well trained women and whose toilet (attire/ garments) and ornaments examined should be appointed as entertainment maids by a king.[3] They should attend to him with such works as serving with fans, water, and perfumes. *Mānasōllāsa*, recommends employing women in the royal households for cleaning rice and serving food, washing feet, massaging, dressing hair, applying unguents and for providing entertainment with programmes of music, dance, instrument playing.[4] The medieval dance treatise *Nṛittaratnākaramu* of Jāyapasēnani suggests that the king should be attended upon by maids alone while he watched programmes of music and dance and there should be a woman who is perfectly talented in these arts in order to explain the significance of the programme to the king.[5] Contemporary epigraphical and literary evidences throw much light on the different duties of women in the royal households.

The wetnurse is entrusted with the duty of bringing up the infant prince/princess to the early years of its childhood. Preferably old and experienced women are appointed for the purpose. *Dādi* is the term associated with these women. Epigraphical and literary references provide more details of the post and the importance attached to it.[6] Women attendants of the palace performed tasks like giving oil or scented bath to the king, massaging hair or other parts of the body, cleaning grains or such other works in the royal kitchen.[7] A record mentions the donor as the son of *Aḍupulotteḍi Aṅgāṅḍi* (one who massages the feet) of king, Kulottungachoḍa Deva.[8] Women are appointed sometimes to look into the catering services of the royal kitchen. An undated epigraph from Amarāvati refers to the wife of Prolaya as *Vaṅṭala* Kāmasāni, probably incharge of royal kitchen.[9] Serving meals for the members of the royal family, specially the king, is also one of the duties of women attendants of the palace. Such women who arrange the meal plates for the king are referred to as *Taḷiya*.[10] It appears that the court of Prataparudra II, the Kakatiya emperor had 3,200 women attendants.[11]

Women alone are appointed as guards for the inner apartments of the palace and as personal body guards for royal women.[12] *Mānasōllāsa*, prescribes elderly and experienced women to supervise the work of the maids of the palace.[13]

Āndhra Mahābhāratamu mentions a post, *Sairaṅdhri*, (a woman engaged to decorate the queen). According to Tikkana, often women who are deserted take up this job. They stay for a specific period in the harem. Their duty is to decorate the queen and the job requires perfect talent in arts like hair dressing, beautification processes and making different kinds of garlands.[14] This post probably had its origin in Vedic period. No specific payment is prescribed but she was maintained within the palace and was given a respectable treatment.

Women belonging to *Bōya, Eṛuka, Cheṅchu* communities too are appointed for various services in the royal palaces. *Bōya* women wrap clothes to the palanquins, while their husbands were the palanquin bearers.[15] The services of *Eṛuka* women were utilised to learn the plans of rival political powers in the war fields.[16]

Details regarding the mode of payment, amount of salary paid to each of these women employees are however not available. It appears that they are maintained out of royal income and residential accommodation is also provided to them within the palace compound. Moreover, the children or husband of these women were assigned administrative posts such as *Talāṛi* and *Daṅḍanāyaka*. An inscription dated

A.D. 1235 records grants made by a royal servant and son of the wetnurse of king Kōṭ a Maṅmaketa.[17] Another similar reference indicates that the husband of one Itasāni, a servant of Ganapatideva was the horse-man of the king.[18]

(b) Other General Occupations

During medieval times, professions are mostly caste oriented. The contemporary sources provide us with evidences of women's direct involvement in most of them. The village fairs and *tiṛunāḷḷu* held near the temples and pilgrim centres provided sufficient market ground for carrying out their economic activities. In addition, some of them are involved in selling their goods in the streets of the cities and towns. The contemporary literature provides abundant examples of women vendors. *Krīdābhirāmanu* refers to women of *Teliki* community whose traditional occupation is extraction of oil, selling hair oil made of *Saṁpeṅga* flowers (Michelia Champaka).[19] From the same work it can be gathered that few women sold herbal medicines and cosmetics for beautification in the *Maila-saṅta* (market for the out castes).[20] Women selling flowers are termed as *Pushpalāvikalu*.[21] Generally they sold flowers in the streets of the city during evening or twilight hours. At times they also ran shops to sell flowers.

In *Keyūrabāhucharitramu*, a *vaisya* girl is described as selling oil in exchange to rice in the shop.[22] Srinatha's *Cātu* verses refer to women running shops in the village fair to sell fruits like mangoes,[23] betel leaves,[24] bangles,[25] etc. Poor widows of brahman community stitched meal-plates with broad leaves and earned money by giving them in the houses of brahmans.[26] In addition inns and rest houses are run by poor and destitute women mostly of brahman community. *Krīdābhirāmamu* refers to *Pōotakūḷḷa illu* (inn) maintained by brahman widows where delicious food was offered at cheaper rate.[27] The work further refers to a rest house called *Tammaḍi sāni Maṅdiramu*.[28]

Women belonging to *Mēdara, Eṛuka, Cheṅchu*, *Sabara* communities too probably made monetary use of their craft skills. *Mēdara* women were experts in basket weaving.[29] *Eṛuka* women were proficient in future telling.[30] *Sabara* and *Cheṅchu* women probably earned their livelihood through selling tanned animal skins, combs, false hairs and other forest products.[31] Women of *Dommari* and *Goṛaga* classes were expert jugglers. *Krīdābhirāmamu* depicts them as performing gymnastic feats in the streets of Ōṛugallu.[32] They were very clever tumblers and tight rope dancers exhibiting their skills as they travel about. Some of them sold date mats, cane baskets and combs of horn and wood.[33] *Basavapurāṇamu* refers to a *golletha* (*Bōya woman*) selling milk, curd and butter in the streets.[34]

Literary and epigraphical sources refer to maids employed for domestic works like bringing water,[35] cooking,[36] etc. The elite class, concubines and wealthy courtesans are the employers for those maids. The maids of concubines and courtesans are supposed to acquire sufficient knowledge in fine arts and instrument playing.[37] *Basavapurāṇamu* mentions women in bonded labour.[38] Their occupation seems to be permanent for the family of the maid based on the term *Ilupuṭṭubānisa* found in *Paṇḍitārādhyacharitra*.[39] Large monastic establishments running residential schools, choultries attached to the temples too employed women for petty works like cleaning grains and vessels. An epigraph from Drākshārāmam registers a grant of 3 *kuṅchamulu* of rice, 1 *jīvita māḍa* and 3 *chinnālu* as salary for the two women employed for pounding rice grains, cleaning vessels and to bring water in the *Kuloṭṭuṅga Choḷa satramu* attached to the temple.[40] Another epigraph, also from the same place records grants of lands in lieu of salary to two women for pounding rice in the temple choultry.[41]

While these occupations are characterised by the direct involvement of women in earning money for the family, certain others like domestic service, rearing cattle, bringing up children, assisting their husbands in craft occupations and agricultural processes remained as supplementary roles as they are not recognised as works or paid jobs. Palkuriki Somanatha, in his *Basavapuṛāṇamu* gives a detailed description of how medieval women brought up their children, their care for the infants and concern about the general ailment of small children.[42] A mother's voice is considered important in deciding issues like marriages of children.[43]

Within the artisan tradition too women played a passive role in assisting their husbands in the preparatory processes. Their work is not a full time wage employment as production was not commercial. The woman worked in a joint endeavour with her husband. For example, if a potter turns the wheel and moulds the clay into shapes, his wife paints them and dries them.[44] Similarly in other fields like weaving,[45] dairy farming **(Plate II a, VIII b)**,[46] oil industry,[47] fishing **(Plate I b)**, nut processing,[48] and such other domestic craft occupations, women's subsidiary role went un-noticed and remained hidden. Thus, her contribution to the income of the family did not come to light.

Similar is the case of agricultural processes wherein a woman's contribution is inevitable at every stage of crop production. Planting of seeds, weeding of plants, husking and winnowing of paddy and such other sundry jobs were done entirely by women.[49] *Kumārasaṁbhavamu* contains a description of young and unmarried girls keeping a watch over the paddy fields to drive off the birds and other stray animals.[50] Literary works refer to women singing songs while engaged in agricultural activities such as pounding the grain.[51]

The occupations of family women are thus direct as well as indirect economic activities. In addition, midwifery and nursing, are the other professions taken up by women who are elderly and experienced. The Gōḷakimaṭha established by Viśveśvara Śiva Dēsika at Malkāpuram had one *Prasūtiśāla* (maternity home) attached to it. Though no other details are available in the grant, it can be assumed that women were probably working in the said maternity home as mid-wives and carrying out the duty of attending to child-birth.[52]

Women as *Bhōgastṛeelu* (Entertainment Maids)

All ancient works including Dharmasastras, mention a separate class of women working as entertainment maids. It was a part of the traditional culture of having women with a separate social status for the purpose of providing enjoyment to men. To this category are included the courtesans, concubines and the prostitutes. Their professions are recognised by law and are brought under its protection by framing rules of succession, maintenance and such other property rights, distinct from those of family women. Laws are also made for protecting them from the dangers of their profession.

In the medieval period, the increasing feudal character of the state necessitated the king to be more authoritative on local chiefs. The existence and stability of the kingdom depended on the king's exercise (exhibition) of right and might. He had to undertake wars for the purpose, assume titles, extend patronage to religious institutions, scholars and poets. Along with these, it became a regular practice to maintain a number of beautiful and talented women as courtesans in the courts or as concubines in the harems. The prowess of the king is reflected in the number of women in his harem, thus creating a great political significance to the institutions of courtesans and concubinage. Gradually the men of elite as well as common sections of the society too maintained women besides lawfully wedded wives. While courtesans and concubines of the king enjoyed higher social status and privileges, prostitutes could not claim so. Even the classical tradition depicts them as money minded. Thus it appears that there are three categories of entertainment maids, courtesans, concubines and prostitutes.

Courtesans

The appointment of a group of dancers in the king's court was a customary practice of the ancient and medieval times. Āndhradeśa too is no exception to this. They are referred to as *Vārāṅganalu*,[53] *Vāravilāsinulu*,[54] *Gaṇikalu*.[55] Vatsayana defines *Gaṇika* as a woman expertised in all 64 arts.[56] *Mānasollāsa* ordains that the

Ganikas along with women of royal family, dancers, priests and feudatories are to attend the king's assembly on special occasions.[57] The very presence of the courtesans brought gracefulness to the court. Ekamranatha mentions that there are as many as 8000 *Biṛudu Pātralu* (courtesans whose profession is to sing/dance in courts to the tunes in praise of the king) and 500 entertainment maids in the court of Prataparudra.[58] Though exaggerating, but th efigure indicates the popularity of the dancers in the courts of medieval period.

The contemporary literary sources indicate that every royal court had a contingent of courtesans whose *Nṛityagāna Vinōdamulu* is a daily routine in the court.[59] Girls proficient in fine arts were appointed for the purpose. Courtesans were one among the tributes paid by the feudatories to their overlord. Instances from *Siṁhāsanadvātriṁsika* refer to the vassals sending girls as part of their tributary payments offered to their lords.[60]

The courtesans lived in separate streets in the capital cities. Their houses were well furnished and beautifully decorated giving great appearance to the city itself. Literary and epigraphical references show that capital cities like *Vikramasiṁhapura*,[61] *Tsandavole*,[62] *Amarapuramu*,[63] were appearing graceful because of the beautiful houses of the courtesans. This is suggestive of the higher socio-economic status of these women. They were a class by themselves due to the nature of their profession. They received specialised training through teachers appointed for the purpose.[64] Their higher social status and greater economic independence is reflected in their patronising scholars, poets and involvement in religious services through gift making.

Concubinage

On the origin of this institution, N.Venkataramanayya says, "The existence of courtesans in large numbers in the courts of kings and nobles and those attached to temples must have fostered its growth and encouraged people to form irregular unions with members of this community without any social opprobrium".[65]

The kings maintained rich, learned women and those skilled in fine arts as their concubines in the harem. They are variously referred to as *Bhōgastrēelu*,[66] *Bhōgamahishi*,[67] *Lañjapeṇḍlamu*,[68] *Lanjiya*,[69] *Vārakanta*,[70] etc. No social stigma is attached to this practice. Even the kings and nobles patronising concubines took pride in assuming such titles as *Vāranāri manōrañjana*,[71] *Rāya vesyābhujaṁga*,[72] *Vāranāriyauvana Vasaṁthudu*,[73] *Kāminījana Manōvallabha*,[74] etc. as indicated in the contemporary epigraphs. A Telugu Choḍa chief from Cuddapah region claimed that he was *Vilāsavibhavabhōgapuraṅdara*, and *Chāturvidha Kāminī - janaratīśvara*.[75] Another record from Drākshārāmam gives the epithet of the king as *Vāravanitājana Chitta Bhavudu*.[76] This gives support to the argument that patronising concubines is considered as a status symbol of royalty during the period. This practice of the kings is followed even by petty ruling chiefs and nobles.

The harlots lived in separate localities called *Āryavāṭikas*. Their houses were beautifully decorated with paintings, ornate furniture, soft beds, decorated foams, comfortable chairs, large mirrors and painting halls. They dressed themselves in the most elegant manner.[77] Patronising scholars, poets, painters, musicians, holding literary assemblies, contributing to the state's development through their munificent grants to religious and charitable institutions were part of their regular activities.[78] Prataparudra's concubine Māchaldevi was a famous woman. She commanded a great respect in the society and was described as *Pratāparudra dharaṇisopatta Gōshtipratishta Pāriṇa*.[79] Kota Keta's concubines gave grants to Buddhadeva at Amarāvati.[80] The concubines of the kings took no hesitation to call themselves the *Bhōgastṛeelu* of the ruling chiefs. Even their children who were generally appointed in the royal service claimed identity through them. The donees of Gaṅjam plates of Gōkarṇa and Māturа grant of Nārāyaṇa claimed themselves as *Veśya Vamsodhbhava*.[81] The concubines demanded money in the form of *Uṅkuva*, while their men participated in the wars. It is quoted in *Palnāṭi Vīracharitra* that Syāmāṅgi, the concubine of Bālachandra (son of Brahmanayudu) demanded a silk saree and Rs.12,000 as *unkuva* at the time of his leaving for the war field.[82] She claimed that the amount was charged as she had to accompany him to the heaven as *velayalu*.[83] *Unkuva* forms a part of *stridhana*, a woman's property.[84]

Despite their economic stability and social security in royal courts as courtesans and concubines, there was a need for their legal security and protection. Dharmasastras provide maintenance allowance for the concubines of the deceased besides recognising their sons as illegitimate heirs to the parental property.[85] They also made strict regulations to check the irregularities of the practice. Yājñavalkya prescribes a fine of 50 *panas* against a person cohabiting with the concubine of another.[86] Generally patronised by the men of elite section as part of their privileges, these concubines enjoyed a higher socio-economic status whereas prostitution differs from this in its operational manner.

Prostitution

Commonly referred to as *Veśya, Vārāṅgana, Velayālu, Laṅjiya,* these women constitute a professional group by themselves. At times there is no clear distinction between a concubine and a girl who practices prostitution as a profession. They trace their origin from the heavenly nymphs called *Apsaras*.[87] Not a single procession whether of political, social, religious or of festive significance advanced without the programmes by the girls of this group.[88] Raṅganātha Rāmāyaṇamu refers to a *Gaṅikānikāyamu* (an association of *Gaṇikas*) on the occasion of the marriage of Lord Rāma with Sitā.[89]

Women following the profession lived in separate localities of the cities called *veśyavāṭikas*. The Thousand pillar temple inscription of Hanumakonda describes one such *vesyavatika* of Ōṛugallu.[90] A similar account is given in the literary work, *Krīdābhirāmamu*.[91] *Pratāparudracharitra*, quotes that there were about 1,27,000 houses of *veśyas* in Ōṛugallu.[92] The figure seemed to be too high, but, at the same time is suggestive of the wide spread nature of the profession. Contemporary poets described prostitutes of the temple city of Drākshārāmam in their works.[93]

The material prosperity achieved through stabilised feudal political relations during Kakatiya rule in Āndhradeśa could have given rise to the amorous nature of the class of elite. The rulers and their officers needed company of women even during times of war to provide them with relief through their programmes of music/dance and to give them strength and relaxation of the mind. Common men too followed suit. The Saivite movement recognizing the *Paṅchamakāras* as forms of devotion to God, accorded a sort of religious legitimation to this practice.[94] Saivite scriptures identified one's sexual pleasure as that belonging to the Lord, it being one form of devotion of God.[95] *Basavapurāṇamu* reflects that Basaveśvara, used to send presents, delicious food preparations to the Saivite priests who spend their whole day in the company of prostitutes.[96] From the various sources we gather that there were about 12,000 such priests who were referred to as *Miṅḍa Jaṅgamas*.[97] The large number only indicates the wide religious sanction by the sect to prostitution.

From the very young age a harlot is trained properly, the syllabi of which is designed in such a way as to make her occupation profitable. In addition, they are supposed to eat little, observe vows for prosperity, learn tricks to deceive men and earn more money.[98] The most important guide and mentor for a harlot is her mother. The *veśyamātha* teaches her daughter that money, costly garments and precious ornaments are compulsory for women following this profession.[99] She trains her daughter to be specific regarding matters of money and makes efforts to prevent her from being carried away by the promises of *Magalaṅjiyalu* (men who try to save money through deceiving the innocent prostitutes), or by religious sentiments.[100] She keeps guard over her daughter and protects her from unpecunious customers.

However, the practices of the mothers of the girls are not held in esteem by many of the contemporary poets. They highlighted the greediness of the *Veśyamātha* with great contempt. This shows their male bias as they have not reflected the fear and foresight of the mother for the security of her daughter based on the age bound and temporary nature of their profession. They do not have any other occupation except utilising their youthfullness for earning their livelihood. Once they cross their youth, their plight becomes miserable. Moreover, in the continuous expansion of the institution they have to face competition in their profession from the youngsters. A girl has to accumulate profits to the maximum extent possible during this period of her life. Having realised this need, the *veśyamātha* guides her daughter to be particular in demanding money from the customers. This is evident from the story of *Chatuṛika*, in *Kēyūrąbāhucharitramu*, who very cleverly organised her profession and earned money.[101] *Daśakumāra charitra* mentions *Kuṅṭineelu* probably women brokers.[102] The fee collected from the customer is referred to as *Rōyi*. It can either be in cash or kind. As long as the contract for which *Rōyi* was paid holds good, the girl can not entertain any other person.[103] Generally the amount of *Rōyi* depends on the demands of the girl. *Krīdābhirāmamu* quotes one *Kaṛnāṭi veśya* demanding *satīhātakanishkamu* (one sari and some amount of gold) and another *veśya* asking for two *sonnāṭaṅkamulu* (two gold coins).[104] Sometimes their demands were so high that a person had to mortgage landed property.[105] *Paṅḍitārādhyacharitra* contains another practice called *Vāḍapottu* wherein men of a particular street enter into a specific contract with a harlot as regards the person who should visit her. The girl was thus maintained by the men of that street.[106]

The dangers of the profession and its temporariness lead the prostitutes going for unfair means of earning money. *Krīḍābhirāmamu* refers to a *veśyamātha* sending her daughter to another person after collecting fee from a person. The maid of the girl was asked to entertain the latter. For controlling such practices the state appointed officers and a separate court was established for the purpose, which is referred to as *Jāradharmāsanamu*.[107] The Koṛavi inscription and *Vijñaneśvaramu* of Ketana mention laws made by the state to punish greedy mothers of the harlots and to control their unfair practices of earning money.[108] Generally a specific amount of fine is levied on the accused together with such punishments as cutting the nose, ears or shaving the head.[109] At the same time laws are also made to protect women from the evil attempts of men. It is declared that for women of this class having sex with men is not a sin.[110] A customer who promises to pay the amount to a *veśya* but fails to comply with is penalised with double the amount to be paid to her and an equal amount as penalty to the king.[111] Similarly, for impersonification, one gold *masaka* is to be paid.[112] Fines are also imposed for causing physical injury to the girls.[113] Thus, the protection offered is dual, protection of prostitutes against exploitation by customers and society and protection of the public from the treacherous or dubious nature or the prostitutes.

The contemporary literature provides instances of certain *veśyas* religiously inclined towards Saivism. They took *Dīksha* from *Jaṅgama* priests and dedicated the whole of their life in their service, not entertaining any other customer. Such girls were respected and accorded motherly treatment from the disciples of the priests, who gave them initiation.[114] Through references in the literary works of the period it appears that courtesans and concubines of elite men enjoyed recognition in the society whereas prostitutes had to struggle hard to earn money. Moreover, the state collected a tax on the mirrors used by the girls of this community.[115]

Women in Temple Service

By medieval times, the temple achieved great institutional status linking itself closely with the rise of devotional sects. It became a principal site for sect activity. The temples are provided with support and protection by the ruling warrior groups.[116] This involved a diverse body of functionaries with substantial pilgrim participation. In turn the temple culture firmly established the agrarian feudal order. The rise of devotional bhakti literature of the times too is suggestive of the new feudal class relationships and the corresponding ideology. The deity in the temple is equated with the king and a parallel world of authority is reconstructed on the spiritual plane. Ritual worship in the temple is conceived on the same lines of ritual services offered to the king. Thus, attempts are made to authenticate and legitimise the new feudal polity of the period through a parallelism between the deity and the king.[117]

Since, the temple and God are homologised with royal court and king respectively, the *dēvasthāna* maintained the same bureaucracy as that of the *Rājasthāna*. This aspect gains further support from the inscriptional references indicating interchangeability of women in temple service with those of the king's court. An inscription from Srikalahasthi temple registers orders of a king transferring a dancing girl and her descendants from his service to the temple.[118] Another record from Mukhalingam temple mentions that Vāsama, the *Guḍisāni* of Madhukisvara temple was also the *Lañjiya* of Doḍḍapanāyaka, an officer of the Velanāḍuchoḍa king Rajendra Choḍa.[119] This interchangeability can be understood in terms of the ritual exchange of honours between the king, his officers and the temple in the feudal political background.

The God and the king had to follow elaborate rituals before they start their routine. The temple rituals are of two types – *Aṅgabhōga* (the general worship services) and *Raṅgabhōga* (the ritual services specially in the *Raṅgamaṇṭapa* built for the purpose daily or on festive occasions). Women are employed in both categories, however, in large numbers in the latter.

Big temples of the period in Āndhradeśa like Pālakolanu, Chēbṛolu, Drākshārāmam, Siṁhāchalam maintained as many as 300 to 500 temple girls. They are generally donated by the kings, vassals or their generals. 30 daughters from the *Nāyaka* families of Kaliṅga maṇḍala were donated to the temple at Mukhaliṅgam by an officer of Eastern Gaṅgas to execute various deeds specified in the record.[120] General Jāyapa donated 300 girls of the age of 8 years to the temple at Chēbṛolu.[121] Another record indicates the donation of a girl called Bhaṅdramu Akkama as *sāni* to the temple at Velpūṛu by Ganapatidevaraja, son of Kōṭa Bayyaladevi. Lands and gardens were also donated by him as *vṛitti* to her.[122]

Sometimes girls are brought from different places of the country and are given employment in the temple as in the case of the Viśveśvara temple at Malkāpuram where the singers were brought from Kashmir.[123] Apart from these, it is also observed that many women enter into temple service for employment probably for the sake of the shares in temple property and a portion of *prasādamu* of the deity offered to them in lieu of their services in the temple. A merchant at Elēśvaram donated his two grand daughters to the temple.[124]

The temple girls are commonly termed as *Sānulu*, *Sāni Saṁpradāyamuvāru*, *Guḍisānulu* or sometimes indicating the numerical status as *Munnūṭi Sānulu, Pedamunnūṭi Sānulu, Sāni Munnūru*, etc.[125] The term does not indicate any caste status, though an inscription from Simhachalam relates them to the sudra caste.[126] *Pātra* is another term used generally to denote the dancing girls of the temple.[127] *Dvādasa Sēva Vilāsini* refers to women performing 12 prescribed duties.[128] The various services into which temple girls are recruited and details of their payment are shown in the Chart IV.

It appears that women temple employees performed a variety of functions in the temple both of *Aṅgabhōga* and *Raṅgabhōga* services. They are paid generally in kind, with a share in the temple property, a part of the *prasāda* offered to the deity. Occasionally they are paid in cash. Sometimes the donors specify the manner of enjoying share in the temple lands by the temple girls and deposit certain money in the temple treasury for their maintenance. Further it is seen that most of the lady temple professionals of the temple appear to be married. But certain services of *Raṅgabhōga* needed elaborate and intensive training from childhood, through a dance master, for which purpose, they are generally dedicated to the temple service unmarried and young.[129]

After passing through a prescribed test conducted on completion of training, they are inducted into actual service which involved singing and dancing on particular occasions of worship both in the morning and night and performing special programmes on festival days.[130] The professional and marital status of the temple girls is generally reflected in the grants given by their relatives, father, husband or sons claiming matronymic identity.[131]

Due to their continuous service requirements at the temple for most part of the day, these temple women are provided with quarters in the vicinity of the temple. The locality is termed *Sānivāḍa*.[132] Epigraphical references indicate that temples like Srīkūrmam, Kollūṛu, Nādiṅḍla, Juttiga, Ghaṅṭasāla, Chēbṛōlu had separate quarters built for the temple dancing girls.[133] Chēbṛōlu inscription of general Jāyapa records construction of two rows of double storeyed buildings for 16 lady temple attendants.[134] Pillalamaṛṛi inscription of Rēcheṛla chief Nāmireḍḍi records construction of houses to temple girls in the fort of Pillalamaṛṛi where the temple of Eṛakeśvara was constructed by him.[135]

It is further observed that the services of these temple girls are hereditary.[136] They enjoyed a higher socio-economic status as revealed through their grants, which included not only cash or kind but immovable property too. Their sons are generally appointed in the royal service. The two sons of Sokkama, the *naṛtaki* of Paṅḍīśvara temple were in the service of the king Goṅka II and her daughter Kāmidevi was one of the queens of the king.[137] Similarly, the son of sāni Bayyāṁbika, of the same temple was in the service of the king Goṅka II.[138]

The expansion of temple building activity, the presence of temple girls in large numbers in most of the temples together with their higher socio-ritual status necessitated an organisational operation for them. They formed into a professional guild called *Sānula Samayamu* or *Sāni Munnūṛu* which was found in every big temple of Āndhradeśa. The different activities of the guild are shown through Chart V.

These include, maintaining temple properties, supervising the grants or other endowments of the temple, mobilising temple resources (through leasing out the lands, animals, etc.) in addition to determining the rules and procedural aspects of the services of the temple girls who were members of the guild.[139] Gradually, their association became a part of the temple administrative functionaries of the higher-rank referred to as *Mānulu* and figured in most of the matters relating to the appropriation of temple property.[140]

Thus we can say that the involvement of women in economic activities was more prominent in medieval Āndhra. Ketana's *Vijñaneśvaramu,* the legal digest of the period giving permission for women to enter into contracts with the prior consent of their husbands is worth mentioning in this connection.[141] Moreover, contemporary epigraphs contain ample references to the involvement of women in gift making as part of their attempt to gain religious merit.

Can this be taken to mean the economic independence of women? It is doubtful, as Dharmasastras, quote that the wages earned by a woman on her own exertion are not included in her property but they become part of the joint property of the family. However, they have provided for certain rights to women on property both inherited and acquired in the form of gifts given to them on specific occasions such as marriage. Therefore, to understand the extent of economic independence enjoyed by women more clearly, it becomes necessary first to study the rights on property allowed to them by tradition and to understand a woman's domain on the same.

Property Rights

The evolution of women's property rights has witnessed several stages. Initially, a woman is regarded as an item in the movable property of her husband and is along with sons, slaves considered as money less.[142] They were given away as gifts to the priests in lieu of their services or sold as slaves to clear the debts made by their husbands.[143] By the first century of Christian era, the Dharmasastra writers made it very clear that wife and children are not to be tendered as objects of gifts or sale under any circumstances.[144] Āpasthaṁbha's theory of wife and husband as the joint owners of the family property secured minor rights for a wife but they were conditional as she had no right to spend money or incur normal expenditure even on household without the consent of her husband.[145] Among the other Smṛti writers, Yājñavalkya came forward with more liberalised principles regarding property rights of women. *Mitākshara*, a medieval digest on the same further enlarged the scope of women's right over property.

There are two sources of property for women, inheritance and acquired (*strīdhana*). Inheritance can be the property that is inherited by a woman as an heir to the parental property. Different views are expressed by the legal text writers on this issue. From Manu, it is known that a daughter cannot become an heir to the paternal property under normal circumstances.[146] She can become so only when she is duly appointed by her father in the absence of male issue with a view to beget a son through her, who shall take on to the estate of his grand father besides offering funeral cake to him. Such an appointed daughter is called *Putṛika*.[147]

Mitākshara, on the contrary, gives a different picture on this issue. It says that the property shall pass on to the successors depending on their relationship with the owner of the property. They are of two categories – those who get share through *Apṛatibandha dāya* (sons, grand sons, great grandsons … who are presumed as coparcenors to one's property by birth) and those who get their share through *Sapṛatibandha dāya* (wife, daughter and such others who become owners of the property only after the death of the owner.[148] Thus, in the absence of male heirs, the wife (widow) becomes the first heir. Next to her in order of succession are, daughter, mother, father, brothers, their sons or persons of the same *gōṭra*, disciples, co-students in the respective order.[149] It is here that a great change is brought by Vijñāneśvara by making widow as the first heir of her sonless deceased husband's property, provided she be pious, chaste and religious minded.[150] It appears that the laws of *Mitākshara* were closely followed in Āndhradeśa, as the same is translated into Telugu by Ketaṇa as *Vijñāneśvaramu* which formed the basic source of law during Kakatiya period.

Both Manu and Vijñāneśvara converge on the issue of daughter's nomination as natural heir, providing maintenance allowance to the widow of the deceased to the extent that her share in the property shall be equal to that of the sons' and setting 1/4th of each son's share towards marriage expenses of unmarried daughters.[151]

One of the Mukhalingam temple inscriptions refers to the distribution of property of a deceased *desi* trader among his heirs. The widow was provided maintenance allowance and some amount was set apart for the marriage expenses of unmarried daughters.[152]

Mitākshara further states that the ownership of a woman on such property is complete in all respects whether the heir belonged to *Apṛatibandha* or *Sapṛatibandha* category. In other words, the holder of the property had the rights of *Dāna* (giving in charity), *Damana* (overpowering-destruction), *Bhōga* (enjoying), *Vinimaya* (consuming), and *Vikṛaya* (selling).[153] Questioning Manu's theory of dependence of a woman on man at every stage of her life, Vijñāneśvara states that she may be dependent on her male counterpart due to her weak physical nature, but that should not fall in the way of her economic independence or her claims to parental property of what so ever kind.[154] In the case of the community of temple dancing girls and those women whose profession is prostitution, daughters become the *Apratibandha dāya* holders (natural heirs) and succession is in the female line. Sons become *Sapratibandha dāya* holders.[155] Concubinage too is brought under the cover of law as discussed earlier.

Besides property obtained through inheritance, women also acquire property through various means. The origin to the acquisition of property by women can be traced to Vēdic times. The wedding hymns of *Rgvēda* indicate that gifts are to be sent to the bridegroom's house with the bride and over such articles the wife is the mistress.[156] Ornaments, costly dresses and household articles constitute those and they are generally kept under the control of women. Gradually, such kinds of property went on increasing in extent and value necessitating the early jurors to be specific on the claims on such property, which is otherwise called *Strīdhana*.

Manu defines *Strīdhana* as the six folded property of a woman obtained through gifts before the *nuptial* fire on the bridal procession, what was given in token of love, and what was received from her brother, mother or father.[157] This concept is elaborated greatly by the jurors Yajñavalkya and Kātyāyana,[158] *Mitākshara*, accepting these earlier definitions of *strīdhana* included property received through inheritance, gifts given by husband out of love, the amount due to her at the time of his second marriage superseding her and the property acquired through general methods of earning such as *Ṛikhta* (inheritance), *Kraya* (purchase), *Saṁvibhāga* (partition), *parigraha* (chance) and *Adhigama* (adverse possessions). The bride price (*ōli* or *sulka*), *uṅkuva* and *Aranamu* too are included under woman's property.[159] The evidences from Dharmasastras are supported by plenty of contemporary literary and epigraphical sources.

An epigraph dated A.D. 1255 recorded a gift of a land containing *Pōka* trees as *strīdhana* by Achanta Sūraparāju to his daughter. This *strīdhana* is referred to in the grant as *Araṇamu*.[160] The Bayyāram, Niḍigoṅḍa and Kuṅdavaram inscriptions refer to the villages Bayyāram, Niḍigoṅda and Kuṅdavaram as *araṇamu* lands given to the donors Mailama and Kuṅdama at the time of their marriage with Natavāḍi chief Rudra.[161] *Palnāti Vīracharitra*, refers to *araṇamu* on many occasions. At the time of the marriage of Mahadevarāju, a Haihaya chief of Palnad, the bride's father gave several cows and many bōya servants as *araṇamu* to the bride.[162] On the occasion of Mailama's marriage with Anugurāju, her father, the Velanāḍu chief Goṅka gave *Palanātisīma* as *araṇamu*.[163] Similarly, Anugurāju's son Mallarāju was married to Kālāchūri princess Sirādevi who brought 1000 cows, 1000 sheep and the necessary bōya attendants as *araṇamu* along with her.[164] Nannechoḍa, in his *Kumārasaṁbhavamu*, mentions that Parvati's father gave several valuable presents to her in lieu of her marriage with Lord Śiva.[165] *Raṅganātha Rāmāyaṇamu* also has a reference to *aṛaṇamu* paid to Sitā by her father in lieu of her marriage with Lord Rāma.[166]

Ōli, Uṅkuva are the other terms found in the contemporary literary sources as well as in the epigraphs. These correspond to the *Sulka* or the bride-price which is included under *strīdhana* by the legal writers. However, it appears that the demand seemed to be very high from the parents of the girls. Because of this, the caste associations decided the amount of *Ōli* to be paid to the bride's father. An epigraph from Malleśvara temple, Vijayawada records one such arrangement made by the *Telikivēvuru* of the regions of Koṅdavīḍu, Koṅḍapalli and Rājamahēndravaramu. It is decided that for the first marriage, the *Ōli* should be 21 *chinnamāḍalu* (gold coins) and certain amount of silver.[167] *Palnāṭi Vīracharitra* also has a reference to this practice. At the time of Balachandra's marriage with Manchala, the bride's mother demanded huge sums of money towards *ōli*.[168] *Uṅkuva* too finds frequent mention in the contemporary literary works.[169] Generally, it is the amount paid by the groom to the bride or her parents at the time of marriage.[170] However, the use of the term is often associated with the business of prostitution in terms of the money paid to the mother of the girl.[171]

The treatises on Dharmasastras and moral literature not only dealt with the property rights and possessions of women but laid some restraints and limitations on their appropriation. For the sake of deciding the dominion of a woman on her *stṛīdhana*, the property received by her is divided into two categories based on its source (a) *Saudāyika* that which is received by a woman whether as a maiden or as a married woman, form her parents or husband and over which she had complete control and (b) *Non-saudāyika*, the property received by all other means. On this she has only the right to enjoy.[172] A maiden is free to dispose of *Saudāyika* as well as *non-saudāyika* property at her pleasure.[173] A widow too can dispose of every kind of *strīdhana* including movable property but not immovable.[174] However, she can alienate a portion of immovable property towards religious purposes or for *śraddha* rituals for her husband.[175] A married woman, if her husband is alive can dispose of at her pleasure only *Saudāyika* property.[176] The husband's rights on *strīdhana* also are determined by this division. The *non-saudāyika* property is subject to husband's dominion during his life and may be taken by him even when there is no distress.[177] If, however, the property is of *saudāyika* category, he has no domain except under certain circumstances of distress, disease, famine or religious purposes.[178] For all other purposes he is liable to return the same. No other person has any right to use it under distress or otherwise.[179] If he takes away the ornaments by force, he is liable to be punished in the courts.[180]

The succession to *strīdhana* again varies according to the marital status of a woman and the form of marriage. Generally, *strīdhana* devolves in the line of females only.[181] The order of succession to *strīdhana* except for *Sulka* and maiden's property is :

(1) unmarried daughter,

(2) married daughter who is indigent,

(3) married daughter who is well provided for,

(4) grand daughters through daughter,

(5) daughter's son,

(6) sons,

(7) son's sons,

(8) husband (in approved form of marriage), and

(9) *sapiṇḍas* of husband[182]

The paternal gifts given to the deceased women can be claimed by the husband in the event of failure of daughters provided the marriage is one of the approved forms.[183] Nādiṇḍla inscription records an interesting issue of parent's claims on a married woman's property after her death and reasserts the husband's right on the same.[184] Guilds like *Teliki Samayamu* as in the above instance decide such issues. However, if the marriage is not approved by the legal traditions, the property claims can be made by the parents.[185] The *Sulka* and maiden's property has a separate course. Maiden's property generally devolves on brothers and parents. *Sulka* (bride-price, *oli*) too can be claimed by the brothers or parents and the husband has no dominion on the same.[186]

Thus, a considerable regard is shown to the economic needs of women. Though Vijñāneśvara did not intend to give women, the full rights of disposal over the immovable property, both inherited and acquired, they are to a limited extent economically independent as revealed from the extensive inscriptional evidences registering grants by women of all classes of the society. We even have few instances of the purchase of lands by women paying suitable price and donating the same to the deities. A record from Nilakaṇṭeśvara temple, Nārāyaṇapuram registers grant of a piece of wet land to the temple by Nāgava, a *Sānikāpu* woman.[187] It is mentioned in the record that she bought the same by paying a suitable price. Another record refers to the purchase of land by one Komaṛasāni, though details are not given.[188] An epigraph mentions that a couple obtained sale deed of a piece of land on which both their names are written as partners of the property.[189]

As the purpose is religious for which both husband and wife enjoy equal status, it is very difficult to arrive at the economic independence of women. The case of temple girls too can not be viewed in isolation to the temple and their economic independence is always related to their status in the temple and their conditions of service. In this connection, the observation of Dhrama Kumar is worth mentioning, "In the medieval period there existed no legitimate private property rights worth the name as the king reserved the right of eviction of land for certain reason".[190] Thus, even the male coparcenors had no unrestricted right over their self acquired property.

Thus, it is evident that women in medieval Andhra society maintained their space in practicing professions and acquired legal protection against exploitation at different levels in the society. In a Dharmic society like India, where a happy culmination of public and private domains of men and women respectively is aimed at for a happy family life, though the roles are gender specific, interchangeability of roles in terms of professions is not an unseen process atleast in the case of women belonging to weak sections of the society.

This provision of women's space in professions and property rights is further strengthened by the changes and social perceptions of men and women which demanded a change in the syllabi of education to suit the contemporary socio-political needs.

REFERENCES

1. Monika Vonder Meden and Kathee Myers, 'The Hidden Talent, Women Creators and Inventors' in *Women's World*, No. 10, (US June, 1986), pp. 5-8.
2. Buhler, *Laws of Manu*, VII, verse 219.
3. *Ibid.*
4. Sōmeśvaradeva, *Mānasōllāsa*, (Trans.) S. Visvanathasarma, (Hyderabad, 1961), 3rd canto, Chapters, 1,4, 13, verses 956, 958, 993, 1529, 1530 and 1531.
5. Jāyapa Sēnani, *Nṛittaratnākaramu,* translation by Rallapalli Ananta Krishna Sarma, (Hyderabad, 1969), Chapter VIII.
6. We find references to wet nurses in the literary works of the period like *Kēyūrabāhucharitramu, Siṁhāsanadvātṛmsika, Kumāra saṁbhavamu*, etc. They are supposed to maintain the secrecy of the personal matters of king. Generally they were treated with much respect and their children were appointed in important posts

of administration. In the epigraph they figured as donors of lands. Devakabbe, the wet nurse of Iṛivebeḍeṅga granted 70 Ḍṛammas and land at Choppadaṅḍu, wherein a tank was constructed. (*IAP : KD*, No. 8).

7. *Mānasōllāsa*, Chapters, 1,4, 13.
8. *SII*, Vol. IV, No. 1249.
9. *Ibid.*, Vol. VI, No. 240.
10. *Ibid.*, No. 178.
11. *Pratāparudracharitra*, p. 46.
12. A.S. Altekar, *The Position of Women in Hindu Civilisation*, (Delhi, 1962), p. 180.
13. Jyotsna K. Kamath, *Social Life in Medieval Karnataka*, (Delhi, 1980), p. 119.
14. Tikkana, *Andhra Mahābhāratamu*, (Virata, Udyoga Parvamulu), (ed.), K. Laxmi Ranjanam and Divakarla Venkatavadhani, (Hyderabad, 1970), Ist canto, verses 289-335 give a detailed description of the responsibilities of the post of *Sairaṅdhri*.
15. K. Chengalraya Chetti, *Āndhradeśa Sāṅghika Āaṛdhika Charitra*, (A.D. 1300-1600), (Tirupati, 1991), p. 198.
16. Ambati Subbaraya Chetti, 'Kakatīyulanāti Saṁghika Charitra' in *Kakatiya Samchika*, (Hyderabad, Reprint, 1992), pp. 141-149.
17. A.R. 484 of 1913.
18. A.R. 558 of 1925.
19. *Krīdābhirāmamu,* verse 102.
20. *Ibid.*, verse 77.
21. *Ibid.*, verse 173, also Nannechoda, *Kumārasaṁbhavamu*, (ed.), Korada Mahadeva Sastri, (Hyderabad, 1987), 8th canto, verse 122.
22. *Kēyūrabāhucharitramu*, 2nd canto, verses 11-15.
23. Veturi Prabhakara Sastri, (ed.), *Cātu Padya Maṇimañjari*, (Hyderabad, 1988), verse 314, p. 134.
24. *Ibid.*, verse 313, p. 134.
25. *Ibid.*, verse 353, p. 144.
26. *Ibid.*, verse 325, p. 136.
27. *Krīḍabhirāmamu*, verses 161-166. The details of the food preparations are given in verse 166.
28. *Ibid.*, verse 273.
29. *Ibid.*, verses 68-69.
30. K. Chengalraya Chetti, *Op. cit.*, 1991, p. 65.
31. Palkuriki Somanatha, *Sri Paṅḍitārādhyacharitra*, (ed.), Chilukuri Narayana Rao, (Madras, 1939), Paṛvata Prakaranamu, Jōgula Naḍakalu, pp. 235-236.
32. *Krīdābhirāmamu*, verses 143-144. The woman belonging to Goṛaga caste was able to take out the nose-ring put in a tub of water with her nose and with her back facing the tub. Simialrly, she was able to string the black beads into a chain within no time.
33. Edgar Thurston and K. Rangachari, (ed.), *Castes and Tribes of Southern India*, Vol. II, (Madras, 1987), pp. 185-190.

34. Palkuriki Somanatha, *Basavapurāṇamu*, (ed.), Nidadavolu Venkat Rao, (Madras, 1952), 2nd canto, pp. 41-42.
35. *Ibid.*, 4th canto, Nimmavva Katha, pp. 103-105.
36. *Ibid.*, Siriyāḷuni Katha, pp. 100-102.
37. *Ibid.*, 3rd canto, Mugdhya Sangayya Katha, pp. 50-53. The harlot asks her maids to bring various musical instruments and to play different tunes together with singing and dancing to entertain the devotee of Śiva, who came to her house.
38. *Ibid.*, 4th canto, Piṭṭavva Katha, p. 115. Also 3rd canto, Nāṭyanamittaṅḍi Katha, p.66.
39. *Paṅditārādhyacharitra,* Purātana Prakaraṇamu, Gurubhaktāṅḍāri Katha, pp. 78-83.
40. *SII*, Vol. IV, No. 1015.
41. *Ibid.*, No. 1288.
42. *Basavapurāṇamu*, 3rd canto, Bejjamahādevi Katha, pp. 58-61. There is a detailed description of the way in which small children were given bath, the procedure for feeding them and steps to be taken to prevent the general ailments like indigestion, cold, etc.
43. *Ibid.*, Also see Nannaya, *Āndhra Mahābhārtamu*, Ādipaṛvamu, 8th canto, verse 254. At the time of the marriage of Draupadi, importance was given to the mother's voice which was equated by the poet to that of *Vidhāta* (creator). A similar opinion was conveyed through *Kumāra Saṁbhavamu* also at the time of the marriage of Parvati.
44. Papul Jayakar, 'Handi Crafts' in Tara Ali Baig, *Women of India*, (Delhi, 1958), pp. 212-220.
45. *Catu Padya Maṇimañjari*, verse 31 pp. 139-140.
46. K. Radhakrishna Murthy, *The Economic Conditions of Medieval Āndhradeśa,* (Tirupati, 1987), pp. 131-132. The idea is also based on few sculptures depicting women feeding animals, milching cows and churning curds, available from the temples of Srisailam & Tirupati.
47. *Krīdābhirāmamu,* verses 102-103 contain the description of a Teliki woman moving along the mortar probably while pressing the oil.
48. Though there are no exact references for the involvement of women either directly or indirectly in this industry, we can presume that women played their part in cleaning the nuts and processing them. Because, we find plenty of references in the inscriptions of the period to the gardens of *Poka* trees (areca nut) and thus it could be one of the popular occupations of the period.
49. Generally, these works are associated with the beliefs in the fertility cult prevalent among the village people and was reflected in the songs sung by them. And therefore, they are performed only by women (An interview with Dr. Nayani Krishnakumari).
50. *Kumārasaṁbhavamu,* 7th canto, verse 92.
51. These songs are commonly called as *Taṛuvōja*, Arudra, *Sc nagra Āndhra Sāhityam*, Vol. I, (Madras, 1977), p. 77.

52. *SII*, Vol. X, No. 395. It is quite possible that Śaivism, during its process of propagation into the common sections of the society, opened up maternity homes for their help and could have recruited women as midwives for providing assistance during the course of delivery. However, this assumption can not be proved as there are no evidences for the same in the contemporary inscriptions or literary sources.
53. *Pratāparudracharitra*, p. 47.
54. Maineni Krishnakumari, 'Rājarāja Devendravarmuni Yudhapura Tāmrasāsanamu', *Bharati* (Jan, 1986), pp. 30-33.
55. *Kēyūrabāhucharitramu*, Ist canto, verse 57.
56. Vatsyana, *Kāmasutra,* I. 3.20,quoted in P.V. Kane, *History of Dharamasastra*, Vol. III,1974, p. 639.
57. Someśvaradeva, *Mānasōllāsa*, I p. 155, verses 3-5, quoted from Jyostna K. Kamat, *Op. cit.*, 1980, pp. 115-116.
58. *Pratāparuḍracharitra*, p. 45.
59. *Ibid.*, p. 47.
60. Koravi Goparaju, *Simhāsanadvatṛmsika*, (ed.), Gadiyaram Ramakrishna Sarma, (Hyderabad, 1982), 2nd canto, verse 131 and 11th canto, verse 172.
61. Ketana, *Daśakumāracharitra*, (ed.), Kandukuri Viresalingam, (Madras, 1975) Ist canto, verse 11.
62. *Ķeyūrabāhucharitramu*, Ist canto, verse 18.
63. Maineni Krishna Kumari, *Op. cit.*, pp. 30-33.
64. P. see Chapter '5' for more details.
65. Nelaturi Venkataramanayya, *The Eastern Chalukyas of Vengi*, (Madras, 1950), p. 287.
66. *SII*, Vol. V, No. 290-252.
67. *Ibid.*, Vol. VI, No. 55.
68. *Ibid.*, Vol. V, Nos. 249.
69. *Ibid.*, Vol. VI, Nos. 1083 1090.
70. *Ibid.*, No.210.
71. *Ibid.*, Vol. X, No. 258.
72. *Ibid.*
73. *HAS*, Vol. XIII, Vardhamānapura Inscription of Malyala Gunḍadanḍādhisa.
74. *SII*, Vol. X, No. 258.
75. *IAP : CD*, (Hyderabad, 1977), No. 159, pp. 241-248.
76. *SII*, Vol. IV No. 1039.
77. *Kridābhirāmamu* depicts the description of the house of Machaldevi, the concubine of Prataparudra II in verses 183, 187, 191, 192, 193 (pp. 50-55).
78. *SII*, Vol. VI, No. 669 refers to Viramba, *Prēyasi* of king Nṛisimha donating a kitchen to the temple at Panchadhārala.
79. *Krīḍābhirāmamu*, verse 180.

80. *Epigraphia Indica*, Vol. VI, No. 15A.
81. *AR*, 1952-53 (1958), No. 7.
82. *Palnāti Vīracharitra*, pp. 341-344.
83. *Ibid*., p. 341.
84. *Uṅkuva* is another term for *Sulkamu* or the bride-price. Also referred to as *Oli* in certain circumstances. It is the money given by the bride-groom to the parents of the bride. It is a part of *Strīdhana* in the sense of *Sulkamu*. (*Saṁgrahāṅdhra Vijñāna Kosamu*, pp. 174-179). We find references to this term in the other literary texts of the period like *Kumārasaṁbhavamu*, 7th canto, verse 136, *Daśakumāracharitramu*, 6th canto, verse 51, *Raṅganātha Rāmāyaṇamu*, Bālakaṅḍamu, p. 55, etc.
85. Nārada, Kātyāyana, Yāgñavalkya are the earlier Smṛiti writers who argued on this point. *Mitakshara* provides further details of the maintenance to be provided to the concubines of the deceased. For more details, P.V. Kane, *Op. cit*., Vol. III, 1974, pp. 808-812.
86. *Ibid*., p. 812.
87. *Ibid*., p. 638.
88. B.S.L. Hanumatha Rao, *Āndhrula Charitra*, (Guntur, 1983), p. 282.
89. *Raṅganātha Rāmāyaṇamu*, Bālakaṅḍamu, line 75.
90. P.V. Parabrahma Sastry, *Kakatiya Sasana Sahityamu* (Hyderabad, 1981), Thousand pillar temple inscription, p. 7-16.
91. Such streets where prostitutes live are also referred to as *Bhōgamu Vīdhi*. *Krīḍābhirāmamu*, verses 114-117.
92. *Pratāparudracharitra*, p. 43.
93. *Paṅditārādhyacharitra*, Purātana Prakaraṇamu, Gurubhaktaṅḍāri Katha, p. 80.Also, *Catu Padya Manimanjari*, pp. 121-126.
94. According to R.S. Sharma, *Paṅchamakāras*, the five orgiastic rites of Tantric religion are introduced into Saivism due to socio-political changes of the medieval period. For details R.S. Sharma, 'Material Milieu of Tantricism' in R.S. Sharma, (ed.), *Indian Society, Historical Probings, Essays in memory of D.D. Kosambi*, (New Delhi, 1984), pp. 175-189.
95. K. Satyanarayana, *A Study of History and culture of Andhras*, Vol. II, (Delhi, 1983), p. 76.
96. *Basavapurāṇamu*, 3rd canto, Mugdhasaṅgayya Katha, pp. 50-53. Also, 3rd canto, pp.48-49. Basaveśvara, without any hesitation, concedes to the demand of one such *Jaṅgama* priest, and gives with pleasure, the silk sari of his wife.
97. R.N. Naṅdi, 'Origin of Virasaiva Movement' in *IHR*, Vol. II, No. 2, (Delhi, 1976), pp.32-46.
98. *Daśakumāracharitramu*, 5th canto, verse 1028. Hemadri, in his *vrata khāṅḍa* of *Chāturvarga Chintāmaṇi*, mentioned one *Vāravrata* to be observed by the girls for prosperity in their profession. H.V. II, 541-548, quoted from P.V. Kane, *Op. cit*., Vol. VI, Part I, 1975, p. 417.

99. *Daśakumāracharitramu*, 6th canto, verse 114.
100. *Kumārasaṁbhavamu*, 8th canto, verses 136-144.
101. *Kēyūrabāhucharitramu*, 2nd canto, Chaturika Katha, verses 42-74.
102. *Daśakumāracharitramu*,5th canto, verse 49.
103. *Paṅḍitārādhyacharitra*, Purātana Prakaraṇamu, Malhaṇa Katha, pp. 84-86. Also Gurubhaktāṅḍari Katha, pp. 78-83.
104. *Krīdābhirāmamu*, verses 91, 286, 290.
105. *Ibid.*, verse 245.
106. *Paṅditārādhyacharitra*, Purātana Prakaraṇamu, Gurubhaktaṅḍāri Katha, pp. 78-83.
107. *Krīdābhirāmamu*, verses 265, 272.
108. *Vijñāneśvaramu,* Prāyaschitta Kāṅḍamu, verse 110, Also, *HAS*,Vol.XIX, Wg 3, Koṛavi, pp. 135-138.
109. *Ibid.*, Also, *Krīdābhirāmamu*, verse 270.
110. P.V.Kane, *Op. cit.*, Vol. III, 1974, p. 638.
111. *Matsyapurāṇa*, 227-144-146 quoted from P.V. Kane, *Op. cit.*, Vol. III, 1974, p. 481.
112. *Ibid.*
113. *Vijñāneśvaramu*, Prāyaschitta Kaṅḍamu, verse 113.
114. *Basavapurāṇamu,* 3rd canto, Mugdha Sangayya Katha, pp. 50-53.
115. Gade Narsing Rao, 'Chāḷukyula Kalamnati Rajyanga Paristhithulu' in *Rajaraja Pattabhisheka Saṁchika*, (Rajahmundry, 1922), p. 132. *Andhra Mahabharatamu*, *Santiparva*, 6-88 also refers to tax on prostitutes.
116. Burton Stein, 'Social Mobility and Medieval South Indian Hindu Sects' in Burton Stein, (ed.), *All the King's Mana* : *Papers on Medieval South Indian History*, (Madras, 1984), pp. 282-301.
117. M.G.S. Narayanan and Veluthat Keshavan, 'The Bhakti Movement in Medieval South India' in D.N. Jha, (ed.), *Feudal Social Formation in Early India*, (Delhi, 1987), pp. 348-373.
118. *Inscriptions of Āndhradeśa*, Vol. II, Part I, (Tirupati, 1968), No. 669.
119. SII., Vol. V, No. 1083.
120. *TIAP*, Vol. I (Srikakulam Dist), No. 264.
121. V. Yasodadevi, 'A History of Andhra Country', *JAHRS*, Vol. XXV, p. 147.
122. *SII*, Vol. X,No. 344.
123. *Ibid.*, No. 395.
124. Abdul Waheed Khan, *A Monograph on Yélēśvaram Excavation*, (Hyderabad, 1963), No. 25, p. 62.
125. The term 'Sāni' is very frequently mentioned and with various meanings in the contemporary inscriptions. It was used as a suffix to the married women in the sense of *Svāmini* (wife) or to denote the courtesans or the temple girls. The term *Munnūru* refers to 300 probably indicating the numerical status of the group. As their post in the temple appeared to be hereditary, we find another usage - *Saṁpradāyam Sānulu*.

126. *SII*, Vol. VI, No. 1202.
127. Girls whose function is exclusively dancing and those who expertised themselves in the art of dancing are called *Pātṛa*. We find several references to this term in the contemporary epigraphs in connection with providing *vṛittis* to them. For instance *SII*, Vol. VI, No. 1052.
128. *Ibid.*, Vol. X, No. 74. For more details regarding the 12 services which are supposed to be performed by the girls, see Alladi Vaidehi, *Āndhrula Saṁghika Āardhika Charitra*, (Madhya Yugam) *(A.D. 1000-A.D. 1250)*, (Hyderabad, 1978), pp. 61-62.
129. *Saṁgrāhaṅdhra Vijñāna Kōsamu*, Devālaya Nṛityamulu, pp. 708-717.
130. *Ibid*, The Syllabi of education for a temple girl is discussed in the next chapter.
131. The donor of a record from Tsandavole was the son of the *Guḍi Sāni* Bānāṁbika and he was also employed with the king Kulōttuṅga Choḷa Goṅka. *SII.*, Vol. IV, No. 1130, Similarly other references like *SII.*, Vol V, No. 1027, Vol. X, No. 5, 189, Vol. VI, No. 169 and many more are of the same nature, given by the children of the temple girls. A record from Mukhalingam temple registers a grant by the father of *Guḍi Sāni*, (*TIAP*, Vol. I, (Srikakulam Dist.), No. 165), and another from the same region records a grant by the husband of Sāni Mādali Rekama, (*SII.*, Vol. V, No. 117).
132. *AR*, No. 164 & 1893, (*SII*, Vol. IV, No. 989).
133. *SII*, Vol. IV, 989, Also, Vol. X, Nos. 5, 107, 110, 115, 116, etc.
134. V. Yasoda Devi, 'A History of Andhra Country', *JAHRS*, Vol. XXV, p. 147.
135. B.N. Sastri, *Rēcheṛla Reḍḍy Vaṁsa Charitra, Sāsanamulu*, (Hyderabad, 1989), Pillalamarri inscription, No. 5.
136. M. Ramarao, *Inscriptions of Āndhradeśa*, Vol. II, (Tirupati, 1968), No. 135.
137. V. Yasoda Devi, 'A History of Andhra Country', *JAHRS*, Vol. XXV, p. 146.
138. *Ibid.*
139. A record from Siṁhāchalam, mentions the various regulations of the guild. It is stated that if these instructions are not obeyed properly the girls would be expelled from the guild. (*SII*, Vol. VI, No. 1202).
140. The term *Māni* refers to a person having a vow of celibacy. The temple administrative functionary containing male members, together with the female functionaries form the unit *Sānulu Mānulu*, which takes care of the temple properties. Please see Chart V for more details of their functions.
141. *Vijñāneśvaramu*, Vyavahāra Kāṅḍamu, verse 61.
142. A.S. Altekaṛ, *Op. cit.*, 1962, p. 213.
143. *Ibid.*
144. *Ibid.*, p. 214.
145. S. Bhattacharji, 'Economic Rights of Ancient Indian Women', in *EPW*, March, 2-9, 1991, pp. 507-512.
146. Bühler, *Laws of Manu*, IX, verse 134.

147. *Ibid.*, IX, 127. Also, for a detailed description on the issue, Arudra, 'Puṭrika Elānti Kūtuṛu' *Vyāsapiṭham*, (Vijayawada, 1985), pp. 54-59.
148. *Saṁgrahāṅdhra Vijñānakōsamu*, pp. 174-179.
149. *Ibid.*
150. The chastity of a widow's life is given great emphasis. It is stated that she should observe fast, make gifts in the name of her husband and perform such other good deeds and lead a virtuous life. Then only she would become the heir of her sonless deceased husband's property. P.V. Kanc, *Op. cit.*, Vol. III, 1974, pp. 735-738.
151. Buhler, *Laws of Manu*, IX, 118.
152. *TIAP*, Vol. I, (Srikakulam Dist), No. 35.
153. *Saṁgrahāndhra Vijñāna Kosamu*, pp. 174-179.
154. *Ibid.*
155. *Ibid.*, Also G.R. Kuppuswamy, *Economic Conditions in Karnataka (A.D. 973-A.D. 1336)*, (Dharwar, 1975), FN 126, 'A note on Mitākshara' p. 40.
156. A.S. Altekar, *Op. cit.*, 1962, p. 218.
157. Buhler, *Laws of Manu*, IX, 194.
158. Yajñavalkya is the foremost among the promoters to the cause of women's property rights. Kātyāyana defines *Strīdhana* as the property acquired through—*Adhyagni* (nuptial fire), *Adhyāvāhanika* (bridal procession), *Pādavaṅdanika* (doing obeisance at the feet of elders), *Prītidatta* (out of love), *Sulka* (bride price) and *Anyādhēyaka* (received after marriage). *Mitākshara* includes a wider range of definition, making *strīdhana* as applicable to all kinds of money that belonged to a woman.
159. *Saṁgrahāṅdhra Vijñana Kosamu*, pp. 174-179.
160. *SII*, Vol. X, No. 349.
161. *IAP : WD*, No. 57, 58 and *Epigraphia Andhrica*, Vol. I, 'Bayyaram Tank Inscription of Kakati Mailama', pp. 71-94.
162. *Palnāṭi Vīracharitra*, p. 139.
163. *Ibid.*, p. 24.
164. *Ibid.*, p. 56.
165. *Kumārasaṁbhavamu*, 7th canto, verses 139, 140.
166. *Raṅganātha Rāmāyaṇamu,* Bālakāṅḍamu, p. 67.
167. *SII*, Vol. VI, No. 797.
168. *Palnāṭi Vīracharitra*, pp. 341-343.
169. *Kumārasaṁbhavamu*, 7th canto, verse 136.
170. *Raṅganātha Rāmāyaṇamu, Bāla Kaṅḍamu*, p. 55.
171. *Daśakumāracharitramu*, 6th canto, verse 51. Also, *Palnāṭi Viracharitra*, pp. 341-344.
172. N. Aruna Kumari, 'Concept of Stridhana in Mitakshara' in *PAPHC*, 8th Session, (Kakinada, 1984), pp. 42-44.
173. P.V. Kane, *Op. cit.*, Vol. III, 197, p. 784.

174. *Ibid.*
175. Generally permission from the king or the members of village assembly or elders is necessary for such an act. *Andhra Pradesh Government Report on Epigraphy*, 1965, No. 4 records the confirmation of the grant of land by one Srimahādevi by the king, while her husband Vijayaditya predeceased her.
176. P.V. Kane, *Op. cit.*, Vol. III, 1974, p. 784.
177. *Ibid.*, p. 785.
178. *Ibid.*
179. *Ibid.*, p. 787.
180. *Vijñāneśvaramu*, Vyavaharakāṇḍamu, verses 53, 54.
181. *Ibid.*, verse 138.
182. *Mitākshara* on Yaj. II,145, quoted from P.V. Kane, *Op. cit.*, Vol. III, 1974, p. 794.
183. Buhler, *Laws of Manu*, IX, 196. *Mitākshara* also agrees with Manu on this issue.
184. *SII, Vol. X, NO. 221.*
185. *Bühler, Laws of Manu*, IX, 197, *Mitākshara* too opines the same.
186. P.V. Kane, *Op. cit.*, Vol. III, 1974, p. 793.
187. *SII*, Vol. X, No. 654. Also, *Ibid.*, Vol. VI, Nos. 967 & 979 are of the same nature.
188. *HAS,* Vol. XIX, Km. 17, Ramakrishnapuram.
189. *SII*, Vol. V, NO. 1014.
190. Dharma Kumar, 'Private Property in Asia? The case of Medieval South India', in *CSSH* Vol. XXVII, No.2, (April, 1985), pp. 340-366.

CHART - IV

RECRUITMENT OF TEMPLE GIRLS – SERVICES – PAYMENT – DETAILS

Sl. No.	Donee Temple	Employer/ Donor	Names of Temple Girls	Nature of Work	Details of Vṛitti alotted	Date of Inscription	Source
1	2	3	4	5	6	7	8
1.	Paṭṭabhirāma temple Narasampet	Manmaganda gopala	1. Kōṭi Kēśavadāsini 2. Koṭṭāri Kēśavadāsini	For performing the yearly Gaṇḍagopala Tiṛunāḷḷu in the Chaitramāsa at Kōṭyadona	20 puṭṭis of dry land in Paḍumuvāra Gaṇḍa Siddhapuram and 20 khaṇḍikas of land	A.D. 1297	No. 661 SII Vol. IV
2.	--do--	Kommanamatya	1...mmaka, D/o Kota Betana 2. Peraka, D/o Prolana	For supplying ghee of one mānika daily	3 kh of land to each of the girls	A.D. 1151	No. 676
3.	Yāminiśvara temple	Jāyama, D/o Pedamunnuṭi Samara Modali Bētināyaka	2 lady employees of the choultry attached to the temple	For grinding rice, dals, to clean mealplates and to bring water	3 kuṇchas of rice, 1 jīvitamāḍa and 3 chinnas for each of them	A.D. 1084	No. 1015
4.	Mulasthaneśvara temple Nadinḍla	Chōḍeraju	A list of temple girls is given in the record	Singing and other Raṅgabhōga services	Lands were given to individual employees as specified below : (1) 4 singers to each of them 4 puṭṭis of land, together 16 kh of !and. (2) Goḍavukāme-2 kh (3) Bōya Vidda	–	No. 663

1	2	3	4	5	6	7	8
					vallabhi 3 kh (4) (lost) 3 kh (5) Dāḍepōju Mācha 2 kh (6) (lost) 4 kh (7) Koṭe Nāga - 3kh (8) Surama (9) Vennaka 3 kh (10) Sabbedāra 3 kh (11) Palledama 3 kh (12) Gokana Sūra 2kh (13) Gaḍiyanabūma 3kh (14) Vemaka Eṛiya 3kh (15) Komma Eṛiya 3kh (16) Podarabolla 3kh (17) Tantrapāla Vardanamka 3 kh (18) Kāmakuppa 3 kh (19) Gasada Komma 3 kh (20) Poyigāramu Kendamara Kanne 2kh		
5.	--do--	Manma manḍa	A list of temple girls is given in the record	Raṅgabhōga functions, singing, dancing, instrument playing, Chāmara kolupu, etc.	Individual land grants were given to the girls based on the nature of services	–	No. 677
6.	Bhimesvara temple Draksharamam	Kuḍiyāṅḍu Kāpi Raṭṭaḍi	4 lady employees of the choultry attached to the temple (names not given)	For grinding rice	For one lady 1 māḍa and some salary (details lost) for three other ladies land (particulars lost)	–	No. 1288

1	2	3	4	5	6	7	8
7.	Narendreśvara temple, Krāṅza	Dārapanāyaka and Jāmenapeggaḍa	2 sāni kāṁpu women	For supply of ghee of 1 mānika daily to burn the perpetual lamp @ 1 mānika by each woman	5 Kulōttuṅga gadyas for both of them	A.D. 1155	No. 996
8.	Srikurmam	Viśvanātha dēva	Sanulu of the Temple	–	3 Gāryalu	A.D. 1309	No. 1214 SII Vol. V
9.	Bhimeśvara temple, Koṭyadona	Kulottunga Choḍa Goṅka	Chanḍika, Nāga, Rāmaka, Ammaka, Gaṅga, Dāmaka, Umayaka, Nakka	Worship services to the deity	3 kh of land to each of the employee	A.D. 1151	No. 613
10.	Rājanārāyaṇa temple Bhimavaram	Not clear	Brammaka, daughter of Eṛṛiyaka	Sānivṛitti	Certain amount of temple land in Puligunta village, Prolinadu.	–	No. 62
11.	Bhimeśvara temple, Chāḷukya Bhimapuram	Vishṇubhaṭṭāraka	(1) Sāni Nāyaghava Eṛṛiyaka, Dārakava Prola, Eṛṛiyaka kosani, Prolava Gonnaka (2) Chimmaka Amkava, Sankava Vāsiki, Ayanava Kommaka, Rājamava Valleka, Eṛṛiyaka Bhadiri, Eṛṛiyaka Keti, Kuchamana, Eṛṛiyaka, Eṛṛiyaka Pella, Mauryaka Dāmava, Mēḍava Komarava,	Chāmara kolupu Dancing and other Raṅgabhōga services	4 kh of Cheluka land, 4 kh of Garuvu land to each of the employees in the Pulinguṇṭa village, Prolināḍu	–	No. 82

1	2	3	4	5	6	7	8
			Pampava cheeḍi, Rākapa Eṛṛiyava, Eṛṛiyaka Sankava, Ayanapa koṇḍaka				
12.	Koppeśvara temple, Palivela, Razole	A minister of Velanāṭi Choḍa	3 Dancing girls	Dancing	Land of 30 kh, 10 kh for each of the dancing girl	–	No. 105
13.	Srikurmam	Queen Gangādevi and Sita devi	1. Naṭṭava Talāsāni 2. Surasāni, D/o Kusanayana 3. Bāsāsāni D/o Singārini (Probably from the families of temple dancing girls only)	Dancing, Alāvaṭam kolupu, and Chāmara kolupu on both times morning and evening	Daily prasāda of 1 Kuḍuṭamu, 1 Appa and 1 Viḍiya, salary of 1 Gaṇḍamāḍa to each of the employees.	A.D. 1349	No. 1225
14.	Rājanārāyaṇa temple Bhimavaram	Kommarāju Raṭṭaḍikam (8 of such Nāyakas)	Nitya Peṛṛayaka, Melunāyaka Muchhiyaka, Ganoju Neṛṛiyama, Peṛṛiya, and other male members	Dancing and other Raṅga bhōga services	4 kh Chelika land and 4 kh Garavu land to each of them.	–	No. 80
15.	Simhachalam temple	Narasimhanātha	Akkasāni, Anyasāni and Bunnasāni	Chāmara kolupu and Dancing	2 kunchas of prasādamu and 10 Padmanidhi gaṇḍamāḍas deposited in the treasury.	A.D. 1369	No. 740 SII Vol. VI

1	2	3	4	5	6	7	8
16.	--do--	Military General from Kaḷiṅga	Sampradāyamu Tantrasāni	Chāmarakolupu	Prasādamu of Appas and Viḍiyas and 2 puṭṭis of land near lake in Lakumavūru in Oḍḍadi country.	A.D. 1113	No. 751
17.	--do--	Siriya Mudasiri	Polama, D/o Gangabhōgena Tarasani	--do--	1 kuncha of prasādamu containing Appas and Viḍiyas and 3 Padmanidhi mallamāḍas	A.D. 1113	No. 756
18.	--do--	Chilama Sahasamalla	Mudunaṛakha D/o Chiṭṭasāni	Not clear	2 kunchas of prasādamu daily and 4 puṭṭis wet land behind Mrempeḍa lake.	A.D. 1371	No. 772
19.	--do--	Varadana Peggaḍa of Oddadi	Anyasāni, Kūnasāni, Prātasāni, Varadasāni	Chāmarakolupu and keeping Raṅgoli twice in a day	10 Ganḍamāḍas, one kuncha of prasādamu for each of the girls	A.D. 1375	No. 797
20.	--do--	Nārāyaṇa Senapati	2 singers and 4 laṅjalu (prostitutes) of Sāni Saṁpradāyamu	To sing Maṅgaḷagitamulu	5 Nibandhas (not specified)	A.D. 1291	No. 904
21.	--do--	Kaliṅga Pariksha Śankarajiyana and his wife	Naṛṛuva Nachnapa	For applying sandal wood, holding mirror and to keep raṅgoli etc.	5 Padmanidhi ganḍamāḍas and 1 kuncha of prasādamu daily	–	No. 1099
22.	--do--	Kaliṅga Pariksha	Daughter of the dancing girls	For Nāmasaṅkirtana throughout the day at	A vṛitti of 4 Nibandhas and 20	A.D. 1374	No. 1134

1	2	3	4	5	6	7	8
		Dharma dāsajiyar	together called sānulu with individual	every service in the temple. This includes instrument playing such as viṇakolupu, taḷadāri, gāṇi kolupu	Padmanidhi gaṇḍamāḍas deposited in the temple treasury for all of them. In addition, the following individual vṛittis (share in the daily prasādamu) 1. Kunamu Naṭṭava savarāsāṇi (viṇa) 1 kuncha 2. Eṛṛasani (tāḷa) aḍḍa 3. Eṛṛasani (Gāṇi kolupu) 1 aḍḍa and kunchas 4. Pinasirigāsāni - (viṇa and tāḷa) 2 kunchas 5. Sirigasāni D/o Naṭṭapa (gāṇikolupu) 2 kunchas (4 Nibandhas could be 4 kunchas of Appas, Viḍiyas, and salary of 13 (18) Gaṇḍachinnas for one year).		

1	2	3	4	5	6	7	8
23.	Bhimeśvara temple Cheṛṛakūru	Kota Keta	(1) Mogali Surama, Patra Kāmaka Āvajamudāse	Kāmabhōgamu (dancing, music)	1 kh of land for each of them	A.D. 1209	No. 207
			(2) Prolama, Pota, Anyama, Pina anyama	--do--	10 Na. of land for each of them		
24.	Simhachalam temple	Narasimha bhārati	(1) Savarasāni, Ekkasāni, Potasāni, Nachhasāni, Akkasāni, all daughters of dancemasters (ladies) Koḍyasāni, Pinakoḍyasāni, chingasāni, chiṭṭasāni (other dancing girls,probably of the above families only)	Nāmasaṁkirtana at both times of the day	5 kunchas of prasādamu. In addition, an amount of 10 Gaṇḍamāḍas was kept in the temple treasury	A.D. 1359	No. 890
			(2) Bhumipiraṭi, Nachisāni D/o Narasimha, other names are not clear	For various attending services (Attendants)	8 kuḍumus of prasādamu.		
25.	--do--	Bayyamadevi	Tallasāni, Tiruva sāni Aṛijasāni	Chāmara kolupu	2 kunchas of prasādamu and 10 Gaṇḍamāḍas	S. 1297	No. 901

1	2	3	4	5	6	7	8
26.	--do--	Kaliṅga Pariksha Yogikshara jiyana	1. Naṭṭuva Keḷasāni, Saṁpradāyamu chiṭṭasāni 2. Kasyakāra chiṅgi	To sing Maṅgalagita mulu daily --do--	2 māḍas, 5 chinnas --do--	A.D. 1375	No.939
27.	--do--	Varadagiri Sripāda	1 mukhari and 2 lañjalu	--do-- at both times of the day	6 Nibandhas (details not given)	A.D. 1337	No. 941
28.	--do--	–	Vaṛadāchi	To bring one pot full of water for Tiṛumajakāla service	10 māḍas and 1 kuncha of prasādamu	–	No. 980
29.	--do--	Daṇḍa Sivadasa pasāyita	Sānulu of the temple (no. not specified)	Viñjāmara at both the times and for other Raṅgabhōga services	1 kunchamu of prasādamu daily	A.D. 1307	No. 1000
30.	--do--	Gaṅgadevi	(1) Arjunasundara Jamunasundara, Kañchisundara, Gaurasundara, Lakuma, Arjuna sundara, Rājasundara, Satusundara, (2) Māṇikasundara, Mugdhasundara, (3) Tārasundara, sanimāṇikasundara (4) Kañchisundara (5) Yamunasundara (6) Jānakasundara, (7) Umasundara (8) Tulasamadu (9) Pirāṭṭidevi	Bhōga Service (1) Pātralu - dancing (2) Mādati Katyalu (inst. playing) (3) Singing (4) Inst. playing (kaṅsya laṭamu (5) -do-(saṅkhu) (6) -do-(Āvajamu, Bhēri) (7) -do-(mihuri) (8) -do-(Brahmamuhuri),	Houses and garden lands for all these employees.	A.D. 1350	No. 1052

1	2	3	4	5	6	7	8
			(10) Maṅka, subhadra, Eḍḍa, Pātra, Māṇikalu	Sumanta Kāhaḷi) (9) Inst. playing - Chāmarakolupu (10) Inst. playing Kāhaḷi			
31.	--do--	Dāsapaṇḍita	10 beautiful, virtuous girls, Tallama, Damiraḍḍipirṟāṭi, Kālipirṟāṭi, Mruggupirṟāṭi Pāṭiborgekunama, Chiṅge, Chudama, Pinna Tiruvama, Kunama, Chingama (along with 2 instrument players - men)	For Gita goshṭi (Singing)	Certain amount of grain as salary and garden lands.	–	No. 1137
32.	--do--	–	100 dancing girls names of all were given in the record	Singing and dancing	… details lost.	–	No. 1197
33.	Mahamalleśvara temple Vipparla	Allaḍa Pemmayadeva Mahārāju	Sānulu (names not given)	Raṅgabhōga	10 Kh of land in the west of Jālamuri Teṛuvu	A.D. 1264	No. 588
34.	Someśvara temple Inumeḷḷa, Vinukoṇḍa	Kālapanāyaka	--do--	--do--	10 kh of land	A.D. 1250	No. 602
35.	--do--	--do--	--do--	--do--	--do--	–	No. 603

1	2	3	4	5	6	7	8
36.	Śankarasvāmi temple, Koṇidena	Tribhuvana malladeva choḍa	Naṭṭavula Seṅke & others (Details lost)	--do-- (Probably dancing)	1 kh of land	A.D. 1147	No. 608
37.	Simhachalam temple	Nārāyaṇa Pradhāni	Ubhyasaṁpradāya mulavaru (names not given)	Singing Maṅgaḷagitālu from morning to night	4 Nibandhas (details not given)	A.D. 1296	No. 982
38.	--do--	Vidyādharuḍu	Jiyaneḍi Kommaya, Chiṭṭayaneḍi Gaṅgu, Saṁpradāyamu Chuḍi piraṭi, Koṭinachyāriketa	Chāmarakolupu, 2 chāmaras on both occasions, morning and night.	At the rate of 16 Gaṅḍamādas - total 16 māḍas in the treasury and 2 kunchas prasādamu	A.D. 1358	No. 1028
39.	--do--	Dharmadāsa jiyana	Kuṭarigopali	Holding mirror and keeping raṅgoli	2 kunchas of prasādamu, 6 Appas and 8 chinnas as salary	A.D. 1374	No. 1128
40.	--do--	Paṁḍaleṅka, Viśvanatha jiyana sons of Dharmadāsa jiyana (royal officers)	Balasaraswathi Tripurasāni, Kuppasāni (Grand daughters of temple dancing girls)	Chāmarakolupu for both times of the day	2 Nibandhas after depositing 10 Padmanidhigaṅḍa māḍas. Salary for them is Appas, Viḍiyas every month, 8 chinnas as salary per year and 8 paṟṟukalu.	A.D. 1374	No. 1130
41.	Rāmasvāmi temple, Ikkuṟṟu, Narasaraopet	Mallināyaka	A girl who plays instrument Maddela	Instrument playing	2 kh land.	A.D. 1166 SII Vol. X	No. 159
42.	Guntūra temple	Mandāḍi Nāmmināyaka	Different girls with individual	Instrument playing, keeping Raṅgoli etc.	1 kh of land to Saṅku Malle	A.D. 1168	No. 164

1	2	3	4	5	6	7	8
		and his relatives	grants		10 na of land to Muggu mṛṛeka and Polama		
43.	Rajeśvarasvāmi temple, Peda Koṇḍūru, Tenāli	Rāma	Melināyani Komarama and Guḍisāni Ketama	For maintaining the lamp	Some amount of land	A.D. 1173	No. 189
44.	Veṇugopālasvāmi temple Pedapalakalūru	King	Temple girls with individual grants	for providing entertainment to the God (Bhōgamu)	5 kh to Naṭṭavula Sure 2 kh to Nallamgete 2 kh to … name lost 2 kh to Kunṭamu Kāsaka There may be other beneficiaries too whose names are not complete, multilated grant	–	No. 238
45.	Velpūru temple	Gaṇapatideva rāja son of of Koṭa Bayyamadevi	Bhandaramu Akkama (Dedicated to the temple by (king)	Dancing the donor)	A vṛitti of 2 kh dry field, 1 mar. of wet land, a house site and a garden	A.D. 1254	No. 344
46.	Kodanḍarāma svāmi temple, Kopparam	Kannarachoḍa deva and his brother (minister) (3) Gāyaki Gaura	(1) Nartakitilaka Padmavati (2) Bogakhya Pātra (4) Pamarika Eṛriyaka (5) Chāmara holders and Dvādaśaseva Vilasinis	Dancing 5 kh and 4 -do- Singing Chāmarakolupu and 12 other specified functions	12 kh and 6 vṛihi kh 4 kh and 2 vṛihi kh 6 kh and 4 -do- 48kh and 24 -do- (for all of them together) the land is in two villages, Biḍepalli of Kammavishaya	A.D. 1115	No. 74

1	2	3	4	5	6	7	8
47	Maheśvara temple, Dumbaṟṟuta, Narsarao pet	Kapeyanāyaka a general of Manḍerāju	Naṭṭavula Kete Potasāni Proli, Kāpasāni Ravva, Manneva Vennaka, Vese silataka (and other male employees)	Dancing Music, instrument playing	6 kh and 1 maṟtuṟu land 3 kh land for each of them. This is out of 100 puttis of land given to the temple by the donor)	A.D. 1132	No. 89
48.	Karṇamoti temple, Nadiṇḍla	Manmamanḍaya raja (a subordinate of Kulottuṅga Choḍa)	Dancing girls and instrument players the names of all are given in the record. Based on the names profession can be understood, for eg. singer Jakke, Naṭṭavulu Dādepoju Malle, Śankhudhāra Kanne, Maddaliya Kāme etc. Sometimes their caste status can also be understood as Bōya Buddana Suraka, Mādirāju Māraka Basivisetṭi Pochaka, Sāni Muppasāni Pochaka, etc.	Bhōgamu of the Lord which includes dancing, singing and instrument playing	For Naṭṭavulu Malle, 6 kh of land Maddaliya Kāme and 2 singers 4 kh and for others 3 kh of land in Nadiṇḍla	A.D. 1139	No. 107

1	2	3	4	5	6	7	8
49.	Anaṅteśvara temple, Chirumāmiḷḷa, Guntur	Kulottuṅga Choḍa Goṅkarāju	Names of about 13 girls is given. Few of them are dancers, others musicians and singers. One is a dancer Naṭṭava Bāre. Maddaliya Dāve, Maddaliya Kāve are instrument players.	For services of dancing singing, and instrument playing	Naṭṭava Bare, 6 kh of dry land Maddaliya Dāve, Kāve 4 kh of dry land, Singer Loke 4 kh of dry land for others 3 kh of dry land. Goḍavu Neṟṟiyama and Toṅta Dāme were given 1 kh land each.	A.D. 1161	No. 148
50.	Choḍeśvara temple, Mopaṟṟu	Paḍavālu Goṅka, a general and his wife Gokāṁbika	8 dancing girls called sānulu Modalisāni Prolama Potana, Ketama, Mārama, Prolama, Nandama, Bhimama, Choḍama. Their fathers' names are given. Few of them are from the same family	Trisaṅdhyala Kolupu	1 kh and 10 na of land to each of them.	A.D. 1170	No. 171
51.	Venkaṭeśvara temple, Durgi	Nāmadeva paṇḍita feudatory of Kakatiya Ganapatideva	Maddelavāru, Pātralu, Siṁhaṇyethalu, Mokhari (Raṅgabhōgamu Unit)	Raṅgabhōgamu Services	Land grants to each of them from the total lands granted to the temple by the donor	A.D. 1251	No. 334
52.	Viśveśvara temple,	Rudramadevi Kakatiya	Temple sānulu with names and	Probably for Raṅgabhōgamu. The	1 kh and 10 tūmus of land to each of	–	No. 396

1	2	3	4	5	6	7	8
	Malkāpuram	queen (gift executed by Kasiśvara Siva Ayyaṅgāru on the orders of the royal priest	individual grants. Names with their father's names are given such as Prolaṇḍi Seṭṭi's daughter Samnala Akkāsāni, Nalamarasāni D/o Nalladeviseṭi, Viśveśvara Māṇikya D/o Samayamantu, Goḷagiri Māṇikya D/O Aṇḍāri and 12 other dancing girls whose names are given.	term Sānivṛitti is given the indication. Individual duties are not specified.	the lady employees		
53.	Gopinātha temple, Dugya	Jannigarāja Subordinate of Rudramadevi	Dancing girls, singers and instrument players, called pātralu, paḍeḍi siyāṇethalu, etc.	Aṅgaraṅgabhōga services	(1) 5 pātras to get 2 kh of land. (2) 10 singers to get 2 kh 10 na of land. (3) Aṅgāraka - 5 Na. (4) Suvāsi - 5 Na. and also grants of land to Virapatiṅdla vāru, vāru, Jeganṭala Dhavala Sankula vāru, Ekasaṅkula vāru etc. (probably	A.D. 1269	No. 422

1	2	3	4	5	6	7	8
					the instrument players, both male and female).		
54.	Cholagañga Mādhavadeva temple, Vizianagaram	A relative of the king Anantavarma devara	Bedisānulu and instrument players	Probably for Rañgabhōgamu	Lands with all emoluments in the village of Tātāram in Talāṇḍa -12	A.D. 1153	No. 707
55.	Śaktiśvara temple, Nūtakki, Guntur	Kandravāṭi Bhimarāju	1. Aya 2. Bole 3. Bolaka d/o Ketana 4. Aḍumaka d/o Erṛiyana 5. Vatiyaka 6. Kona 7. Ketaka d/oApana	Dancer Singer	3 kh — lost 2 kh --do-- --do-- --do-- 1 kh	–	No. 102
56.	Gopālakrishna temple, Inugurṭi	Queen Kāketa Mailalamahā devi	Singers	Not specified in the grant	Houses for the singing girls and certain Nibandhas specified	A.D. 1221 IAP : WD	No. 59
57.	Prasanna Viśveśvara temple, Elkurṭi	Malla, great grand son of Bhāskaramantri	Bhōgamvāru (18 of them) who include singers, dancers, flutists, drummers, Jalajakaraṇḍa vāru (appear to be both male and female)	Entertainment to God	8 marturus of land	–	No. 74
58.	Tripurāntaka Mahādeva temple, Pottapāḍu	Tripurāntaka, feudatory of Rudradeva	Guḍisānulu	Damaged	Damaged	A.D.1219-20	Darsi (57) NDI Part II

1	2	3	4	5	6	7	8
59.	Gopiśvaradeva temple, Tammalūru	Mallaṇadevi Ammaṅgāru, a relative of Mādhavadeva rāju governor of Addanki sthala.	--do--	Aṅgaraṅgabhōgamu	A portion from the dryland, a paṭṭi field, two marṭuṛus paddy field and a flower garden	A.D.1272-73	Darsi (72)
60.	Chennakeśava temple, Chandaluru	-lost-	Tirupaṇidāsi, Dantamma, Melunaṅkoni, Naṛaventuchu, Pātra Bayyaka	Not specified probably dancing	600 kuṇṭas for Tirupaṇidāsi and for others, 200 kuṇṭas	–	Ongole (24)
61.	Veṇugopālaśvami temple, Velaparla (Konṭridona)	Mahāmaṇḍale śvara Tribhuvana malladeva Choḍa	Dancing girls	Probably dancing	A portion of the lands of village Volupāra.	A.D.1148-49	Ongole (142)
62.	Aniyaṅka Bhimeśvara temple	Dirghāsivāsi	Davalapa, d/o Dirghāsivāsi	Protection of lamp	It appears that the lady was dedicated by her parents to the temple as Sani. Vṛitti is not specified	A.D.1085	B.N.Sastri, Mukhaliṅga devālaya Charitra-Sāsanamulu No. 19
63.	Nāmeśvara temple, Pillalamaṛṛi	Nāmireḍḍy the Recherla chief	—	Raṅgabhōgam vāru (both male and female) of whom the ladies include dancers Pātra Sitama, Pārvati, Muttama, Singers Tripuranama, Jakka,	A house site for each of these ladies in the fort of Pillalamaṛṛi, permanent for them	–	B.N. Sastri, Recherla Reḍḍi Vaṁsa charitra Sāsanamulu, No.5

1	2	3	4	5	6	7	8
				Brammaka, Māraka Raṅgabhōgamu to the Gods			
64.	Attili, Tanuku Tq.	Chāḷukya Bhiṁa	Cākaya D/o Mallapa	Dancing girl in the temple	1000 acres arecanut garden 105 kh wet land and a house site	–	IAD Vol.II Part I No.118
65.	Kāḷahasti	Kulottuṅga Choḷa	A dancing girl and her descendents	Not specified, probably dancing and recreation to God.	She was transferred from the king's service to the temple.	–	No. 699
66.	Vāsukiṛāvi Someśvara temple Juttiga	–	Prola and other sānulu (300 of them)	Dancing and providing recreation to the deity	Appointed for services as hereditary	–	No. 138
67.	Yeleśvara svāmy temple	Devasaranu Maṅkiseṭṭi	Virapa and Nāgapa, the grand daughters of the donor	–	The girls were dedicated to the God and the gift was handed over to the priest	A.D.1271	A Mono graph on Yeleśvaram Excavations No. 25
68.	Mailāradeva temple	Meḍeyabhaṭlu	Singers and other lady employees	Singing, keeping Raṅgoli, etc.	Singers - 5 Gadyas Raṅgavallivāru-1 māda Rākātavāru - 3 Gadyas	A.D.1146	B.N. Sastri Sāsana Saṁputi : Bollepalli Sāsanamu
69.	Mulasthaneśvara temple, Tāḍikoṇḍa	Paṁdāṁbika	Bhōgaṁvaru	Aṅgaraṅgabhōga services	2 kh of dry land, and wet land	A.D.1266	Epigrahia Andrica : Vol. V, No. 13

1	2	3	4	5	6	7	8
70.	Prasanna Vallabha	Rearrangement of the grant made by Viriyala Nagasānamma and others	--do--	--do--	1000 paṭlu of rice	A.D.1236	Hyd. Arch. Series : No. 19, Pammi
71.	Pachala Someśvara temple	Mailamāṁba	--do--	God's personal enjoyment, singing, vocal and instrumental music, dancing	Gālpuṭlu and 1 kh. mar. of land	A.D. 1124	No. 13 Pānugal No. 36
72.	Srikurmam	–	Kattula Bhūmasāni	Chāmara kolupu	Salary of 1 māḍa, prasāda of one tūmu, Appas (25) and Viḍiyas (30)	A.D.1379	T I A P Vol. I, No. 319
73.	--do--	Gaṅgamadevi	Sitavallabhi	For Nāmasaṁkirthana morning and evening	Salary of 2 māḍas, prasāda of 1 māḍa Appas, 1 m. and Viḍiyas	A.D. 1341	No. 303
74.	Aniyaṅka Bhimeśvara temple	King	Gaṅgamanāyaku ṛālu	Raṅgavṛitti	30 puṭṭis of land	A.D.1155	No. 127

CHART - V

ACTIVITIES OF THE GUILD OF TEMPLE GIRLS

Sl. No.	Temple	Employer	Name of the	Activities Guild	Vṛtti Allotted/Payment	Date of Inscription	Source
1	2	3	4	5	6	7	8
1.	Pushpagiri	Certain Jiyyars names not clear	Sānulu	Protection of the sale deed executed by the Jiyyars	Damaged record, Particulars not available	A.D.1303 No. 164	IAP : CD
2.	Pushpagiri		A lady named as Puṛasāni was mentioned as a partner of the sthanapatis Aiśvajiya Būye and Beiḍe	The grant registers sale of the shares of the members of the association in the temple wells, paddy fields, and the villages by one of them duly obtainng the permission of the other three including Sāni to the other Jiyyars. They obtained 100 Valūri Gadyānas through this sale		A.D.1260	--do-- No. 136
3.	Chiṛumāna Mallikārjuna temple	Kāmanāyaka and Devināyaka, sons of Golapuṅdi Kesima Nāyaka	Temple Sānulu (Bhōgaṁvaru)	For performing dancing	4 paṭṭas of paddy field, a field called Kaluvachenu, highlevel fields in wet lands, 1000 kuṅchenaṅga, 4 paṭṭas dry land in Penōmani field measuring about 4000 kuṇṭas	A.D.1285 Atmakur (25)	NDI, Part I

1	2	3	4	5	6	7	8
			the record.	For worship services They were given permission to lease the lands to kāpus, in which case, the kāpus treat it as sarvamānyamu and not make the fields going waste without cultivation. Details regarding distribution of shares among temple employees is also given. The dancing girls are probably the executors of this deed. The lands of the temple are given to them for executing the gift particulars given in	Paḍḍy field of 750 kuṅṭas, in Anāgidachenu and dry land of 400 kuṅṭas in Gṛaddakuṅṭa Revaṭa		
	Nilakaṅṭheśvara Swāmi temple Guḍlūr	Choḍadevachoḍa Mahārāja Mallidevarāja and Chikkirāja	Moṅkaṭisānulu	For performing worship services. They should lease out the low land in the lands attached to the temple treasury for a half share of the produce to their friends	4 pattas of dry land and low land in the paddy field at Nilamakatta Devar a bandaruvu (paddy field belonging to the temple).	A.D.1237-38	Kandukur (22)
5	Chennakeśava temple, Chāndalūru	–	Sāni mānyam (sānulu)	For Raṅgabhōga probably. Shares to each of them were given. The rest for lights and other services, details of which were lost.	4 pattas of dry land	–	Ongole (24)

1	2	3	4	5	6	7	8
6.	Vāsukiṛāvi Someśvara temple Juttiga		Sāni Munnuṛu	Protection of a lamp		15th year of Chalukya Vishnuvard hana	Inscriptions of Āndhradeśa Vol. II Part I No.123
7.	--do--		--do--	--do--		17th year of --do--	--do-- No. 124
8.	--do--		--do--	--do--		17th year of --do--	--do-- No.125
9.	--do--	A dancing girl	--do--	--do--		A.D.1141	--do-- No. 128
10.	--do--	Kolani Okkettugaṇḍa	--do--	--do--	Gift of taxes Manniyatiṛu, Payiḍi, etc.	A.D. 1125	--do-- No. 132
11.	--do--	–	Sānulu and 72 Niyōgas of the temple together with the priests, Srikaraṇam, Tambaḷis.	Allotment of vṛitti to one Annapasāni. Their consent was important for obtaining vṛitti in the temple property.	–	A.D.1277	--do-- No. 136
12.	Sahasraliṅga Gaṇapati temple	Royal preceptor of Prataparudra	Non brahmin priests and one Govindadāsi	Preparation of sale deeds		A.D.1313	HAS, Vol. Vol.XIII No. 16
13.	Mukhalingam temple	King Anaṅtavarma	Devagaṇikas along with male members of the	Headship over the singers and dancers of the temple association	–		TIAP, Vol.I No.10
14.	Srikurmam	Sāhasmalla, Sānteśvara, officers of king	Saṁpradāyamu Sānulu (30 of them repetition from	Execute the various arrangement made by the donors regarding	Grain at the specified rate per year and share in	A.D.1250	No. 264

1	2	3	4	5	6	7	8
		Viranarasiṁha	Kaliṅgāmaṅḍala, all from Nāyaka families	allotment of shares to temple servants from the land grant made by them. (30 puṭṭis of areca garden and 103 māḍas)	the daily offerings made to the deity is the salary for these girls.		
15.	Agasteśvara temple, Kāza, Guntur	Bollināyaka	Sānulu Mānulu		10 kh of land	A.D.1269	SII, Vol.IV No. 707
16.	Kaḷyāṇa keśava temple Kṛāṅza	Bollināyaka	--do--	Angaraṅgabhōga	10 kh of land		--do-- No. 705
17.	–	Saṁbhudeva	Sānulu and Mahājanulu	Protection of lamps given by donor	–	–	--do-- No. 918
18.	Mulasthāneśvara temple, Dendulū	Malyapṛaggaḍa	Sānulu Mānulu	For looking after various duties of the temple	30 units of low land˙	A.D.1233	SII, Vol. V No. 194
19.	Ksheerārā meśvara temple	Suryārkuḍu, a royal officer	Sāni Munnūṛu	Naṭṭava, Nāvajava vṛitti has to be maintained	7 Nishkas	–	--do-- No. 162
20.	--do--	Guṁdāṁbika	--do--	Protection of the lamp and running of the same	--do--		--do-- No. 161
21.	--do--	Goṅka	--do--	--do--		–	--do-- No. 160
22.	Koṇidena	Reḍḍi, Nūṅkiṣeṭṭi	Sānulu Mānulu	Performing regular worship services	–		SII, Vol. VI No. 605
23.	Bhimeśvara temple, Koṭyadona	Kulōttuṅga Choḍa Goṅka	--do--	--do--	Jonna pṛalūṛu village in Kammanāḍu		--do-- No. 610
24.	--do--	--do--	--do--	--do--	Individual vṛittis		No. 613 given (lands)

1	2	3	4	5	6	7	8
25.	Bhāvanārāyaṇa temple, Pṛeṁ palli	King	Sānivaṁśānva yamulu (Sāni Saṁpradāyam 30 members)	Maintenance of a grant of feeding 5 brahmins and offering prasāda to them	Individual grants were given.	–	--do-- No. 200
26.	Nāgeśvara temple Pedakaḷḷapalli	–	Sāni Munnūṛu	Protection of lamp grant	–		--do-- No. 84
27.	--do--	Jñanōttama Śivadeva	--do--	--do--	–	A.D.1236	--do-- No. 86
28.	--do--	Wife of Ballanarendṛa	--do--	--do--	–	A.D.1154	--do-- No. 67
29.	--do--	Sōmaladevi	--do--	--do--			--do-- No. 88
30.	Nāgeśvara temple, Chebṛōlu	Jakkanarāju		--do--		A.D.1153	--do-- No. 101
31.	Nāgeśvara temple, Peddakaḷḷapalli	Chinnamakkā che	--do--	--do--		A.D.1281	--do-- No. 85
32.	--do-- Chebṛōlu	W/o Paṅḍan dādhipa	--do--	--do--		–	--do-- No. 116
33.	--do--	Maṅḍabhūpāla	--do--	--do--		A.D. 1118	--do-- No. 117
34.	Śankaradeva temple, Koyadona	Tribhuvana malla Pottapichoḍa	Sānulu Mānulu	Raṅgabhōga Services	Ballikuṛuvu land in Kammanāḍu	–	--do-- No. 624
35.	Someśvara temple, juttiga	Kolaniya kettu gaṅḍaḍu	Sāni Munnūṛu	To maintain the perpetual lamp	Vṛiti of a local tax called Manniyatiṛu	A.D.1125	SII, Vol. X No. 83
36.	Jaladhiśvara temple, Ghaṅṭasāla	Koṭa Kommiśeṭṭi	--do--	--do-- and for supply of Ghee	10 Rājarāja, māḍas were kept under them	A.D.1144	--do-- No. 115

1	2	3	4	5	6	7	8
37.	Rāmaliṅgaśvami temple, Chilumūṛu	Reḍḍi Muppa nāyaka	Sānulu Māṇulu Mānulu	–	Individual land grants, Nāvunūru	A.D.1154	--do-- No. 130
38.	Keśavadeva temple, Bejawāda	Rājendra Choḍaya Rāju	Sānulu-Mānulu	For performing worship services and to maintain lamps	Land grant	A.D.1174	--do-- No. 192
39.	Agasteśvara temple Kolakalūr	Amaṛināyaka	--do--	--do--	A field of 2 kh	A.D.1241	--do-- No.292
40.	Malleśvarasvāmi temple, Lāmu, Guntur	A servant of Rudradeva	--do--	–	Gift of land	–	--do-- No. 539
41.	Rāmeśvara temple, Chaṁchalūṛu	Kulottuṅga Choḍa Goṅka	--do--	Bhōgamu of God	Individual land grants in Chāṁchalūṛu	A.D.1135	--do-- No. 97
42.	Agasteśvara temple, Guntur	Pandeyarāyu	--do--	Havirbaliarchanalu (Worship services)	Gaḍḍipuṁḍi land in village	A.D.1158	--do-- No.144
43.	Rāmasvāmi temple, Sri Rāmapuram	Pṛoliya Peggaḍa	Sāni Munnūṛu	Nityanaivedya Services (worship services)	Lands, garden, without taxes	A.D.1170	--do-- No. 173
44.	Rāmaliṅgeśvara temple, Siripuram	–	Sānulu Mānulu	Performing various worship services like lamp, entertainment, offerings and other services	Individual lands at Daṅḍakaṭṭa of Sripuram village, a lake and palm garden, 100m. of land without taxes.	A.D.1171	--do-- No. 177
45.	Chimmiśvara temple, Mallavṛolu	Chānaya nāyaka	Sāni Nibaṅdhas	–	Several lands as individual grants	A.D.1280	--do-- No. 451
46.	Rāmaliṅgasvami temple, Vēlpūṛu	Sons of the Mānulu	Sāni Munnūṛu	Maintenance of lamp		A.D.1112	--do-- No. 70

1	2	3	4	5	6	7	8
47.	- --do--	Son of	--do-- Bhimanāyaka	--do--		--do--	--do-- No. 71
48.	Chennakeśava Svami temple, Kommūṛu Bāpaṭla	Nemmaūṛi	--do--	--do--		A.D.1191	--do-- No. 80
49.	Someśvara temple, Juttiga	Prōlipāva, a dancing girl	--do--	--do--		A.D.1141	--do-- No.110
50.	Jaladhiśvara temple, Ghaṅṭasāla	Somarasa	--do--	--do--		A.D.1159	--do-- No.145
51.	Rāmaliṅgeśvara temple, Vēlpūṛu	3 Mānis of the temple	--do--	--do--		A.D.1200	--do-- No.208
52.	Anaṅta, Bhōgeśvara temple, Kollūṛu	Bōyi Jivaṛu	Sānulu Mānulu	Maintenance of a lamp		–	--do-- No. 216
53.	Rāmaliṅgeśvara temple, Masulipaṭnam	Pōliseṭṭi	Sāni Mannūṛu	--do--			--do-- No. 229
54.	Rāmaliṅgeśvara temple, Vēlpūṛu	–	--do--	Const. of a pillar in the temple		A.D.1255	--do-- No. 348
55.	Vāsukiṛavi Someśvara temple, Juttiga	Eṛadevaya	--do--	Maintenance of a lamp		A.D.1221	--do-- No. 268
56.	Dharaṇikoṭa, Guntur	–	Refers to an arrangement made between the priests and temple sānis regarding shares in the temple lands which was written in the presence of			–	--do-- No. 366

1	2	3	4	5	6	7	8
			the king Maṁmakoṭa Gaṇapatideva and the Karaṇālu of the village				
57.	Simhachalam	Refers to the agreement/order passed by the Sānisaṁpradāyamu of the temple which is binding on every member of the guild failing which punishment would be expulsion from the guild. (The guild was supposed to be of Sudra caste)				–	S.I.I., Vol. VI, No.1202

CHAPTER 5

Women and Education

Dharmaśāstras gave ample space for educational rights of women despite their treatment as a dependent gender and secondary to men. In the early times a learned daughter was preferred to an unworthy son. Upanishads contain rites to be observed by a householder who desires to have a learned daughter.[1] *Kāmasūtra* of Vātsāyana prescribes that a woman should study *Chatusshashṭi Kaļās* (the sixty four arts) before she attains youth. Among these are included riddles of words, chanting from books, in addition to singing, dancing and painting.[2] All these tend to indicate the literary progress achieved by women of ancient period. But the same cannot be said to be true of the Sūtra period where attempts were made to curtail freedom of women and her educational rights. A learned daughter meant her proficiency in domestic work.[3] Manu's theory of dependence of women and his declaration that women and sudras are not permitted to read Vedic scriptures[4] could have further negated the chances of her education.

Several works of medieval period too express similar feelings. Sōmadevasūri in his *Yasastilaka*, opines that it would be risky to educate women.[5] Mañchana, in his *Kèyūrabāhucharitramu* declares that under no circumstances, a woman should be given permission to move out of the house frequently or to develop contacts with the neighbouring women.[6] He fears that such a woman spoils her money, caste and life. *Mitākshara*, well known for its liberal economic rights of women, contains no clear reference to female education.

On the other hand, the importance of educating sons was well recognised specially among the brahman families. Koṛavi Goparāju in his *Siṁhasanadvātriṁsika* indicates that in the brahman families, an illiterate son was a murrian on the caste.[7] He further describes the concern of parents for the education of their sons which would give the man understanding power and provide them sufficient knowledge for the well-being of an individual.[8]

It appears, thus, that importance of education was recognised for men rather than women. More emphasis is laid on a woman's submissiveness in the family. It was felt that there was no necessity for a woman to be educated formally. She was required to be skilled in the matters of devotion towards her husband. In the opinion of Manu, marriage is her initiation ceremony and service to her husband is equivalent to the service to the preceptor.[9] As observed by Abbe J. Dubois, A Hindu woman should know how to cook and look after household affairs. Courtesans, who dance in temples and at public ceremonies and prostitutes were the only women who are allowed to learn.[10]

The Indian kinship relations and family structure being patrilineal, duties of men and women are demarcated almost clearly. There exists a clear division of labour between the two sexes. A man has to maintain the legality and prestige of the family and a woman has to carry the same to the future generations, thereby their roles becoming public and private respectively. While this created a need for formal education for men, non-formal education on various household traditions was considered important for women so that they can maintain the structural continuum of tradition.

A formal education can be defined as the mode of learning through close personal contact of the pupil with the teacher, through his stay with the teacher as a member of his family, stern discipline and control of emotions.[11] Dewey refers to education as a formal or institutional education which is a regular programme of training for a specific period.[12] A specific syllabi is out lined for this system. On the contrary, non-formal education begins right at the home level with parents as instructors regarding code of conduct, behavioural pattern, knowledge about tradition, religion, customs of each caste, etc. No specific syllabi is framed or any pattern of instruction. Generally non-formal education is imparted to the child through oral media like riddles, songs, tales or suggestions regarding good conduct and well behaviour. Age is not a determined factor in this. Both men and women are supposed to develop an awareness in these matters. However, a woman has more scope towards non-formal education irrespective of the class to which she belongs, as she is a tradition bearer, primarily responsible for protection and integration of the family system. Dharmasastras hold that certain *Acāras* (traditions) are to be learnt only by and from women. Sōmeśvaradeva's *Abhilashitārtha Chintāmaṇi* states, "A teacher is greater than the initiator, the father is greater than the teacher, but the mother is much greater than the father".[13]

The above discussion asserts the space given to women in traditional society. At the same time depending on the contextual needs, formal education was also provided to her as in the case of women of elite group and those who took to various professions. The syllabi, however varied according to the nature of profession and the tradition they inherited. The issue of educational rights of women can thus be discussed under two broad heads : Formal education and Non-formal education. Under each category, provisions of educational space to both elite and folk categories of women is discussed.

Formal Education

The socio-economic and political conditions of the contemporary times necessitated women's involvement either directly or indirectly in the state affairs. Owing to the prevalence of feudal elements in contemporary state and polity, there was a need for formal education with specialised training in state and warcraft alongwith arts and letters for women of royal families.

The need for educating girls on formal lines was well recognised in political circles and of the class of elite. The manner in which children, both boys and girls were brought up was distinctly varying when compared to the corresponding picture in middle class families. Due to the feudal character of medieval state, most of the kingdoms were short lived and depended for their continuous existence on the power of control exercised by the kings. It was here that a woman's involvement was made essential in her role as a queen, as a co-regent or as a guardian to the minor-king.

The general branches of learning prescribed for the children of royal families include : science of polity, state-craft and different war-fare skills like horse-riding, elephant-riding, and science of archery.[14] According to *Daśakumāracharitramu*, kings are supposed to acquire knowledge in medicine, astrology, expertise knowledge in Dharmasastras, Purāṇās, Āgama texts of various sectarian movements, interest in science of music and other fine arts, philosophy and prodigy.[15] In addition, they should also know the art of reading and writing, understand the idea and concept of God and are supposed to develop a virtuous character.[16] *Pratāparudracharitra* outlines the syllabi comprising different branches of learning prescribed for royal family members in the form of an age-wise curriculum.[17] Kakatiya queen Rudramadevi learnt various arts of state craft and archery.[18] Her knowledge in military science is well exemplified in her great victory over Yadava forces. The following chart gives us an idea about the literary talents and interests of women in Āndhradeśa.

CHART VI : LITERARY ACHIEVEMENTS OF WOMEN

Sl. No.	Reference	Name of the Woman	Description as Given in the Inscription
1	2	3	4
1.	SII Vol. IV, No. 1313	Rājādevi, W/o Kona Mummaḍirāju	Best among the women of royal families
2.	-do- No. 1156	Gauramadevi	Famous scholar in music
3.	-do- Vol. V, No. 1179	Piṛatyaṁbika, W/o Nṛisiṁha Bhaṭṭōpādhyāya	Having an increased knowledge in Bhaktigñāna (Devotion)
4.	-do- Vol. VI, No. 189	Wife of Velanāṭi Goṅka	Best known for her various virtues and was considered as a teacher to the young.
5.	-do- No. 740	Wife of Kaliṅgadaṅḍa Somanātha mahāpisāti	Listens to Vedās, Śāstrās and Puṛānās everyday
6.	-do- No. 1180	Sivarāṇi, W/o Minister of Gaṅga lineage	Described as Kaliyuga Saraśwathi (Goddess of learning)
7.	-do- Vol. V, No.1177, 1179	Piṛāṭṭi Sōmidevamma	Described as the one who is interested in Vedās, Śāstrās and Puṛānās.
8.	-do- Vol. X,No. 1047	Ghaṅṭasāla Kāmaka, D/o Prolināyaka	Described as a jewel among women of the city, Ghaṅtasāla
9.	EI, XIII, pp.150 ff text verse 19 quoted from C.V. Ramachandra Rao, Administration and Society under Eastern Gangas and Suryavamsa Gajapathis.	Chaṅdrikadevi, D/o Aniyaṅka Bhima III	Described as learned in music and also as a seat of sport in skilful practice of the arts of musical measure, beating of time and the dance having a soul inspired in devotion, from her childhood.
10.	HAS, Vol. XIX, No.4 (Kmm)	Aytama, W/o Viṛiyāla Annaya	Obtained proficiency in learning, moral science and was soft spoken.
11.	Epigraphia Andhrica, Vol. V, Tāḍikoṅḍa inscription	Paṁḍāṁbika, the queen	Described as Goddess Saraśwathi holding vina

1	2	3	4
12.	B.N. Sastry, Kanduri Chodulu: Sasanamulu, Charitra, Pānugallu Inscription pp.135-139	Mailaṁbika, W/o Kandūri Toṅḍarasa Choḷa	Described as Apara Saraśwathi, Goddess of learning.
13.	Idem. Mahabubnagar Jilla Sarvasvamu, Inscription Nos.35, 42 pp.942-43, 954-56.	Mannādevi, W/o Chāḷukya Vikramāditya VI	Had a title Abhinava Saraśwathi. She is stated to have possessed the art of writing lucid verses.
14.	-do- No. 63 pp.990-91	Mallahaṇi Devi, D/o Padmaladevi	Described as Vidyadhari, learned woman.
15.	-do- p. 183	Laxmidevi, W/o Chāḷukya Vikramāditya	Scholar in all branches of learning and state-craft.
16.	SII, Vol. IV. No.1032	A woman	Described as one who is soft-spoken, pious in all her acts and activities.
17.	-do- No. 676	W/o Kommāmātya	She is like the mythological cow. Kāmadhenu to poets and learned men. Also she herself is a learned woman who follows a true traditional path.
18.	-do-No. 1040	A certain woman (name not clear)	Described as Vanitālalāma, greatest among women.
19.	-do- No. 1043	Suramadevi, W/o Oḍḍāḍi Arjunadeva	Described as Vanitōttama, greatest among women.
20.	-do- No. 1218	Valyama, W/o Veṅgi Goṅka	Described as a jewel among women.
21.	-do- Vol. V, No. 106	W/o a minister	Described as virtuous and beautiful.
22.	-do- No. 161	Guṁḍāṁbika	Patronised learned men.
23.	-do- No. 647	Kāmidevi	Ajewel among women of the family. Praised as a virtuous lady.
24.	-do- No. 175	Rājāṁbika	One who increases the honour of the family. A follower of good traditions and pious woman.
25.	ARE, 1965, No. 169	Somaladevi	Described as Sahaja Vedāṅgi, one who is interested in learning Vedās.

We observe that learned women are often equated to the Goddess of learning, Saraswathi. They are described as having great interest in listening to discourses on religion, Purāṇa literature and participating in the literary programmes held by poets and scholars patronised by them.[19] Further, it appears that not only women of political circles but those of the elite sections of the society and women of the class of courtesans too were receiving the benefits of formal education.

However, information is not clear as regards the mode of learning. The popular education centres of the period namely *Agrahāra,*[20] *Ghaṭika*,[21] temples and monasteries[22] were catering to the needs of the students who are often mentioned in the inscriptions as *Vidyārthulu* (students) without gender specification. Moreover, they impart residential mode of instruction. Therefore, it is not certain that girls are studying at these institutions. Probably, they are taught through special teachers appointed for the purpose. A brahman, Cenavelabharum Bhadramaya was appointed as the preceptor for imparting religious education to Bayyama Devi daughter of Pātra Potarāja Jiyana.[23] Similarly a record from eastern Āndhra region belonging to the Eastern Gaṅga kings mentions another brahman teacher of the queen-mother by name Valalēṛu Timmaya.[24] Brahmans of Valalēṛu family were probably appointed by the elite classes for imparting formal education to their girls.[25]

The women who prevailed in the society as courtesans, concubines, prostitutes and temple girls also appear to have had their formal education to increase their professional perfection.

Courtesans were dancers in the royal courts and concubines were patronised mostly by kings and nobles. They were supposed to gain proficiency in the arts of music and dance pertaining to both *Mārga* (sanskritic) and *Dēśi* (native) styles. Besides their profession of court dance programmes, they were also used as instruments in the political strategy. This necessitates their knowledge in matters of state-craft atleast theoretically, though the same might not be put by them into actual practice. Thus, few variations can be found in the syllabi of education given to girls of these classes when compared with that of princely families.

Literary and epigraphical evidences reflect the skill in education attained by the courtesans and concubines of kings and their officers. The concubine of Rajendra Choḍa (Velanadu chief) is described as virtuous and learned. She is praised by the scribe as *Kāmadhenu* (the mythological cow) to the poets and learned men.[26] The *Bhoga Stree* (concubine) of Eastern Chalukyan king, Chalukya Bhima, Chakava is described as adept in music and one who hailed from a family of musicians.[27] Her father Mallapa had a title *Tuṁbura*. An earlier inscription of the same dynasty registers grant of a village, Kaluchumbaṛṛu in *Attilināḍu Vishaya* to one Arhanaṅdin, a Jain preceptor of Chāmekaṁba the concubine of the king.[28] The courtesan of Rāyapanāyaka called Trōlama is referred to as an ornament to the class of courtesans. She had a title, *Gaṇikā Vibhūshaṇi*.[29] Mācaladevi, the concubine of Pratapa Rudra II is another well noted personality of her period. Her house was supposed to be one of the beautifully decorated houses in the capital city, Ōṛugallu with huge painting halls. She was always busy in participating in the intellectual debates and learned assemblies which were held within the compound of her house.[30] The description of court dances in different literary works is a further indication of the perfectness achieved by the courtesans in the fields of dance and music.

The education of girls following the profession of prostitution is also more or less designed in the same pattern as in the case of courtesans and concubines. They come into contact with men of different cultures and of varied interests. In the absence of a constant (permanent) family system, they had to accumulate money sufficient for their livelihood through maintaining continuous associations with men. For this, they had to excel themselves in all branches of learning which would be of interest to the males with whom they come in touch. Their proficiency in fine arts makes them survive firmly in the competition among the followers of this institution. Therefore, their syllabi of learning was co-related with the interests of men of all classes and is designed in such a way as to keep them distinctly away from the family ladies. They are supposed to learn *Nāṭyaśāstra* of Bharata, *Kāmasūtra* of Vatsāyana, instrumental music, singing, clay-modelling, painting, etc. The contemporary literary evidences give us an idea of the importance of clever behaviour in case of these girls, to entertain men.[31] As in the case of girls of royal elite, even these were trained in the respective fields at home alone by teachers appointed specially for this purpose.[32]

The training of the temple dancing girl starts at the age of 5 years.[33] This training is by a dance master called *Nāṭyāchāṛya* appointed either by the temple or by the donors. The Chēbṛōlu inscription refers to the appointment of a dance master by the donor general Jāyapa to train girls who were dedicated to the temple at the age of 8 years.[34] An epigraph from Simhachalam temple refers to the appointment of Raṅganātha Vāggēyakara who had titles like *Abhinava Bharatāchārya* and *Tōḍaramalla* indicating his proficiency in the branches of dance and music, to impart instructions in both the fields to the temple dancing girls.[35]

Initially she is given training in physical exercises and massaging the body with specific oils. This course is referred to as *Mallamu*. The duration of this is about 6 months. Later on, various traditional dance styles and the local patterns (*Mārga* and *Dēśi*) are taught to her. Simultaneously she is given thorough instructions in music, script both of Sanskrit and Telugu languages and an idea about the different worship and ritual services offered to the temple deity. Based on the nature of the temple to which she is attached, she is required to learn either Saivite or Vaishnavite Agama texts.[36] By the time she attains the age of 14 years, the girl completes her course and acquires an idea of the nature of duties to be performed by her in the temple. She would be declared eligible for the temple service only when she clears the test conducted by her master. Failing which, she has to lead the life of common harlot.[37] Possibly for the sake of this long and elaborate training and instruction they were dedicated to the temple service at an early age and were provided with residential accommodation in the vicinity of the temple.

Non-formal Education

Sufficient evidences are not available to arrive at an understanding regarding the provision of space for common women towards formal education. However, all of them enjoyed benefits of non-formal education which again is varied in accordance with the needs of the section to which they belonged.

Apart from formal education, women of elite groups are also receiving sufficient training from their elders in matters concerning state-craft, political diplomacy, code of conduct, or any other relevant subject.

Rudramadevi learnt political diplomacy from her father.[38] The greatest Saivite preceptor Viśveśvara Śiva Dēsika was her teacher. *Nāyakuṛālu Nagamma* was a great diplomat. Sīlama had vast knowledge in the science of war-fare and Dharmasastras. The details of the educational skills of women of ruling elite are clearly exhibited through their acts of counselling as discussed under various heads in the earlier chapter on polity.

Non-formal education in various professional skills was imparted to girls belonging to the class of concubines and prostitutes by their mothers. They train their daughters in matters of painting, drawing, decorating the compounds of their houses, etc.[39] In addition, they also taught them various beautification processes, preparation, and use of cosmetics, medicines, skill in dressing and ornamentation, developing clever behavioural patterns in order to earn more money and such other aspects concerning their profession.[40] The literary works of the period are abound with references to the mothers of *Vēśyas* making suggestions to their daughters regarding these issues. The elderly women of these classes also help the *Vēśyamāthas* while training the young girls.[41]

The aspects of non-formal education relate to the preservation of family system. They are applicable mostly to women of middle classes in comparison to the others. Their learning requirements are only perfection in domestic affairs. As A.S. Altekar observes, "The ladies of cultured families were expected to cultivate the love of sport, arts of music and dance, painting, gardening, garland-making, toy making, house decoration, etc."[42] In her day to day life, the girl becomes perfect in all these through personal experience and observation. In addition, the girls were taught at home the traditional mode of worship, performance of religious observances and rituals, their importance specially to married women, the behaviour towards elders and husband.[43] *Siṁhāsana Dvātṛmsika* mentions that Malayavati, wife of Jīmūtavāhana had learnt the arts of music and instrument playing to enliven her husband's mind and traditional worship practices to pray for her husband's long life and for a happy and fruitful married life.[44]

Nannechoḍa, in his *Kumārasaṁbhavamu* gives an idea about the different aspects of non-formal education for girls such as garland making, stringing of rosaries, necklaces, making wreaths of flowers and leaves, dance and music, making dolls and toys of mud, ivory and glass, cooking variety of dishes and the preparation of drinks.[45] Further, every girl was taught in the traditional arts of painting and decorating floors with beautiful floral and geometrical designs of various patterns. The contemporary literature is abound with several such references to women decorating the compounds of their houses with exquisite floral patterns using a preparation of rice flour. The art is referred to as *Raṅgavalli* (Rangoli) **(Plate VII b)**.[46] On festive occasions and on functions like royal marriage, every street was decorated with colourful *Raṅgavalli* designs.[47] Most of the women had medicinal knowledge in the common ailments of children and seasonal health disturbances.[48] Cosmetics and beauty aids were prepared at home with herbs in kitchen garden and grains and cereals used in kitchen.[49] Such traditions are carried through generations by women only. Since, house is the basic unit of society for learning in which mother is the informal teacher and mentor for children. The contemporary literature contains copious references to mothers giving instructions to brides regarding their behaviour in the in-law's house. Menaka, the mother of Parvati instructs her daughter how to behave in the husband's house after marriage.[50]

King Janāka directs his daughter Sita regarding the code of conduct and behaviour to be followed by her in the marital home.[51]

The occupations like weaving, spinning, extraction of oils, selling, etc. are caste oriented and mostly hereditary. Therefore, there were no separate vocational educational institutions for the members of artisan class in these occupations. Though, few Saivite monasteries had provided facilities for vocational education,[52] children learnt these skills through their elders. Every one found a teacher in their father or the elder member of their community or sometimes even the guild. This was also true with the womenfolk of these classes. Though direct references are not available as regards the standard of education of artisan women, it can be presumed that they obtained professional skills in their respective crafts, as suggested by the story of a *vaisya* girl in *Kēyūrabāhucharitramu*.[53] The *vaisya* wanted an intelligent and clever bride for his son and the men sent by him in search of one, found her selling oil in exchange to rice in the shop. Description of various artisan and peasant women in *Krīdābhirāmamu* suggests the nature of occupational skills learnt by them traditionally.

Women belonging to *Mēdaṛa* (basket weavers) class were skilful in the art of basket making.[54] *Karṇāṭi* women knew the method of preparing medicine useful in the art of making love.[55] Women of *Teliki* (oil monger) community learnt extraction of oil from *Sampenga* flower (Gold flower) and preparation of hair oil with it.[56] Girls belonging to *Goṛaga, Dommari* (wandering communities) and such other classes were expert jugglers.[57] They learnt various gymnastic feats through their elders.[58] Women belonging to forest dwelling groups like *Śabara, Cheṅchu* had knowledge in tanning the animal skins and making toys and dolls with them.[59]

However, these domestic and occupational skills learnt at home by women proved to be of great help to them, since they utilised their proficiency in their respective fields to earn and to supplement the income of their husbands. Widows of poor brahman families, who were experts in cooking and preparing leaf-plates made use of their skills to earn money.[60] Similarly, women who gained proficiency in garland making and decoration of floors through *Raṅgavallulu*, took employment in the temples.[61] Women of herdsmen class made money from their domestic skills such as preparing butter-milk, extraction of ghee, butter, etc. Despite these variations in the aspects of learning based on socio-economic differences, women of all classes appeared to have received benefits of religious education and knowledge of Dharma. The bhakti movement in Saivite and Vaishnavite traditions which pervaded all sections of the society provided ample space to the women's participation in religious rituals and observances in public domain like *Bhakta Kūṭavulu* (religious gatherings), pilgrimages along with their menfolk. They tried to extend their religious sanction for their denial of their husbands if they do not belong to their religion.[62] They further rejected the concept of purity and pollution of women on certain occasions for they considered that practice as a way of keeping them at a distance from important events in the society.

The Śaivite literature too, with its thrust on reorganising the society, tried to give more religious freedom for women and attempted to bring these changes at the family level. By giving importance to the use of common dialects (*Dēśi*) in literature, the Śaivite poets, made possible for women to understand religious principles clearly. The temples and other religious institutions like monasteries arranged for discourses in Vedas, Epics, Purāṇas and Āgama literature daily or occasionally in the evenings wherein women's participation was not opposed.[63] They also held assemblies of devotees for which women were allowed entry.[64] Thus elaborate religious education was also open to women which helped bringing to light their involvement in religion.

References to women devotees and their accounts in *Basava purāṇamu, Paṅḍitārādhyacharitra* bear ample testimony to this. The poet mentions that women participated in the literary assemblies arranged by devotees on festive occasions.[65] He also quotes certain devotional songs sung by women during their daily activities.[66] He describes women visiting sacred Saivite shrines like Srisailam along with their husbands as pilgrimage. During their journey, they sang songs in musical tunes. Some of the songs include – *Tummeda Padamulu, Gobbi Padamulu, Prabhāta Padamulu, Valēśu Padamulu, Vennela Padamulu* and so on.[67] Nannechoda, in his *Kumārasaṁbhavamu* describes the interest of forest dwelling women to know the doctrines of Saivism. He describes them as singing *Gauḍa Gītamulu* and *Aṅkamālikalu* while they were pounding *Veḍuru biyyamu* (bamboo-rice).[68] In *Krīḍābhirāmamu*, there is a mention of a widow reciting six cantos of Ramayana in the night in a sweet melodious voice.[69]

Palkuriki Somanatha in his *Paṅḍitārādhyacharitra* gives an episode of a brahman widow, Poraṅḍla Sūrasānamma, a devotee of Lord Śiva. She invites devotees of Lord Śiva to her house and was involved in discussions with them on various issues regarding Śaivite religion.[70] She visits the house of Mallikarjuna Paṅditā-rādhya, a famous preceptor of Ārādhya Śaivism and gives him the *Dīksha* (initiation) of Śaivism.[71] When brahmans of the *Agrahāra* objected to this behaviour of hers which according to them is not traditional, she convinces them with her knowledge in Śaivite philosophy.

According to an account in *Basavapurāṇamu*, Suggulādevi, queen of Desiṅga Ballaha is involved in the discussions about the greatness of Saivism and its doctrines along with her preceptor. She was responsible for conversion of her husband and other Jain devotees to Śaivism.[72] Similar is the story of Vaijakavva, wherein she opposed her husband's belief in Jainism.[73] The bhakti tradition offered opportunity to women to understand the essence of Vedas and Vedic literature through different doctrines of Śaivism and Vaishnavism. The contemporary socio-political conditions necessitated such awareness among the common folk among which women were considered as pivots in the family.

Thus, the type of education provided to the girls and the curriculum of the studies varied with respect to the status, profession or need. The case is same even with men, as in general, the educational system of medieval period is caste oriented and profession oriented. Emphasis is laid more on religious education by all people. The categorisation of educational system of medieval Andhra into formal and non-formal types is done for the sake of convenience and to understand the motive behind such a system. The system of learning was modelled to preserve the family system and kinship relations wherein, men and women exist complimentary to each other but not contradictory. It was necessary for every girl irrespective of the class to which she belonged, to receive non-formal education to keep her role continuous in bearing the tradition of the family and further to act as a carrier of the same to future generations in her role of a mother. However, in the case of royal women, formal education becomes necessary as they had to maintain a structural continuum in the political relations along with men. Similarly, the need for earning a comfortable livelihood in the absence of family system made the a concubines and prostitutes to attain skill in fine arts. The educational training of a temple girl enabled her to achieve perfect skills in both Sanskritic and local traditions and thereby serve as a medium of synthesis between the two. Artisan women and women of weak sections of the society had to acquaint themselves with occupational skills to supplement their family income.

The bhakti cults, more prominently Śaivism made an attempt to bring religion closer to the common masses. In its attempt, it provided religious education to all members of the society irrespective of class or gender differences and is thus helpful in bringing female voice in religion. While it is further to be ascertained here, whether this is a new change brought about by the sect or bringing to light the earlier provisions of religion, it is almost certain that there was a great religious literature as a consequence to this development. Works like Hemadri's *Chāturvarga Chinṭamani* laid more emphasis on performing religious observances, vows, making gifts to achieve materialistic benefits. Most of them were aimed at sanctioning longevity of married life and welfare of the family members. As such women's participation became more conspicuous.

REFERENCES

1. *Brihadāraṅyaka Upanishad* prescribes a rite for a householder desirous of having a learned daughter.
   अथ य इच्छेदुहिता में पण्डिता जायेत।
   (Br. VI.4-17), quoted from P.V. Kane, ***History** of Dharamasastas,* Vol. II, Part I, 1974, p. 366.
2. *Ibid.*, p. 367.
3. It appears that from the time of Saṅkarāchārya, women were prevented from learning the Vedas and hence, the change in understanding the meaning to the term.
   दुहितु: पाण्डित्यं गृहतंत्र विषयमेव वेदेऽनाधिकारात्।
   (Sankarabhashya), quoted from P.V. Kane, *Op. cit.*, 1974, p. 366.
4. Bühler, *Laws of Manu*, IX, 3.
5. K. Suryanarayana, *History of Minor Chalukya Families in Medieval Andhra Desa*, (Delhi, 1986), p. 270.
6. *Kēyūrabāhucharitamu,* 3rd canto, verses 225, 226.
7. *Simhāsanadvātṛmsika,* 4th canto, verse 166.
8. *Ibid.*, 8th canto, verse 138.
9. Bühler, *Laws of Manu*, II, 67.
10. Abbe J. Dubois, *Hindu Manners, Customs and Ceremonies,* (Delhi, 1985), p. 337.
11. P.V. Kane, *Op. cit.*, 1974, p. 369.
12. Dewey, 'Democracy and Education', pp. 7-11 quoted from Pandharinath H. Prabhu, *Hindu Social Organisation*, (Bombay, 1990), p. 102.
13. Śomeśvaradeva, *Abhilashitārtha Chintāmaṇi*, part I, line 115 quoted from Vaidehi Krishnamoorthy, *Socio-Economic Conditions in Eastern Deccan, (A.D. 1000-A.D. 1250),* (Hyderabad, 1970), p. 69.
14. Ancient scriptures including the Epics directed a king to obtain proficiency in three Vedas, metaphysics, state-craft, economics, military science, alphabets and arithmetic, besides gaining great experience in elephant riding, horse riding, fighting techniques, etc.
15. *Daśakumāracharitramu*, 2nd canto verses 115, 116. Also, *Raṅganātha Rāmāyaṇamu,* Bālakāṇḍamu, p. 19.
16. *Daśakumāracharitramu*, 3rd canto, verse 20.
17. *Pratāparudracharitra*, p. 37.

18. *Siddheśvara Charitra*, p. 126.
20. *Agrahāras* are famous centres for Vedic education during medieval times. An *Agrāhāra* is a grant of land given by a king to brahmans in lieu of their scholarship. The epigraphical references suggest that brahmans from various countries like Draviḍa, Karnata, Ahichhaṭra, Lāṭa, Gauḍa, Kāshmira, etc. are invited to settle in Āndhradeśa and were given munificent grants in the form of *Agrahārās* by the ruling chiefs. Their duty is to impart Vedic education. *Vīrachoḍa Chaturvēdi Maṅgaḷam* was the most famous among the *Agrahārās* of Āndhradeśa. The Hanamkonda Inscription of Rudradeva mentions that in the houses of the brahmans of *Agrahārās,* even the parrots joined students in reciting Vedas, Vedaṅgas and all appropriate subjects. It is also stated that beautiful histories were sung in *Pāda* order. Vedas, Vedaṅta philosophy, *Vyākaraṇa* (grammar), Astrology, Theology, Puranas, Medicine, etc. are the other subjects taught here.
21. *Ghatika* is also another educational centre of medieval Āndhradeśa imparting Vedic learning. *Ghaṭika Samaṅvaya* was the chief co-ordinator of this institution. In every *Ghaṭika,* provision is made for residential accommodation for the students and teachers. In addition, there is library called *Saraswathi Bhāṅdāgāramu* helping the students to obtain detailed knowledge in various branches of learning. In Āndhra, *Ghaṭikas* existed at Asanapura, Hemavati, Simhachalam, Nāgāyi, etc. One of the Simhachalm records mentions grants to two *Ghaḍasāsi* brahmans who were experts in *Khāṅḍava* and *Taittirīya* branches of philosophy. Khaṅḍavalli and Buthpur Inscriptions too record grants to the teachers of *Ghaṭika*. In addition to Vedas, logic, philosophy, Dharmasastras, sciences like Āyurveda, Dhanurveda, Gandharvavidya, Arthaśāstra, etc. are taught here.
22. Temples and monasteries are popular educational centres of the period. Abundant references to these can be found in the epigraphs available from various parts of Āndhradeśa. Grants are made by one and all to the teachers and students residing in the residential schools attached to the temples as well as monasteries. Daily recitals of Vedic passages, Purāṇic stories of devotees, religious discourses were held in both poetic and verse forms and were explained in the local language for educating the common masses. The contemporary socio-political conditions too are discussed in the temples and monasteries which resulted in the creation of political awareness among people. In addition, the temples appointed dance masters to teach dance and music in both *Marga and Desi* forms to the dancing girls of the temple. Āgama philosophy was taught in the monasteries. Few Saivite monasteries had provision for *Ashṭādaśa Vidyalu* corresponding to the various branches of learning concerning to the eighteen classes of people. Mandaḍa, Malkāpur, Tripurāṅtakam, Elēśvaram, Srisailam were some of the famous Saivite monasteries. Alaṁpuram, Ahobilam, Simhachalam, Prēmpalli, Bāpaṭla, etc. were few of the Vaishnavite monasteries which were prominent during the period in Āndhradeśa.

23. *SII*, Vol. VI, No. 900.
24. *Ibid.*, No. 1118.
25. C.V. Ramachandra Rao, *Administration and Society in Medieval Andhra under the Eastern Gangas and Suryavamsi Gajapathis, (A.D. 1038-1538),* (Nellore, 1976), p. 296.
26. *SII*, Vol. VI, No 210.
वारकान्ताभिरामकीर्तिं विद्योतयन्ती विरिविदुशामर्थिनां कामधेनु:।
27. M. Rama Rao, *Inscriptions of Andhradesa*, Part II, (Tirupati, 1968), No. 118.
28. *Ibid.*, No. 140.
29. *SII*, Vol. V,No. 164.
30. *Kṛīdābhirāmamu*, verses 180-192. She had a title, "प्रतापरुद्र धरणीशोपात्त गोष्ठी प्रतिष्ठा पारीण"।
31. *Daśakumāracharitramu*, 5th canto, verses 12-19. Generally the mothers take initiative to educate their daughters in the arts of clever conversation, art of making love, doing services like massaging the body, giving them the idea of *Purushārthas,* etc. They also make their daughters observe certain vows for prosperity. For more details see *Kumārasaṁbhavamu*, 8th canto, verses 137-144.
32. Generally the mothers or the elderly women teach them various matters of importance to their profession. Instruction in music and dance was given through a teacher appointed for the purpose at the place of residence itself.
33. *Saṁgrahāndhra Vigñānakosamu*, Dēvālaya Nṛityamulu, p. 709.
34. V. Yasodadevi, 'A History of Andhra Country', *JAHRS*, Vol. XXV, Rajahmundry, pp. 52-152. Such dance master is referred to as *Nattuva*. Inscriptional evidences refer to appointment and provision of *vrittis* to these men. See, *SII*, Vol. X, Nos. 144,148, *TIAP*, Vol. I, (Srikakulam Dist.),No. 264, etc.
35. *SII*, Vol. VI, No. 1091.
36. *Saṁgrahāndhra Vigñānakosamu*, pp. 708-709.
37. *Ibid.*, p. 717.
38. Mallampalli Somasekhara Sarma, *Āndhradeśa Charitra, Saṁgrahamu*, (Vijayawada, 1991), p. 43.
39. Jyotsna K. Kamath, *Social life in Medieval Karnataka,* (Delhi, 1980), p. 116.
40. *Daśakumāracharitramu*, 5th canto, verse 12-19.
51. For more details, see *Daśakumāracharitramu*, 5, 6 cantos., *Kumāra Sambhavamu*, 8th canto, *Kṛīdābhirāmamu*, pp. 54-55 and *Keyūrabāhucharitramu*, 2nd canto. Also, P.V. Kane, *Op. cit.,* Vol. IV, 1974, p. 481.
42. A.S. Altekar, *The Position of Women in Hindu Civilisation*, (Delhi, 1962), p. 21.
43. J. Kanakadurga, *Koṛavi Goparaju, Siṁhāsanadvātṛmsika – Mahiḷā Jana Jīvanamu*, (Kothagudem, 1992), p.35.

44. *Ibid.*
45. *Kumārasaṁbhavamu*, 6th canto, verses 36-38.
46. *Raṅgavallulu* are the floral patterns or patterns of different designs made with *Kastūri* (musk), or *Mukṭāphālamu* (white lime) in front of the compounds of the houses. They have a great significance and vary according to the region, environment and other factors like occasion, seasons, etc.
47. *Basavapurāṇamu*, p. 19. On the occasion of the marriage of Basavana, the streets were decorated with *Kastūri, Mukṭā phalamu* patterns of Raṅgavallulu. Also *Kumārasaṁbhavamu*, 8th canto, verse 41.
48. *Ibid.*, Bejjamahādevi Katha, pp. 58-61.
49. *Kumārasaṁbhavamu*, 8th canto, verse 13, gives the preparation of *Lattuka* (a kind of lipstick).
50. *Ibid.*, 9th canto, verses 143-144.
51. *Raṅganātha Rāmāyaṇamu*, Bāla Kāṅḍamu, p. 65.
52. P.S. Kanakadurga, *Kakatiyulananti Samajika Jivanamu* (Vijayawada, 1992), p. 161, 168.
53. *Kēyūrabāhucharitramu*, 2nd canto, verses 8-16.
54. *Kṛīdābhirāmamu*, verses 68, 69.
55. *Ibid.*, verses 77 to 81 give us the uses of the medicine prepared by the woman.
56. *Ibid.*, verse 101. Verses 102-105 give us the description of *Ganulakanne* (Teliki woman).
57. Veturi Prabhakara Sastry, *Catu Padya Manimanjari*, verse 325. Also *Kṛīḍābhirāmamu*, verses 160, 161.
58. *Kṛīdābhirāmamu*, verses 143, 144.
59. *Paṅḍitārādhyacharitra*, Parvata prakaraṇamu, p. 235.
60. For more details, please refer to the earlier chapter "Professions and Property rights".
61. *SII*, Vol. X, No. 74.
62. Mallikarjuna Panditaradhya, *Sivatatvasāramu*, (ed.) Nidadavolu Venkata Rao. (Hyderabad, 1968), verses 231, 232, 233.
63. *Ibid.*, verse 129.
64. P.S. Kanakadurga, *Op. cit.*, 1992, p. 167.
65. Such assemblies are called *Bhakta Kūṭavulu, Paṅḍitārādhyacharitra,* Vāda Prakaraṇamu, p. 117, 118. Also *Basavapurāṇamu*, p. 124.
66. *Basavapurāṇamu*, p. 119.
67. *Paṅḍitārādhyuacharitra*, 'Vāda Prakaraṇamu', p. 118.
68. *Ibid.*
69. *Kumārasaṁbhavamu*, 6th canto, verses 45, 47, 48.

70. *Kṛīḍābhirāmamu*, verse 185.
71. *Paṅḍitārādhyacharitra*, 'Dīksha Prakaraṇamu, Sūrasāni Katha, pp. 29-33.
72. *Sivatatvasāramu*, p. 20.
73. Basavapur*āṇamu*, Tēḍaradāsayya Katha, pp. 157-162.
74. *Ibid.*, 6th canto, Vaijakavva Katha, pp. 163-167.

CHAPTER 6

Religious and Social Observances

Dharmaśāstras prescribe certain rites and ritual practices to be followed in general and specific contexts by men and women for family welfare and continuity of tradition. People believe that one can achieve *Purushārthas* viz. *Dharma* (Peity), *Artha* (wealth), *Kāma* (sensual gratification) and *Mōksha* (liberation) by observing the prescriptions of Dharmaśāstras.

Ritualistic religion of the Vedic times did not provide space for women who were equated to sudras. The latter by virtue of their birth and the former by their being pure and polluted on certain occasions.[1] However, women's space is clearly defined and her participation was made inevitable in performing all household religious rituals and observances. Manu holds that in religious matters, a husband is one with the wife.[2] He cannot even reap the fruits of a pilgrimage without she accompanying him.[3] The Purāṇic religion provided ample space to women and sudras to perform religious observances and celebrations of festivals. According to it, rituals are classified as *Isṭadharma* (what is sacrificed) in which are included the Vedic rituals and sacrifices having no space for women and sudras and *Puṛtadharma* (whatever is filled) in which are included religious observances, like *vṛata, dāna*, pilgrimage, observing fast and performing meritorious and charitable acts or *Saptasaṅtāna* deeds.[4] Rituals under *Puṛtadharma* are allowed to be practiced by people of all sections of the society irrespective of caste or gender.

Vṛata is a mental resolve to do something or refrain from doing something both enjoined as duties.[5] *Vṛatas* are of three types. They are *Nitya* (whatever is given every day), *Naimittika* (given at certain specified time or on account of doing certain acts) and *Kāmya* (given through the desire of securing progeny, victory, prosperity, heaven or wife).[6] *Agnipurāṇa* holds that the objects of this penance are : Dharma, progeny, wealth, beauty, good fortune, virtues, fame, long life, purity, enjoyment of pleasures, heaven and renunciation.[7] *Dāna* or gift giving is a sacred observance promising merit in the other world. *Agnipurāṇa* refers to ten

Mahādānas, gift of gold, horses, chariots, land, house, maids, a bride, a dark brown cow etc.[8] Based on the nature of *dānas* they can be classified as : *Uttama* (of high order), *Madhyama* (of middle order), and *Adhama* (of lowest order).[9] Purāṇas and Smṛtis regulate procedures to be followed in space and time, keeping in view the contemporary socio-political conditions of the land.

In the earlier times the kingship was *heroic* and was legitimised by conducting Vedic sacrifices and rituals. Literary and epigraphical references from eastern Āndhra region give ample evidences to the kings performing sacrifices after their ascent and on completion of their conquests thereby extending ritual control over the areas conquered by them.[10] In other words, the kings legitimised their Kshatriyahood through sacrifices. The gradual changes of the early medieval period like clearance of forests and extension of cultivable fields, system of landgrants to brahmanas and monastic establishments, recruitment of sudras as artisans and agricultural labour and contacts with different forest dwelling communities[11] reflected a change in the form of kingship in accordance with the change in state formation. The kingship was ritual with dual sovereignty, the political and the ritual. As cited earlier, the kings stabilised their political power by coercion and ritual power by conciliation. The synthesis of both gave strength to the kingship. The kings legtimised their ritual power by gift giving. In other words, by medieval times, gift giving replaced sacrifices as the legitimised factor of kingship. This gift giving included land grants to temples, brahmans, monastic establishments, construction activities and the *Saptasantāna* deeds. Along with the kings, their wives and those of manḍalika chiefs are also involved in the process of gift giving further widening their domain in the religious observances.

Further, contacts with the tribal people led to their beliefs and worship practices making their way into Purāṇic religion through brahmanisation and Sanskritisation processes. Kāpālika sect of Śaivism included in it the *Panchamakāras* (five orgiastic rites namely fish, meat, sex, drink and physical gestures) of the tantric religion. Sakti cult became prominent.[12] Shrines for mother-Goddess with various names were built at various places. In Āndhradeśa, temples were built for Goddesses Kākatamma, Mahūramma, Mūsanamma, Pōlērama, Ēkavira at various places.[13]

Festivals and fairs are introduced to propitiate these dieties. However, the description of women in tantric religion appears to be different from that of women in bhakti cults. Tantric practices are aimed at personal liberation by equating family relations and religious practices, where as the bhakti sects, Śaivism and Vaishnavism made an attempt to bring religion closer to women by giving them equal domain and arguing for religious freedom for women. Virasaivism rejected the concept of purity and pollution isolating women on certain occasions from observing religious practices and rituals.

Along with these developments, the Purāṇic religion too underwent certain modifications to suit the needs of contemporary times. Though the main aim of all these observances and rituals appear to be sacred, i.e. securing religious merit of the highest order in the other world, secular and materialistic purposes dominated over the religious observances. The bulk of the *vratas* practised were of *Naimittika* and *Kāmya* nature, i.e. for the purpose of securing some object in this very life.[14] Even in the context of making gifts, the things mentioned in the various orders of merit varied based on the changes in economy, availability of goods and attitudes of people.[15] Thus, the items mentioned in *Adhama* order earlier were considered important in the medieval times. Great amount of religious merit was attached to visiting sacred places through pilgrimage by self or proxy, involving in philanthropic activities which had socio-political significance and celebration in the form of *Tiṛunāḷḷu* (fairs) near temples. *Chātuṛvaṛga Chintāmaṇi* of Hemadri, a contemporary work gives a list of about thousand *vṛatas* and procedures of their observance. He discusses the merits and importance of making gifts, significance of time and place of performance and fruits of such gifts. The popularity of this work in Āndhradeśa is suggested by the extensive epigraphical evidences quoting rulers performing meritorious activities as given in Hemadri's work.[16]

When the contemporary literature and inscriptions are analysed in the light of the above discussion, new light will be thrown on the significance of women's participation in religious observances in space and time. Their objectives were both sacred (aimed at securing religious merit of the highest order such as attaining *puṇyalōka* after death) and secular (aimed at obtaining merits in this life, such as material prosperity, perpetuity of the family, longevity of married life, birth of sons, welfare of the family, etc.). These practices were commonly observed by women of both elite and common groups though they differ in the manner of observance and in the nature of objects gifted to temples in lieu of their performance. For convenience sake, we can group them under two – Religious Observances and Social Observances.

Religious Observances

The different religious practices observed by women, such as *vṛata, dāna, saptasantāna* and under taking pilgrimage to holy shrines are discussed under this head. The purpose of these practices being both sacred as well as secular. They were observed by both elite and common groups of the society.

Vṛta

The objects of most of the *Vṛatas* mentioned in Hemadri's text are concerned with the perpetuality of family life. They are generally undertaken by married women either individually or along with their husbands. Few penances are prescribed for young women and widows too. It is believed that a woman becomes a widow due to her past sins and is eventually responsible for the death of her husband.[17] To avoid recurrence she had to observe certain penances which promise her a longevity of married life in the next birth. Specific vows are also prescribed for the *Veśyas* for a prosperous profession.

References from contemporary epigrpahs and literary sources reveal the popularity of *vṛatas* in Āndhradeśa. Certain practices are oriented towards achieving victory in the war field and bring political stability of the kingdom. Vidyanatha in his *Pratāparudra Yaśōbhūshaṇamu* quotes that Kakatiya queen Rudramadevi observed *Trirātrivṛatamu* before proceeding against Yadavas in the battle field and thus emerging successful in driving away Yadava forces to the banks of river Godavari in the north-west.[18] Kuppāṁbika, wife of Malyala chief Guṁḍa, performed many vows to achieve long span of married life, family welfare and for the good of her husband. They include *Jalasayana vṛata, Lakshmīnārāyaṇa vṛata, Ekādasi vṛata, Asūnyasayana vṛata*, etc.[19] Her Buthpur inscription praises her as a true devotee of Lord Vishnu. It is further stated that she adhered to the procedures mentioned in the Kalpa texts while performing these penances.[20]

Within the patriarchal society, the birth of a son is considered as the most important aspect of married life. It is believed that a marriage becomes fruitful only with the birth of a son who would relieve the householder from the debts of his forefathers.[21] Prominent among several such penances are, *Dāsarieḍla nōmu* (worship of oxen), *Naṁdikēśa nōmu* (worship of bull), *Gajanimma nōmu* (giving lemon fruits as gifts), etc.

Mummaḍamma, the eldest daughter of queen Rudramadevi, performed *Dāsarieḍla nōmu* as per an account in *Siddhēśvaracharitra*.[22]

Basavapurāṇamu gives an account of the importance of *Naṁdikēśa nōmu* in yielding merit of sons. Madaṁba, wife of Maṁdega Mādirāju, complied with several *vṛatas* with an object of begetting a son. Ultimately following the advice of brahmans and elders she undertook the vow of worshipping *Naṁdi* (bull) and fulfilled her desire.[23]

References to the religious practices promising birth of sons can also be gathered from *Palnāṭi Vīracharitra*. Itama, wife of Brahmanayudu, performed several penances for the birth of a son which include *Vīdhivelugunōmu, Gaṛima nōmu, Sañjavattinōmu, Jagajjoti nōmu, Ēkavillu nōmu, Pacchavillu, Naṅdinōmu, Chikaṭiṅṭi nōmu, Kēdāreśu nōmu* and several others. The observance *Gajanimma nōmu* accomplished her longing desire.[24]

All these above practices appear to be native of Āndhra region as they do not find mention in Hemadri's work. Therefore, it becomes difficult to understand the practices of each one of them. However, they are related to the concept of lighting a lamp, an idea linked to the belief that a family without progeny is one without light.

The importance of observing vows is also recognised in the case of prostitutes. The observance of these *vṛatas* ensured material prosperity. Sacred texts quote that these women are supposed to follow the profession in palaces and temples. They should make gifts of cows, fields and gold to brahmans, perform such other penances which are mentioned in the Kalpa texts.[25] Hemadri mentions, *Veśya vṛata* to be followed by the prostitutes.[26] Literary texts like *Kumārasaṁbhavamu, Daśakumāracharitra*, contain ample references to the mothers of *veśyas* suggesting their daughters to observe penances for prosperity.[27]

Epigraphical references reflect the nature of *vratas* practiced by women from middle class which differ from that of the elite women in the mode of observance and the nature of gifts given. An inscription from Drākshārāma temple describes Parākamma, wife of Dṛōṇabhaṭṭa as *Māsōpavāsi*.[28] This observance of keeping fast on specific days of each month is considered to yield highest merit according to *Anusāsanaparva*.[29] Another record from the same place quotes Suraṁbika, wife of Sridharanāyaka as *Suvṛatā* (one who is observing *vṛatas*).[30] *Kṛīdābhirāmamu* has a reference to *Kāmeśvari nomu* performed by a couple for the welfare of the family and for material prosperity.[31]

Gifts are given to temples, brahmanas or to married and unwidowed women in lieu of the performance of the *vṛatas*. Palkuriki Somana in his *Basavapurāṇamu* mentions such women receiving gifts as *Peraṅṭāṇḍru*.[32] However, the nature of gifts varied in accordance with the elite/folk differentiation (Socio-economic status of the women). Kuppāmbika performed the *vṛata* of giving away land every day during *Chāturmāsya*,[33] Sūramadevi, wife of Oḍḍāḍi chief, Arjunadeva gave a village Saṅkubhīmāpuram to God Bhimeśvara at Drākshārāma on account of

Gaurivratamu.[34] The gifts by common women given in lieu of their vows are comparatively simpler and include gifts of lamp, money, etc.

Thus, it is seen that *Vṛata, dāna* and *dakshiṇa* are interlinked. *Vṛata* cannot yield fruits unless gift making accompanied by donation is given.

Dāna

There are two intentions of making gifts. One is the removal from past sins and the other is to achieve religious merit in the future life. In this sense, *dāna* can be termed as a sacred observance. However, gift giving to temples or monasteries serves a secular purpose. Specially when made by members of the royal family. The aspect of gift giving by women of ruling elite has been discussed in the earlier chapter. Making *dānas* also has the effect of acting as a medium of exchanging and redistributing economic wealth.[35] The system of exchange of gifts kept goods and people in circulation in a specific pattern and also acted as means of maintaining political relationship and ranking.[36]

The popularity of the idea of making *dānas* among women in Āndhradeśa can be understood from the number of epigraphical references registering grants to temples, charitable and religious institutions, priests, sectarian leaders, etc. The details are shown in the form of charts in Appendix categorised depending on the nature of gifts into four different units. Chart VII A includes land grants, VII B, the particulars of live stock donated to the temples, VII C contains details of monetary endowments and grants of jewellery and VII D includes all other general grants made by women.

It is observed from the charts that women belonging to different sections of the society figured as donors. The items of gifts however varied according to the socio-economic status of the donors. The grants ranged from villages, gardens, lands to livestock, cash, lamps, food and such other objects. Sometimes consecration of Gods, institution of certain ritual services in the temple and providing *vritti* to the temple employees was also taken up by them as seen from the above charts. Moreover, the nature of gifts indicate the feudal and agrarian economy.

Further, it is seen that gifts are generally made on a certain auspicious occasion or during eclipses to get more benefits as stated in the scriptures.[37]

Sapta Santāna

The term literally means the seven meritorious deeds assuring highest order of religious merit. They include construction of a tank, a temple, dedication of a work, laying a garden, performing marriage, keeping a treasury and patronage of poets.[38] Doing good on one's own regardless of social claims was considered the chief way for salvation.[39] Apparently the acts performed under this head cater to the necessity of proving political sovereignty through ritual means. The persons involved in these activities are mostly women of the ruling elite and their ritual exchanges are embedded in the larger continuum of social and economic relations. It became a means of controlling different power structures of the state by winning followers and by placing the donees under the obligation of submissiveness to the donor political power.[40]

The construction of tanks and canals or laying gardens had great economical value as discussed in the third chapter and it brought religious merit to those responsible for their creation. Construction of a temple or performing marriages too had a marked social significance.

Literary and epigraphical references suggest the active involvement of elite women in performing *Saptasantāna* deeds. *Pratāparudra Charitra*, refers to the dharmic activities of Kakatiya empress, Rudramadevi. She constructed temples to Lord Śiva, gave grants to religious and monastic institutions, ordered for planting trees on outskirts of the capital city, performed marriages of about five thousand brahmans and caused for the construction of several inns and tanks.[41] Itama, mother of Balachandra too involved herself in such activities as noted from *Palnāṭi Vīracharitra*.[42]

The Dharmasāgar inscription of Kākati Mailama[43], Kuṅdavaram[44] and Niḍigoṅḍa[45] inscriptions of Kuṅdamāṁba, both the wives of Naṭavāḍi chief Rudra are also of the same nature. Pillalamaṛṛi inscription of Eṛakasāni wife of a Rēcherla chief Betireḍḍi, gives details of the meritorious activities of the donor.[46] Buth pur record of Malyala Kuppambika too illustrates the dharmic activities taken up by the donor.[47]

It was a common practice among women chiefly of royal class and those of nobility to install a deity in their name, in their husband's, father's or son's name and donate lands or make gifts in perpetuation of their memory.[48] It appears that this was an attempt at co-ordinating religion with the Hero-cult as well as the desire for political flattery. Kakatiya period in Āndhradeśa had several such instances.[49] (Chart VII D).

Women belonging to the common sections of the society too at times involved in constructional activities. These include construction of a *maṅṭapa*[50], a pillar[51] or causing for the plastering of the temple walls.[52] (Chart VII D).

Pilgrimage

Pilgrimages to places of religious importance formed another important feature in the religious life of the people of Āndhradeśa. Puranas have extolled the merits of pilgrimages.[53] A woman is not allowed to undertake pilgrimage on her own but she can do so with the consent of her husband.[54] A widowed woman is required to undertake pilgrimages and spend time in taking dips in the holy rivers in order to avoid widowhood in the next birth.[55] She can perform the *Śraddha* rituals of her deceased husband at pilgrimage centers like Kāśi or Gayā by sending brahmans duly worshipping them and providing them money. For the purpose she can even demarcate a portion of her property. Mogaluṭla grant of Kōṭa Gaṇapamadevi is of the same nature.[56] Women are permitted to perform pilgrimages by proxy as indicated in the grant of Kuppāṁbika wherein she had sent brahmans to Kāsi, Gaya and other sacred places duly rewarding them.[57] While elite women are involved in performing *saptasaṅtāna* deeds and donating lands or making grants to brahmans who visit pilgrim places on their behalf, common women are described in the literary works of the period as personally visiting the sacred places along with their men folk. Alaṁpur, Srisailam, Drākshārāmam, Simhachalam, Srikurmam, Srikakulam are some of the holy shrines within Āndhradeśa to which pilgrimages are undertaken. Taking a dip in the holy waters of these shrines, circumambulating the mountain or temple are considered as forms of religious expression during pilgrimages.

The literary works of the period contain abundant references with regard to this, i.e. women visiting holy shrines within Āndhradeśa. Palkuriki Somanatha in his *Paṅḍitārādhyacharitra* gives description of women visiting Srisailam along with their husbands.[58] Vallabhachārāya's *Kriḍābhirāmanu* contains a description of women visiting Srikakulam on pilgrimage and participating in the *Tiṛunāḷḷu* held near the temple.[59] He describes the child widows of Palanāḍu. This could be an indication of the popular belief that undertaking pilgrimage by a widow promises her longevity of married life in the next birth.[60]

Social Observances

Certain social customs and practices such as marriage, celebration of festivals, the practice of sati, crowning ceremony are also of great politico-cultural significance as discussed below. While the first two involved women of both the higher and lower sections of the society, the latter, restricted to royal women mostly. Again all these appear to be secular but have sacred elements in each category.

Thus we see a thin line of separation between elite and folk or sacred and secular and at the same time an integration of both which is a specific feature of Kakatiya period.

Marriage

Marriage is one of the sixteen *saṁskāras* of life stated in the scriptures. It is a sacred as well as secular observance. Marriage enables a man to perform religious rites and continuation of the family through progeny.[61] It is a necessary ritual in one's life and gives a certain status to woman.[62] Marriage may also be of political nature the significance of which is discussed in the earlier chapter. Child marriages are probably the order of the day in brahman families. According to Haradatta, a twelfth century commentator, the marriageable age for a girl is fourteen.[63] The eight different forms of marriage and the necessary aspects concerning marriage are discussed at length by Ketana in his *Vijñāneśvaramu*.[64] On the occasion of marriage, *Araṇamu* (bride prices) is given to the bride. It ranges from land, gold to livestock and attendants depending on the economic status of the family. *Araṇamu* forms a part of *Strīdhana* or the property of the woman. Besides *Araṇamu, ōli (sulka)* or bride price is to be paid to the bride's parents. Due to the constant demand for higher bride-price by the parents of the girls, the caste guilds had to frame strict regulations.[65] Certain inscriptions refer to specific tax on *Vivāhapu Paṇḍiḷḷu* (the marriage halls).[66]

Sati and Self Immolation

The performance of *sati* by woman has a great political significance. During the period in Āndhradeśa, *sati* is found to be mostly related to royal families. The possible reasons for this could be the miserable plight of the wives of defeated kings. They were either taken as captives by the victorious kings or they were subjected to molestation.[67] Probably, on such occasions to safeguard themselves they preferred *sati*. Performance of *sati* accords a great ritual status for the woman. References to *sati* are found in the inscriptions and literary sources of the period.

An epigraph dated A.D. 1057, from Beteluru records *sati* performed by one Dēkabbe.[68] Another record from Bāpaṭla indicates self immolation of a couple.[69] According to another inscription, Joḍarāja and his wife entered into fire.[70] *Palṇāti Vīracharitra* also has references to *sati* performed by women of royal families in order to avoid insult from the rival side.[71] A sculpture showing a woman cutting her neck in a bid to offer her head probably to God is available among the *Vīragals* preserved in the State Museum, Hyderabad **(Plate III a)**.[72] Under the influence of

Virasaivism, these religious offerings and attempts of self-immolation became very popular. Memorial stones were erected for such men or women. Sati stones are found at places like Tuṛumeḷḷa, Saṅgameśvaram and Kolanupāka.[73]

Celebration of Festivals

There is generally no clear cut demarcation drawn between a *vṛata* or an *utsava* (festival). What are called *utsavas* have an element of religious rites and conversely many *vratas* too have some elements of being a festival.[74] The idea of making gifts on an *utsava* day too converges with the *vrata* occasionally as noticed from the contemporary epigraphs and literature. Women of all sections of the society made liberal grants to the temples on festive occasions or sometimes instituted certain festivals. *Pratāparudracharitra*, contains a reference to *Tiṛunāḷḷu* (fair) held under the guidance of Rudrama in the temple of Ēkavira at Mogali Charla.[75] She also ordered for the celebration of *Tiṛunāḷḷu* for Goddess Kākati, Goddess Mailaradevi at Ainavolu and for Lord Gaṇesa and Oḍḍapalli. The author states that these are instituted by the queen with the view to beget a son who could become a political successor for her. Ketana, in his *Daśakumāracharitramu*, mentions *Kaṅdukōtsava* performed by unmarried girls.[76] Several epigraphs register grants made to temples by women on such recurring festive occasions as *Kāṛtika punnami*[77] *Vishṇu saṁkrānti*,[78] *Tula Dvādaśi,*[79] *Sṛavaṇa Punnami*,[80] *Deepavali*,[81] *Śivarātri*,[82] *Davana Punnami*,[83] etc.

A record from Drākshārāma temple registers grants made to Lord Bhimeśvara at Drākshārāma on the eve of celebration of *Dōlōtsava* (swinging ceremony) on *Davana Punnami*.[84] On the same occasion Oḍḍādi chief Arjuna Deva gave land grants to a woman name Akkasāni as *Nōmu* indicating that she was involved in the festival as part of her individual *vṛata*.[85]

It would be seen that through these festivals generally celebrated at the places of worship, a cultural integration is possible. It is during these occasions many of the folk patterns of dance and music, were incorporated into the Sanskritic style.[86] Moreover, performance of festivals in a great grandeur at the temple suggest an attempt to equate the institution of God and the kingship.[87]

Crowning Ceremony

Among the ceremonies of political importance, crowning ceremony is significant. In a state with more feudal elements it is always necessary for the king or queen to display their power by arranging for the royal functions including the ascent of the throne. This can be considered as an attempt to ritualise the power of the king and serve the purpose of proving the sovereignty. Crowning ceremony is generally associated with assuming epithets, taking the five great musical sounds and claiming descent from one of the Puranic races.[88] The ceremony was performed generally on a large scale in the presence of all feudatories, intermediary officers of the king, the chief priests, and common people. Declaration is made amidst chanting of verses from sacred texts. An attempt to co-ordinate religion with political power is indicated here. The titles of Rudramadevi, namely *Paṭṭōdhati, Mahamaṇḍaleśvara* suggest the crowning ceremony of the princess before assuming charge. In this connection, it is very interesting to note that the illustrious Kakatiya king Ganapatideva happily conducted the birthday celebration of princess Rudramadevi by decorating the capital with proficient courtesans brought from Kashmir as mentioned for the first time in the Malkāpur inscriptions dated 1260-61 A.D.[89]

The categorisation of observances into religious and social, sacred and secular is made for convenience of study and as a part of the attempt to understand the actual significance of these with respect to the contemporary politico-social conditions. Women as bearers and carriers of tradition to the future generations are in close contact with the customs and rituals. Though a woman is not allowed to read Vedic scripture or perform sacrifices, her position in the family as a wife assumes a higher ritual status. Without the association of a wife by the side of him, a husband cannot reap the fruits of a pilgrimage, neither he can perform a sacrifice.

By medieval times changes in the concept of kingship and the influence of bhakti cults brought significant changes in the religious practices. Observance of *vṛatas,* making gifts, involving oneself in philanthropic activities, undertaking pilgrimages or celebration of festivals are understood to have brought religious merit of the highest order. Thus several penances are practiced by women and gifts are made in lieu of their observance. In this connection, it is noted that the line of demarcation between religious and social observances is not much rigid. Almost every religious ritual has both the sacred purpose of bringing religious merit as also a secular idea of acting as a medium of exchange and redistribution of economic products. Similarly social observances like crowning ceremony aim at a secular significance but at the same time are performed amidst chanting of Vedic hymns and are thus sanctified. Women of both the elite and common sections of the society are involved in practising these rituals as observed from the epigraphical references. However, a ray of separation exists between the two in the manner of observance of the ritual or in the object of gift made which is contextual and determined by the socio-economic status.

REFERENCES

1. Women are considered impure during the course of their menstruation and during the period of child birth. During these two phases, they were not allowed to perform any religious function. However, Virasaivism outrightly rejected this concept of pollution by the touch of a woman in her monthly course or child birth.
2. P.V. Kane, *History of Dharmasastras*, Vol. II, Part I, 1974, p. 573.
3. According to Brahmapurāṇa, a householder whose wife is alive and chaste must go on a pilgrimage with her, otherwise he would not reap the fruits of a pilgrimage. Padmapurāṇa also speaks of the same. P.V. Kane, *Op. cit.*, Vol. IV, 1974, p. 568.
4. *Ibid.*, Vol. II, Part II, 1978, p. 889.
5. *Ibid.*, Vol. V, Part I, 1975, p. 1. Various meanings are given as will, command, law, prescribed order, religious duty, worship, obligation, undertaking, religious or ascetic performance or observance, vow or sacred work.
6. *Ibid.*, p. 55.
7. *Ibid.*
8. *Ibid.*, Vol. II, Part II, 1978, p. 869 (Agnipurāṇa, 209, 23-41).
9. *Ibid.*, p. 847. *Uttama dāna* is of highest order. Food, curd, land, honey, gold, butter, oil, protection of cows, horses, elephants, etc. *Madhyama dāna* is of middle order. Vidyadana, grihadana, utensils, medicines, etc. *Adhama dāna* is of least order. Furniture, vessels, lamps, etc. which are worn out and are not of much use.
10. K. Lakshmi Ranjanam and K. Balendu Sekharam, *Āndhrula-Charitra - Saṁskṛiti*, (Hyderabad, 1985), p. 193. The Vishṇukuṅḍin emperor Mādhava Varma IV is said to have performed several such sacrifices.
11. R.S. Sharma, 'Material Milieu of Tantricism' in R.S. Sharma, (ed.), *Indian Society, Historical Probings, Essays in Memory of D.D. Kosambi*, (Delhi, 1984), pp. 175-179.
12. *Ibid.*
13. *Krīdābhirāmamu*, verse 128.
14. P.V. Kane, *Op. cit.*, Vol. V, Part I, 1975, p. 55.
15. Romila Thapar, *Ancient Indian Social History*, *Some Interpretations*, (Hyderabad, 1978), p. 105.
16. *SII*, Vol. IV, No. 1382 refers to a king Allaya Vemabhupa as the one who performed *danas* prescribed in the text, *Chaturvargachintmani* of Hemadri. Buthpur inscription of Kuppambika (*HAS*, Vol. XIII, No. 50) also quotes that she performed the *danas* according to the Kalpa texts. Also, *HAS*, Vol. XIII, No. 24, Gudur.

17. Vijaya Ganapatrao Babras, *The Position of Women During the Yadava Period, (1000 A.D. to 1350 A.D.)*, Unpub. Ph.D. Thesis, Marathwada University, (Nov., 1992).
18. P.S. Kanakadurga, *Kakatiyulanati Samajika Jivanamu*, (Vijayawada, 1992), p. 124.
19. *HAS*, Vol. XIII, No. 50.
20. *Ibid.*
21. P.V. Kane, *Op. cit.*, Vol. II, Part I, 1974, p. 429.
22. *Sri Siddheśvara Charitra*, p. 131.
23. *Basavapurāṇamu*, Ist Canto, pp. 11-12.
24. *Palnāṭi Vīracharitra*, pp. 322-323.
25. P.V. Kane, *Op.cit.*, Vol. V, 1975, p. 417.
26. *Ibid.*, the *vrata* is a worship of Kāmadeva, the Cupid God, for one year. They should make gifts of cows, fields, gold to brahmans and worship Kāmadeva, honour a brahman well versed in Vedas with the gift of a *prastha* of husked rice grains and render their person to him on Sunday when the star is *Hasta*, *Puṣya* or *Punarvasu*. In the 13th month, they should make a gift of bed stead, gold chain and an image of Kāmadeva. This is *Vāravrata* for *veśyas*. (H. VII, 541-548).
27. *Daśakumāracharitra*, 5th canto, verses 13-18.
28. *S.I.I.,* Vol. IV, No. 1096.
29. P.S. Kanakadurga, *Op. cit.*, 1992, p. 123.
30. *SII*, Vol. IV, No. 664.
31. *Krīḍābhirāmamu*, veses 137-140. This is a worship of Goddess Lakshmi with Her seven consorts. A specific song was composed on these seven Goddesses which was supposed to be sung on the occasion of the observance.
32. *Basavapurāṇamu*, 3rd canto, p. 58.
33. *HAS*, Vol. XIII, No. 50.
34. *SII*, Vol. IV, No. 1043.
35. Romila Thapar, *Op. cit.*, 1978, p. 110.
36. *Ibid.*
37. Yajñavalkya smrti mentioned that if a gift is made on special occasion, the merit of the same will be more than the gifts made daily and also at a sacred place like a temple. The gifts made on *Amāvasyas* (New moon day), yield hundred times the reward of making it on any other day, thousand times when made on the suppression of *tithi*, one hundred thousand times when made on the equinoctical day. A gift brings countless rewards on a *Vyatīpata*. Similarly, gifts made on eclipse days, every twelfth day of the month, on the occasion of *saṁkrānti*, etc., become inexhaustible. For this reason, we find that all the grants were generally made on any particular occasion or on festival days. P.V. Kane, *Op.cit.*, Vol. II, part II, 1978, p. 852.
38. *SII*, Vol. VI, No. 100 mentions the *Satasantāna* deeds.
39. A.M. Hocart, *Kings and Councillors*, *An Essay in the Comparative Anatomy of Human Society*, (University of Chicago, 1970), p. 216.

40. Romila Thapar, *Op. cit.*, 1978, pp. 106-107.
41. *Pratāparudra Charitra*, p. 34.
42. *Palnāṭi Vīracharitra*, p. 322.
43. *HAS*,Vol. XIII, N. 1, pp.1-4.
44. *Ibid.*, No. 58.
45. *Ibid.*, No. 57.
46. B.N. Sastry, *Rēcheṛla Reḍḍi Vaṁśa Charitra - Śāsanamulu* 'Pillalamaṛri Sasanamu', No. 6, pp. 72-77.
47. *HAS*, Vol. XIII, No. 50.
48. The Dharmasagar inscription, Kuṅḍavaram and Niḍigoṅda inscriptions and the Pillalamaṛri inscription are of the same nature. The Gods are given various names such as Rudreśvara, Ganapeśvara, Eṛakeśvara, Betēśvara, etc. after the names of the persons in whose memory the consecration is made.
49. *SII*, Vol. V, No. 192.
50. *Ibid.*, Vol. X, No. 56.
51. *Ibid.*, No. 512. For more details kindly see the Chart VII.
52. P.V. Kane, *Op.cit.*, Vol. IV, 1974, p. 567. Accoridng to Vanaparva, men or women of all four castes when they have bathed in holy rivers are not born again. Whatever sins may have been committed by them, they vanish the moment they take a dip in the holy river. Matsyapurāṇa further asserts that *Avimukta* is the highest benefit offered by the practice of making pilgrimages.
53. *Ibid.*, p. 568-569.
54. *Ibid.*, Vol. III, 1974, pp. 735-738. All Dharmasastra writers emphasised upon a widow leading a chaste life by observing fasts.
55. *Ibid.*, p. 569.
56. Dr. N. Ramesan, 'Mogaluṭla Grant of Kota Ganapamba' in *Epigraphia Andhrica*, Vol. IV, pp. 93-102.
57. *HAS*, Vol. XIII,No. 50.
58. *Paṅditārādhyacharitra*, Parvata prakaraṇamu, p. 235.
59. *Krīdābhirāmamu*, verses 204-213.
60. P.V. Kane, *Op.cit.*, Vol. III, 1974, pp. 735-738.
61. *Ibid.*, Vol. II, Part I, p. 429.
62. *Ibid.*
63. *Ibid.*, p. 441.
64. *Vijñāneśvaramu*, Acārakāṅḍamu, veses 95-101.
65. The *Teliki Samayamu* of Bejawada declared that *Ōli* for the first marriage should be 21 *Chinnamāḍalu* (of gold). This had to be accepted by the Teliki community as a whole. *SII*, vol. IV, No. 797.
66. *SII*, Vol. X, No. 314, 406. Also, Gade Narsinga Rao, 'Chāḷukyula Rājyāṅga Paristhithulu' in *R.R.N. Pattābhisheka Saṁchika*, (Vijayawada, 1922), pp. 128-135.
67. P.V. Kane, *Op.cit.*, Vol. II, Part I, 1974, p. 630.

68. *Epigrahia Indica*, Vol. VI, pp. 213-219. Another instance of Sati is found in *Inscriptions of Āndhradeśa,* Vol. II, Part I, No. 972.
69. *SII*, Vol. VI, No. 144.
70. An undated record published in *AR*, 1946-47, No. 155.
71. *Palnāṭi Vīracharitra,* verse 760, p. 242.
72. Inscriptional evidence from *SII*, Vol. V, No. 95, also suggests an attempt of self immolation.
73. P.S. Kanakadurga, *Op. cit.*, 1992, p. 134.
74. P.V. Kane, *Op. cit.*,Vol. V, Part, I, 1975, p. 57.
75. *Pratāparudracharitra*, p. 34.
76. *Daśakumāracharitramu*, 10th canto, verse 14.
77. *SII*, Vol. VI,No. 740.
78. *Ibid.*, No. 647, 992.
79. *Ibid.*, Vol. VI, No. 1331.
80. *Ibid.*, Vol. VI, No. 176.
81. *Ibid.*, No. 726.
82. *Ibid.*, Nos. 84, 86.
83. *Ibid.*, Vol. IV, Nos. 1368, 1373.
84. *Ibid.*
85. *Ibid.*, Vol. IV, No. 1373.
86. P.S. Kanakadurga, *Op. cit.*, 1992, p. 182.
87. This argument is based on the conception of king as the ritual performer and the symbolically integrative character of the temple and the city as given by A.M. Hocart, *Op.cit.*, 1970.
88. It was a common practice among the medieval dynasties to trace their origin from the Lunar or Solar dynasties of the Puranic period. Crowning ceremony is performed amidst great pomp and show to authenticate the power of the king who was crowned. Various epithets, titles are assumed by the rulers which are generally described in long poetic verses of Sanskrit in the inscriptions. An exaggerated version of the same can also be found in the chroniclers' accounts. Rudrama was supposed to have accepted the divine sword, royal symbols and such others at the time of her taking up the charge of the kingdom. For details, 'Hanumakonda Kaifiyat', *Mackenzie Manuscripts*, Vol. XXVI, pp. 56-57.
89. *SII*, vol. X, No. 395.

CHAPTER 7

Dress and Ornaments

Alaṁkaraṇa which includes dress, decoration and ornamentation is one of the sixty four arts meant for learning and practising by both men and women. It is a medium of distinction and identity by which the people and their hierarchies are recognised by mere sight. However, the way of adornment varies contextually depending on the occasion (sacred or secular) and space (public and private). In addition, other factors like ethinicity, occupation, occasional requirements and socio-economic status determine the pattern of costumes and jewellery that was used by medieval Āndhra women.

Ethnic conditions like cultural traits and attributes, climatic and geographical variations influence the food and dress habits of a region. The climate of Āndhradeśa being mostly dry and temperate except in the coastal regions, thin soft cotton attire and simple ornamentation is preferred on normal occasions. However, on important occasions silk clothes and precious jewellery are opted for. Contemporary literature too stresses the need for wearing the dress according to seasonal variations.[1]

The higher social privileges necessitated women from royal families to adopt exhaustive ornamentation on all occasions. They had to take special care to plan their costumes and jewellery wearing as adornment is a symbol for the expression of royal majesty. Contemporary epigraphs reveal the significance attached to ornamentation for royal women through the titles assumed by victorious kings such as *Virōdhirājavanithālaṁkāra Bhaṁgāvaham,*[2] or *Pratinṛupavanitāsṛuti Srōtrābharaṇa Gaurava Vaiphalyam,*[3] *Paravadhūmaṅgaḷa Sūtra Haraṇa*[4], *or Pratyardhi Kānthā Gaḷasūtra Dātra.*[5]

Adornment is also determined by the nature of profession thus becoming functional. The Dharmasastras specify that a harlot cannot gain anything without ornamentation.[6] They prescribe ornaments as tools of trade for *Veśyas* and in the event of any offence on the part of these women, a king can confiscate their property but not their ornaments.[7] This could be due to the nature of their profession, wherein they had to associate with men of different classes. To maintain continuity of their earnings, they had to keep a clear distinction between themselves and the other family women by way of rich ornamentation and beautification.

Contemporary poets highlighted the interest of women towards dressing and adorning specially during marriage, functions, religious observances or going on a pilgrimage. *Daśakumāracharitra* describes women attending a festival, wearing colourful saris and costly ornaments. They decorated their hairs with flowers, applied cosmetics to the skin and their fore-heads were said to contain beautiful and colourful saffron brooch.[8] Pālkuṛiki Somana in his *Paṅḍitārādhyacharitra,* describes the adornment of different classes of women on pilgrimage to Sriśailam, a holy shrine for Saivites. He writes that their attire is a reflection of their class.[9]

The socio-economic status is revealed in the quality of the cloth, metal used for preparing ornaments and the number and value of jewellery. Women from common sections of the society, belonging to the families of petty peasants, agricultural labourers, poor artisan class, small vendors were involved in their family occupations helping their husbands in maintaining the family. Therefore they could not give importance to ornamentation or dressing specially when compared to women of elite. Due to their low economic status, they were not able to procure better clothes or precious ornaments made of gold and silver. Even if they secured these by facing hardships, they may not be able to protect them due to frequent thefts as reported in the contemporary literature. They had to be satisfied with a dress of coarse cotton, ornaments of beads, glass, false corals or shells.

Despite these variations, traditions, customs and belief systems of the society determine the necessity of ornamentation for women irrespective of the class or status. It is a common belief among women that wearing jewellery and decorating the hair with flowers cause longevity of married life.[10] *Maṅgaḷa Sūtra* (the token of marriage which is a chain made usually of gold with two discs of gold attached to it), *Maṭṭiyalu* (toe-rings made of silver) and *Gājulu* (colourful bangles) are considered to be auspicious. These are supposed to be worn by married and unwidowed women alone. Widowed women are not provided with the opportunity of wearing these.[11] In addition, they are not supposed to wear ornaments or adorn themselves as it was probably felt that physical ornamentation may lead to temptation.[12]

Thus, dress and ornamentation besides expressing cultural functions, can also become parameters for studying the social and economic distinctions. The literary, epigraphical and sculptural evidences throw much light on these different aspects viz. dress, ornamentation, decoration, preparation and use of cosmetic in general and specific occasions. These issues are discussed under four heads, Costumes, Ornaments, Cosmetics and beauty aids and Circumstantial attire.

Costumes

Normally the dress of a woman consisted of a sari and a boddice. The length of an ordinary or silk sari varies from six to seven yards. In *Basavapurāṇamu*, it is mentioned that the silk sari of the wife of Basaveśvara was of 12 cubits in length and it took twelve complete years for the weaver to compete the same.[13] It appears that there is a difference in the mode of wearing the sari based on ritual wearing and ordinary wearing. The saris were tied from the right and the hem of border (mantle) was put on the left shoulder by Āndhra women. This practice of wearing the mantle was probably borrowed from Paithan region.[14] The artisan women too tied their saris around the waist in the normal fashion. However, the truss was taken up from between the knees and tucked at the waist.[15] The folds of the sari were many and long.[16] Contemporary literature gives details of different methods in the mode of sari wearing. Srinatha, in his *Catu* verses, describes a woman of *Sātāni* community wearing a *Maḍicira* (pure, unpolluted sari).[17] A brahman lady tied her sari in such a way as the border was turned on the head and was brought on the other shoulder thus looking like a veil.[18]

Some of the fine cloth manufacturing centers in Āndhradeśa were – Masulipaṭnam, Gaṅḍipuram (Gandikot), Jammalamaḍugu, Saḍapa, etc.[19] Further, textiles were specially brought from Poddalapura (Paithan), Chīṛappali (Tiruchirapalli), Nāgapaṭṭaṇa, Coḷadeśa (Coramandel coast), Allikākula (Srikakulam), Siṁhaḷadvīpa (Ceylon), etc.[20] The textiles from Kakatiya kingdom were world famous. Marcopolo, had all praises for the quality of the cotton textiles of Āndhradeśa. The *Ravasellas* (buckrams) of Āndhradeśa were in great demand among the princely families all over the world due to their smooth and beautiful finishing.[21] Their price too was very high. The progressive nature of the industry is further indicated by traders of cloth, silk and muslin forming associations called *Nakaṛas, Dēśi,* Ubhaya *Nānādēśi,* and quite often donating extensively to the deities.[22]

Palkuriki Somanatha in his *Basavapurāṇamu* gives names of fifty six varieties of saries which include those brought from China, Ceylon, Malaya, Kashmir, Varanasi, Gujarat, etc.[23] Forty nine varieties of silk and cotton saris with intricate design pattern and colour combinations find mention in *Siṁhāsanadvātrṃsika*.[24] Srinatha describes *Orayūru* sari.[25] *Orayūru* is a place in Andhra region famous for women cotton saris.

The thirteenth century work *Mānasollāsa* throws a flood of light on the costumes of the Deccan region, the various decorative patterns, colours used for dyeing and procedures of processing. The prototype of figures or designs on the saris were made from *Paṭṭasuṭra* (silk), *Kārpasa,* (Cotton), *Ksauma,* (Linen), *Rōma* (goat wool), etc.[26] Varieties of designs were printed on the saris which ranged from sun and moon patterns and circles or square designs to that of animal and bird figures like swans, parrots, stripes of squirrels, dolls and with borders dyed with the juice of Myrobalan.[27]

Generally the colours preferred by women of the period were the colour of pollen yellow, colour of *ṛuḍrāksha* seed (light brown), pure white, brilliant red and yellow colours with the *Ancalas* having patterns of contrasting colours.[28] Some times the colour of the sari was dark like red, indigo, green or blue with the fields of pallu and Ancalas left white.[29] Courtesans preferred saffron, white, and yellow colours.[30] The saris presented to the deities of various temples include *Velipaṭṭtu Chīralu* (pure white silk saris), *Mañjishta Chīralu,* (bright red), *Vella Chīralu* (white), etc.[31] In *Raṅganātha Rāmāyaṇamu,* Sitā is described as wearing *Chaṅdrakāvi Valvalu* (garments of moon white colour).[32] Nannaya describes *Ūrvasi* as wearing *Chaṅdrikādhavaḷadukulamu* (pure moon white coloured garments).[33]

Women of elite group used fine and costlier cotton and silk saris, boddices either plain or printed and with or without stripes **[Plate III B]**.[34] Their garments were generally made of brocade, i.e., containing raised patterns of gold and silver threads. Their saris contained exquisite borders and intricate designs of parrots, horses, elephants, swans or peacock tails.[35] The dress pattern for the royal women was designed separately. Special care was taken to select perfect clothes for them. *Mānasollāsa* prescribes that the garments of royal women should either be made of silk, cotton, fibre or wool. Prices of the clothes should be very high and care should be taken to see that the colour of the sari and that of the border was perfectly matched and that the colours should not be washed away but should improve their colour after each wash.[36] Traders had to provide the best quality of cloth to the king's family. Failing to do so is a crime as stated by Ketana, in his *Vijñāneśvaramu.*[37] Thus the clothes worn by women of royal families are very much precious and highly rated both in quality and price. Same is the case with the women of aristocracy and wealthy courtesans. According to *Kāmaṅdakamu,* a moral treatise, the courtesans of king's service should wear fine quality textiles only.[38] Their professional requirements of maintaining a clear distinction between themselves and family ladies make them selective at colours, designs as well as cost. Further, it was a common practice among them to demand from their customers whatever sari they had seen with the other women.[39]

Not only the saris but the boddices also were gorgeous and costly with respect to women of elite group. They were stitched with gold and silver threads forming stripes in the silk background. The silk boddices are referred to as *Paṭṭu Kuppasamulu* or *Ṛavikalu* (blouse).[40] Variety of designs are stitched on those with silver or gold *zaṛi* (lace) or with mirrors looking as eyes.[41] Mañchāla, wife of Bālachandra is described as wearing a silk blouse with golden flowers stitched on it.[42] His harlot Sabbama had blouses decorated with silver and gold flowers.[43] Tailors are appointed to stitch blouses for women of higher classes. They are called *Kuṭrapu panivaru*. They live in a separate locality of the city called *Mōhaṛivāḍa*. *Kṛīḍābhiāmamu* has a description of the practices of these tailors at *Mōhaṛivāḍa*.[44] They had to choose the best quality among the selected textiles and to stitch blouses for women of the harem.

The garments of women belonging to the lower strata of the society were comparatively of a lesser price and were of a different category. The material was of coarse variety and generally contained simple design, patterns, like long, small or broad stripes at a distance **(Plate III a)**. In *Kṛīdābhirāmamu*, a peasant woman is described as wearing a thick sari of red colour and having yellow stripes in square design.[45] The blouse was also of same variety and pattern. A woman of *Teliki* community is quoted as wearing *Togaṭu* sari (sari containing lace) and blouse made of cloth having floral designs.[46] *Catu* verses of Srinatha give us description of women wearing tight blouses tied into a knot in the front.[47] Another woman probably of a lower class wore a blouse which was white in colour and had a reddish tinge.[48] However the poor women of the society were longing to wear costumes, what so variety they may be, to protect from nature. In *Siṁhasanadvātṛṁsika*, it is mentioned that a woman feels for her poverty and laments that she herself and her daughters were not having anything to wear.[49] Widowed women are supposed to keep themselves away from colourful and fine quality saris. They were supposed to wear old garments, made of bark.[50]

Besides literature, temple sculptures too reflect the dress of women dwelling in the forests (those belonging to the *Eṛuka*, *Sabara* and *Cheṅchu* clans). Their garments were made of wool, both sari and blouse. Autumnal leaves also formed their lower garments **(Plate IV a)**.[51] The leaves had a red tinge and did not wither soon. The attire of a *Cheṅchu* woman is described by Goparaju in his *Siṁhasanadvātṛṁsika*.[52]

Not only the attire, but temple sculptures and literary references point to the variations in the hair styles adopted by women of Āndhra region. Most commonly, the hair was plaited or braided into twists and the ends were let loose **(Plate VII a)**. Sometimes the hair was turned up and arranged in the form of a *Koppu* (knot) **(Plate I b, IV a, b)**. This arrangement is of many varieties, either tied in the centre or towards one side of the head or in the form of a very loose knot.

The *Catu* verses of Srinatha describe different types of hair decorating patterns. One of his verses mentions a woman of *Sātāni* community singing in the *Srīkākuḷa tirunallu*, had neatly combed her hair and arranged the same in the form of a knot.[53] Another verse quotes a woman whose long black lustrous hair was braided in the form of a *veni* (plait).[54] The *Vārakāṅtalu (vesyas)* of Kaḍidipuram are portrayed as wearing a *Jāṛukoppu* (loose knot).[55]

Decorating flowers in the hair is a common feature observed in relation to women. Flowers are arranged in various styles to look more appealing. Copious references to flowers and women selling flowers find mention in the contemporary literature. *Cārucarya,* a small text by Appanamantri gives details of the popular flowers of Āndhra region. The book also discusses the seasonal variations in the availability of flowers and reasons for decorating them in hair.[56] *Saṁpenga* (maichelia Champaka) is one of the most popular flowers of Āndhra. It was customary for women of Āndhra to decorate their hair with flowers of different varieties particularly on occasions like marriage, festive celebration, attending for fairs or *tiṛunāḷḷu* as indicated by literary evidences.[57]

Ornaments

Ornamentation, similar to dressing is another component of adornment. It has several variational factors both, traditional and occupational (sacred and secular). Besides these, the socio-economic status determines greatly the pattern or number of ornaments and the quality of metal used.

Toḍavulu is a general term used in literature to denote the ornaments.[58] The *Maṅgalsūtra* (marriage token), bangles and toe-rings are compulsory ornaments for married and unwidowed women of all classes of the society. Women of elite groups had taste for costly and valuable jewellery. Boxes called *Alaṅkārupeti* were used by them to preserve their jewellery.[59] Ornamentation as stated earlier is a status symbol for royal women. Even small children of royal family are supposed to wear ornaments like a small chain with a pendant called *Puligoru,* which was stringed with Kuṛuma thread, corals, or conch shells. For hands, bracelets made of five metals were put as a customary practice.[60] Professional necessity determines the style of ornamentation as in the case of courtesans and prostitutes. The ornaments of *Sairandhri,* a maid of the harem whose duty is to decorate the hair of the queen and make different garlands are described in detail in *Virātaparvamu* of *Āndhra Mahābhāratamu.*[61]

Ornamentation is preferred by women of middle and lower classes of the society too. However, the number is less and the metal used in preparation varied from brass, bell metal, (bronze), lead to glass, beads, ivory, conch shells, false corals or bamboo pearls. Moreover, the finishing of ornaments is not fine but coarse. The ornaments of women of forest dwelling communities are made of bamboo pearls, *ruḍrāksha* seeds, false corals or *guṛuviṅda* (red coloured seed with black head) seeds.[62] The maids of courtesans are described in the literary works as wearing bead necklaces, brass bracelets, amulets made of false corals, toe-rings of bell metal, finger rings of shell or bead and coarsc black banglcs.[63] The nature of ornaments of *Cḥanḍāla* woman called Sāmavedi is described in *Paṅḍitārādhyacharitra.*[64] Thus it appears that the type of metal used for ornamentation differs according to the socio-economic status. Gold, silver, precious stones and pearls are generally used in the making of ornaments for women of elite group, while those of common women are made of brass, copper or non metals like glass, beads, false corals and shells.

Manufacturing of ornaments is taken up by traders belonging to the guild *Paṅchāṇamvāru* (traders in five metals). In addition, *Nakaṛa* traders too had prosperous trade dealings in ornaments. *Maṭṭelawāda* in Ōṛugallu is a place famous for silver industry where silver toe-rings were manufactured on a large scale.[65] Golconda is a place famous for diamond mines as suggested by the accounts of Marcopolo.

The variety of ornaments gifted to temple deities indicate the prosperous trade in metals in Āndhradeśa. A record from southern Āndhra region gives the particulars of ornaments given to the Goddess, which include a *paṭṭam* (golden fillet), crescent, *Tiṛumaṅgaḷi* (Probably the marriage token) and a necklace containing pearls, beads, etc.[66] It is further stated in the inscription that the necklace had 8 superior quality of pearls, 528 second class pearls, 2 gold beads, 13 long corals and 40 round corals. An epigraph from Draksharāmam temple registers the grant of two gold bangles studded with precious gems by king Kulottunga Choladeva.[67] Another inscription from the same place records gift of *Sitamaṇibaṅdha*, a bracelet studded with diamonds.[68] Tāḷḷamaṁba, wife of

Rāmapātra presented two gold necklaces to the deity at Srikurmam.[69] Several other inscriptions from various temples in Āndhradeśa, recorded grants of gold or silver jewellery (as shown in the chart VII C).

For the purpose of ornamentation, the head, hair, nose, ears, neck, hands, fingers, waist, legs, and feet received special attention. Contemporary literature provides us a with wide variety of ornaments. A detailed discussion of these is given in the Appendix 'B'.

Cosmetics

Cosmetics are used generally to beautify the skin and to maintain and protect its tender nature. Dressing and ornamentation accompanied by the use of cosmetics completes the process of *Alaṁkaraṇa* (adornment). Similar to the earlier two, even products used under this head are determined by factors like tradition, occasion, profession and socio-economic status, customer beliefs and traditional practices prescribe use of certain anointments as *Haldi* for skin, collyrium for eyes and saffron mark on the forehead compulsory for maiden, married, unwidowed women irrespective of the class variations. Widowed women are not supposed to use cosmetic products. Similarly contextual needs, for example : higher privileges for royal women, professional demands for dancers and prostitues and occasional necessities like bridal make up during marriages influence the use of cosmetics. Thus cosmetics form a regular component of physical beautification of all sections of the society. However, the product and the extent of its application depend upon the socio-economic position. While elite women used costlier anointments, common women prepared cosmetics from the kitchen products and cheap and easily available herbs of kitchen garden. The Moṭupalli inscription of Ganapatideva gives details of cosmetics products which formed important items of trade in Āndhradeśa. They include sandalwood, camphor, musk, borax, etc.[70] The *Nakaṛa* and *Ubhaya nāna dēśi* guilds carried on profitable trade in these items.[71]

Cosmetic are either applied directly or used as anointments to beautify the skin. Of the former category include the mark on the forehead which symbolises a customary tradition, collyrium for the eyes, *Vannu* (lipstick) for the lips and Henna for hands, and toes. Haldi, sandalwood powder, saffron, musk, etc. are used as anointments. Ample reference about their use as well as preparatory process is available in the contemporary literature.

The mark on the fore-head, generally kept at the centre of the two eyebrows is a common feature among Hindu men and women **(Plates II a, III b)**. Sometimes, it varies according to the sectarian differences. Vaishnavites call the mark as *Tirunāmamu* or *Tiruchūrṇamu* (the red powder used by Vaishnavites as a face mark).[72] and Saivites make the mark with the powder called *Vibhūdi* (sacred ashes).[73] In addition to this sectarian mark, women keep varieties of marks on the fore-head according to their taste which include *Kuṁkuma Chukka* (red powder prepared from turmeric, alum, and lime juice),[74] *Nelavaṅka Nāmamu* (a face mark of the shape of crescent).[75] *Nāgarēkha Siṅdhōoramu* (a vermillion face mark of the shape of the snake),[76] *Chukkaboṭṭu* (a small dot),[77] *Kastūri Nāgaboṭṭu* (a face mark made of musk and is kept in the form of curved snake's head),[78] *Ōlagaṅdhamu* (a mark made with turmeric paste),[79] *Haṁsatilakamu* (a mark put in the shape of a swan),[80] *Gummaḍigiṅja Nāmamu* (a mark resembling the seed of pumpkin),[81] etc.

Kuṁkuma (safforn), *Sindhōoramu* (vermillion), *Kastūri* (musk), *Ōlagaṅdhamu* (turmeric paste), *Paṭeerapāṁsuvu* (sandal wood dust), *Saṅkumadamu* (civet), etc. are used for keeping the mark.[82] Widowed women were not allowed to wear this mark. However, they keep the *vibūdhi bhasmamu* on their forehead based on a reference from the story of Poraṅḍla Sūrasāni in *Paṅḍitārādhya Charitra* of Palkuriki Somana.[83] Srinadha in one of his *Catu* verses mentions a widow wearing a mark of *vibhūdi* on her forehead.[84] Special care is given to the eyes. Collyrium was applied to make them look dark black. Sometimes, it was applied in such a way as the eyes look elongated and large. Nannechoḍa in his *Kumārasaṁbhavamu* gives the procedure for the preparation of collyrium with certain herbs.[85] *Alāktakamu* (Liquefied lac), *Pūtakāṭuka* (lamp back Collyrium), are other varieties of anointments mentioned in the literary works of the period.[86]

Literary sources point to the specific anointment referred to as *Vannu* (lipstick).[87] It is similar to lipstick and when applied, make them appear beautiful. It was prepared from home products and certain herbs.[88] However, its use as also of another anointment used for lips, called *Lattuka* (lac)[89] is not always regular but only during occasions like festivals, marriage, etc. On such occasions Henna paste is also used to make the hands and toes look bright red.[90] This was applied in different floral designs and variety of patterns.

Sandalwood powder, musk, saffron are used as face powders.[91] *Makara* (sandalwood paste as a kind of decoration) designs were painted on the cheeks by the courtesans to look more appealing.[92] Though no sufficient details are available to us about the hair care taken by women of the period, it appears from the references in the literature and inscriptions that oil extracted from the *Saṁpenga* (Michelia Champaka) flowers was used as hair oil.[93] *Manasollasa* gives a description of hair oils and shampoos which were supposed to be used by women of royal families and which help their hair look black, long and lustrous. The author says that hair should be washed with paste prepared from the fruits of Amla tree.[94]

Medieval women knew the method of preparing scented powder with the help of various herbal products mixed and made into a paste according to the prescribed proportions.[95] This powder was used as bath powder. Massaging oil was also prepared using the flowers of *Gēdaṅgi* (Pandenus Odoretissimus), *Chaṁpakamu* (gold flower), *Jāji* (Jasminum Grandiflorum), *Punnāga* (Alexandrian Laurel), etc.[96]

However, it is beyond doubt that these cosmetics or beauty aids were used by women of elite sections of the society alone. Common women were satisfied with comparatively cheaper and easily available cosmetic products as haldi, sandal powder and such other domestic items.

Tāṁbul is another food product which was used by women of all categories of the society. It was prepared generally with camphor, aromatic spices mixed with quick lime and was taken along with the betel leaves.[97] Women while going to pilgrimages usually carry the box containing these items. *Tāṁbul* chewing was a daily practice for them. The box is referred to as *Aḍapatitti* (a bag containing necessary items to prepare *tambul*).[98] By chewing this the lips turn red. The *tāṁbul* taken by royal women and courtesans was specially prepared with the best variety of spices.[99] Marcopolo, in his travel accounts enlightens about the regular use of *Tāṁbul* by both men and women in Āndhradeśa.[100]

Circumstantial Wearing

Adornment patterns are both sacred determined by tradition and common to all sections of the society irrespective of class or gender and secular with certain amount of contextuality. Therefore, it is proposed to discuss under this head, the adornment during specific occasions of public domain (royal, professional), private domain (common wearing), and ritual (marriage, sati, war).

The profession of ruling or military requirements like participation in war necessitate functional wearing. It is in this connection, the male attire of Rudramadevi during her rule can be understood. Occupations like dancing in the courts or temples, the profession of prostitution too need exhaustive ornamentation, costlier costumes and specific use of cosmetics. The professions of *Sairaṁdhri* and midwifery too need circumstantial wearing as described in the contemporary literature.

Kriḍābhirāmamu and Srinatha's *Catu* verses throw much light on the general adornment patterns of elite as well as common women. Somana's *Basavapurāṇamu* and *Paṅḍitārādhyacharitra* too provide ample information on the common wearing. It generally meant cotton sari with simple and linear designs, a very simple cotton boddice and minimum ornamentation, i.e. compulsory ornaments alone. Haldi is applied to the skin.

However, rituals and observances demand contextual wearing. Nannechoda describes men and women wearing *Pachhavaluvalu* (yellow colored garments) and *Vīramaḍḍiyalu* (silver toe-rings for the large toe) on the occasion of war.[101] Gona Buddha Reddy describes the attire of a woman performing *sati* in his *Raṅganātha Rāmāyaṇamu*. She was wearing a silk sari with chains and a garland of flowers in her neck. Her hair was made into a knot and she put on a *Sōochakamu* (band like sign) of round pure pearls to signify the event. Similarly on her forehead, an application of sandalwood paste was made. Then she took her husband's body with due decoration, put the same in her lap and proceeded for the grave in a palanquin.[102]

Marriage is a proper occasion for dressing oneself gorgeously. The contemporary literature throws a flood of information about the various items used in decoration of the bride. The preparations of certain products can also be gathered from these accounts. Bridal decoration is a part of the marriage celebrations. For more details on the process of bridal makeup, three texts namely *Kumārasaṁbhavamu* of Nannechoda, *Raṅganātha Rāmāyaṇamu* of Gona Buddhareddy and *Palnāṭi Vōracharitra* of Srinatha are selected the description of which is given in the Appendix C.

It is thus observed that the attire, ornamentation styles as well as use of cosmetics have both sacred and secular features and can be taken as parameters to study the socio-economic distinctions among women during the period under study. The attire of an elite woman is suggestive of her interest towards selecting suitable jewellery and garments to suit the occasion. While the sketch of a common woman, the dress and ornamentation styles are mostly simple. At the same time, there is a marked influence of the features like ethnicity, seasonal variations, professional and circumstantial, necessities certain specific adornment patterns. These variations between elite and common categories are however not carried on to the sacred features where an element of commonality is noticed through compulsory ornamentation irrespective of class variations. The same attempt by the tradition to bridge the gap between elite and folk sections of the society is also reflected in the art forms and amusements.

REFERENCES

1. Someśvaradeva, *Mānasollāsa,* 3-6, 1082 to 1085. The seasonal pattern of dressing was more particular in case of the royal families. According to the author, royal personages including the king should adopt such wearing as to suit the seasonal changes. For example,

   Spring Season – Cotton or fibre garments generally white in colour, thin in texture.

   Summer - Thin, delicate cotton attire.

   Rainy - Red, purple or rose coloured beautiful garments.

   Autumn - Thick fibered garments.

   Winter - Woolen or thick cotton fabrics.
2. *SII,* Vol. VI. No. 124.
3. *Ibid.*, No. 594.
4. *Ibid.*, No. 249.
5. *Ibid.*, No. 74.
6. *Daśakumāracharitra*, 6th canto, verse 114.
7. P.V. Kane, *History of Dharmasastras,* Vol.III, 1974, p. 404.
8. *Daśakumāracharitra*, 10th canto, verse 7, 8.
9. *Paṇḍitārādhyacharitra,* Parvata Prakaranamu, Punyanganala nadakalu, p. 235. Jogula nadakalu, pp. 235-236.
10. Masana Chennappa, *Prachīna Kavyāllo Grāmīṇa Jana Jīvana Chitraṇa,* (Hyderabad, 1991), p. 240.
11. *Āndhra Mahābhāratamu, Ādiparvamu*, 4th canto, verse 230.
12. *Siṁhāsanadvātrṃsika,* 11th canto, verse 147.
13. *Basavapuranamu,* 3rd canto, p. 46.
14. Veturi Prabhakara Sastri, *Telugu Merugulu,* (Madras, 1948), p. 4.
15. *Cātu Padya Maṇimanjari,* (Hyderabad, 1988), p. 132.
16. *Ibid.*, pp. 131, 133, 144.
17. *Ibid.*, p. 133.
18. *Ibid.*, p. 135.
19. S.P. Gupta, *Costumes, Textiles and Cosmetic Coiffure in Ancient and Medieval India,* (Delhi, 1973), pp. 150-151.
20. *Ibid.*
21. K.A. Nilakantha Sastry, *Foreign Notices on South India,* University of Madras, 1939, p. 175.
22. K. Satyanarayana, *A History and Culture of Andhras,* (Hyderabad, 1983), Vol.II, p. 53.
23. *Basavapurāṇamu,* 3rd canto, p. 46.
24. *Siṁhāsanadvātrṃsika,* 3rd canto, verse 188, varieties of saris are mentioned in the verse.
25. Veturi Prabhakara Sastri, *Op.cit.*, 1968, p. 132.

26. *Mānasōllāsa,* 3rd canto, 6th chapter, Also S.P. Gupta, *Op.cit.*, 1973, pp. 150-151.
27. *Telugu Vijñāna Sarvasvamu, Telugu Saṁskṛiti,* Vol. III, p. 1138.
28. *Ibid.*
29. *Mānasollāsa,* 3rd canto, 6th chapter, verse 1076.
30. K. Chengalraya Chetti, *Āndhrula Saṁghika Ārdhika Charitra,* (A.D. 1300-1600), (Tirupati, 1991), p. 61.
31. *SII,* Vol. V, No. 1172.
32. *Raṅganātha Rāmāyaṇamu,* Balakandamu, p. 56.
33. *Āndhra Mahābhāratamu, Araṇyaparvamu,* 1st canto, verse 358.
34. Srirama Murthy, *Social and Cultural Life of the Eastern Chalukyas of Vengi,* (Hyderabad), p. 87.
35. *Ibid.*
36. *Mānasollāsa,* 3rd canto, 6th chapter, verse 1076.
37. *Vijñaneśvaramu,* Prāyaschitta Kāṅḍamu, verse 84.
38. *Sakalanīti Sammatamu,* verse 284.
39. *Basavapurāṇamu,* 3rd canto, p. 49.
40. *Palnāṭi Vīracharitra,* p. 337.
41. *Raṅgñanātha Rāmāyaṇamu,* Bālakaṇdamu, Line 75.
42. *Palnāṭi Vīracharitra,* p. 340.
43. *Ibid.,* p. 337.
44. *Krīḍābhirāmamu,* verse 106.
45. *Ibid.,* verses 134.
46. *Ibid.,* verses 102-104.
47. Veturi Prabhakara Sastry, *Op.cit.*, 1988, p. 132.
48. *Ibid.,* pp. 145-146.
49. *Siṁhāsanadvātṛṁsika,* 8th canto, verse 207.
50. *Krīdābhirāmamu,* verse 214.
51. N.L.N. Acharya, *Bejjaṅki Dēvalaya Silpavisheshalu,* (Siddipet, 1993).
52. *Siṁhasanadvātṛṁsika,* 11th canto, verse 6. Chenchu women are described as wearing *Guṛi japērulu, Pāruṭākulu* as garments and decorated wild flowers in their knots.
53. Veturi Prabhakara Sastry, *Op.cit.*, p. 133.
54. *Ibid.,* p. 132.
55. *Ibid.,* p. 141.
56. Appanamantri, *Cārucarya,* verses 12-20, quoted from Arudra, *Samagrāṅdhrasāhityam,* Vol. II, Kakatiyayugamu, pp. 127-128.
57. *Āndhra Mahābhāratamu*, Ādiparvamu, 5th canto, verse 141. Palkuriki Somana, in his *Paṇḍitārādhyacharitra,* Parvata Prakaraṇamu, (p. 238) gives a list of flowers available in Āndhra during his times. We find references to flowers and women selling flowers in most of the literary works of the period like, *Kumārasaṁbhavamu, Paṅḍitārādhyacharitra,* Basavapurāṇamu, *Krīḍabhirāmamu,* etc.

58. *Daśakumāracharithra,* 6th canto, verse 114.
59. *SII,* Vol. VI, No. 705.
60. *Mānasollāsa*, 3rd canto, 12th chapter, verse 1329.
61. *Āndhra Mahābhāratamu,* Virātaparvamu, 1st canto, verses 290, 291, 292.
62. *Kumārasaṁbhavamu,* 6th canto, verses, 43, 44 to 48. The Poet gives the description of the attire, ornaments of *Eṛuka* and *Sabara* women.
63. K. Chengalraya Chetti, *Op.cit.*, p. 61.
64. Palkuriki Somanatha, *Paṅditārādhya Charitra,* Diksha Parakaraṇamu, Sāmavēdi Katha, pp. 33-36.
65. K. Balendu Sekharam, *Āndhras Through Ages*, Part II, p. 57.
66. *ARE,* 1911, p. 63, p. 15.
67. *SII,* Vol. IV, No. 1190.
68. *Ibid.*, No. 1007.
69. *TIAP,* Vol. I. (SKLM dt).
70. C.V. Ramachandra Rao, 'Āndhrula Samudravyāparamu – Valasalu', (B.C. 600-A.D. 1700) in *Abhinaṅdana,* Spl. issue on 60th birth anniversary of Acharya Tumati Donappa, (Hyderabad 1987), pp. 58-81.
71. K. Satyanarayana, *Op.cit.*, pp. 55-56.
72. Veturi Prabhakara Sastry, *Op.cit.*, p. 143. It is of the pattern 
73. *Ibid.*, p. 141. The pattern is 
74. *Ibid.*, p. 131, 133, 144.
75. *Ibid.*, p. 133.
76. *Ibid.*, p. 134.
77. *Ibid.*, p. 141.
78. *Ibid.*, p. 145. Also. *Kṛīdābhirāmamu,* verse 223.
79. *Ibid.*, verse 134.
80. *Kumārasaṁbhavamu,* 9th canto, verse 4-13.
81. Masana Chennappa, *Op.cit.*, p. 239.
82. Veturi Prabhakara Sastry, *Op.cit.*, p. 148.
83. *Paṅḍitārādhyacharitra, Dikshāprakaraṇamu, Sūrasāni* Katha, pp. 29-33.
84. Veturi Prabhakara Sastry, *Op.cit.*, p. 148.
85. *Kumārasaṁbhavamu,* 9th canto, verse 9, Also, 8th canto, verses 65-66.
86. *Daśakumāracharitra*, 3rd canto, verse 78.
87. *Kumārasaṁbhavamu,* 9th canto, verse 9.
88. *Ibid.*
89. *Ibid.*, 8th canto, verse 65. Also its preparation mentioned in verse 13.
90. *Telugu Saṁskṛti,* Vol.III, p. 1138.
91. *HAS,* Vol. XII, No.9, Koṇḍiparthi Inscription.
92. *Ibid., No. 3,* Hanaṁkoṇḍa Inscription.
93. *Krīdābhirāmamu,* verse 102.

94. *Manasollāsa,* 3rd canto, 4th chapter, verse 993.
95. *Ibid.,* 3rd canto, 4th chapter, verse 985.
96. *Ibid.,* 3rd canto, 4th chapter, verse 974, 977. Also 15th chapter, verses 1813, 1815, 1816, 1817.
97. K.A. Nilakantha Sastry, *Op.cit.,* p. 180.
98. *Paṅḍitārādhyacharitra,* Paravata Prakaranamu, pp. 236-237.
99. *Mānasollāsa,* 3rd canto, 4th chapter, verses 1004, 1009, 1012, 1016, 1017, 1024, etc.
100. K.A. Nilakantha Sastry, *Op.cit.,* 1939, p. 180. In the words of Marcopolo, "All the people of this city have a custom of perpetually keeping in the mouth a certain leaf called *Tāṁbul* to gratify a certain habit and desire they have continuously chewing it. They have these leaves prepared with camphor and other aromatic spices and also mixed with quick lime".
101. *Kumārasaṁbhavamu,* 11th canto, Also Chilukuri Virabhadra Rao, *Āndhrula Charitramu, Madhyayugam,* (Madras, 1912), p. 46.
102. *Raṅganātha Rāmāyaṅamu,* p. 415.

CHAPTER 8

Performing Arts and Recreations

The culture of a given society generally finds its expression in the art forms such as dance (both *mārga* and *dēśi*), musical concerts, street-plays, ballad-singing, puppet shows and amusements both indoor and outdoor. They not only reflect the ventage of the people's feelings but their contribution for the cultural continuum. Besides serving as pastime activities. They also assume a religio-political significance by bringing the religion within the reach of common people and making possible an integration of different cultural forms specially the native and classical.

The processes of Sanskritisation and Brahmanisation enabled medieval rulers to effectively incorporate the pastoral and forest dwelling communities and their deities into the main stream of the society.[1] The medieval *bhakti* sects besides the classical art forms as media for popularising their faith, adopted native or folk art froms like *Peraṇi, Kolāṭamu*, etc. In the same way as the literature of the period reflected a culmination of *mārga - dēśi* traditions,[2] the art forms and amusements too had combination of the two. Thus during the period in Āndhra interestingly a synthesis of traditional and indigenous cultures is reflected in the polity, society, religion and also in the cultural expressions. The performers of dance of *mārga* style were proficient even in *dēśi* pattern and are said to have performed different styles in relation to the occasion. The games and sports which are played by the rulers and the ruled also reflect the same ideology. For example, amusements like hunting besides serving the purpose of protecting the people from cruel animals, acted as a check against the forest dwellers who threatened the border regions, and also as a means of venting their leisure hours. In this chapter, different styles of *mārga* and *dēśi* art forms and other amusements like games and sports that were prevalent during the period of study and the space and contribution of women are highlighted. The discussion is made under two heads viz., Performing arts and Recreations.

Performing Arts

Fine arts like music, dance, instrument playing, etc. progressed greatly in Āndhradeśa during the medieval times. As discussed earlier, the political unification of Āndhra under the Kakatiyas, material prosperity of the state, attempts of *bhakti* sects to bring religion closer to common sections of the society, led to a great cultural progress. Taking from the local processions of the village deities to that of court (royal processions), not a single function was held without the programmes of *Nṛtya* (dance), *gāna* (music), *vādya* (instrument playing) and *vinōdamulu* (recreations).[3]

The kings, intermediary chiefs and temples are the principal patrons of the performing arts. Every court, be it of a chief of smaller order, had a regular contingent of actors, dancers, musicians, jesters, voice entertainers, debators, orators, readers of panegyrics, poets and art critics.[4] Similarly, every temple had provision for musicians, dancers and drummers all of whom constituted the *Raṅgabhōgamu* unit in the temple. They were appointed generally on permanent basis and lands were granted for their maintenance. Temples like Pillalamaṛṛi, Chēbṛōlu, Simhachalam even provided residential accommodation for the dancing girls of the temple.

The importance attached to the programmes of dance and music as daily rituals in the temples is further reflected in the architectural style of the temples of the period. Almost every temple had a *Raṅgamaṇṭapa* (dance hall) attached to the sanctum-sanctorium as seen in the ground plan of the Thousand Pillar Temple, Hanamkonda **(Fig. 1)**. It was built in a circular shape with about 8-10" circumference. The pavement and pillars are made of dolarite stone and were highly polished.[5] The pillars are exquisitely sculpted, with various scenes from Purāṇas, and women in dancing posture. The *Raṅgamaṇṭapa* of Ramappa temple is an excellent example of this type a characteristic feature of Kakatiya period. **(Plate VIII b, IX a).**

Literature related to art also developed. Some important literary works of the period on fine art include, Jāyapa's *Nṛttaraṭnākaramu*, Chāḷukya Jagadēkamalla's *Saṅgītachūḍāmaṇi* and Mataṅga's *Bṛha dēśi*.[6] Besides these, the contemporary literary works like Nannechoda's *Kumārasaṁbhavamu*, Palkuriki Somana's *Basavapurāṇamu*, *Paṇḍitārādhyacharitra*, Gona Budhareddy's *Raṅganātha Rāmāyaṇamu* too contain abundant references to the progress of fine arts in Āndhradeśa. Based on these evidences it can be gathered that there are two patterns of arts, *Mārga* and *Dēśi*.

Māṛga can be defined as the classical tradition that was developed by scholars like Bharata, Kōhaḷa, Nārada, Bhaṭṭu Taṅḍa (Tuṁbuṛa), Kīrtidhara and Abhinavagupta.[7] It was mostly meant for the elite sections of the society. Performances in *Māṛga* style are held before a selected group of audience, within the court, the king and his ministers or other important officers and in the temple, inside the sanctum-sanctorium in the presence of God and chief priests in lieu of specific worship offered to the deity. The themes relate to the greatness of the supreme deity, the king as a representative of God and the language was Sanskrit.

Dēśi can be described as the native style which was easily understood and followed even by the common sections of the society. Jāyapa in his *Nṛttaraṭnāvali*, a treatise on dance defines *Dēśi* as the tradition developed as per the changing wishes of the local ruling chiefs and hence specific to that region.[8] Generally *Dēśi* styles are adopted in the festive processions like *Jātaṛa, Tiṛunāḷḷu*, etc. and outside the sanctum-sanctorum, while the deity in His *utsava* image is seated along with His Consort in the assembly of devotees in the *Kaḷyānamaṅṭapa*. Inspiring stories of devotees from Purāṇas with emphasis on devotion and submission to God are the subject of these programmes. *Nṛttaraṭnākaramu* mentions certain native styles of dance which were popular in Āndhradeśa during the period. They are *Chiṅdu, Hallīsakamu, Pēṛaṇi, Goṅḍli, Prēṅkhaṇamu, Kolātamu, Bhaṅḍikamu, Sivapriyamu, Bahurūpa, Kēḷika, Jōka, Kaṅdukamu, Chāṛaṇa*, etc.[9] These are either native of Āndhradeśa or indigenous tradition of south India. *Goṅḍli* is an antique style of Gonds who resided in Āndhra in the ancient times.[10] *Chiṅdu* is probably brought into Āndhra from Karnātadeśa.[11] *Pēṛani* is performed by the Virasaivites during the festive occasions like *Sivarātri*.[12] *Siṁhalatalu* and *Kolakaniki* are probably of Vaishnavite traditions.[13]

Music and dance form part of the syllabi of education for the children of royal family, temple girls, courtesans, concubines and those following the profession of prostitution. The latter however were required to learn both *Māṛgadharmi* and *Lōkadharmi* as per the demands of their profession. Besides Agrahārās and monastaries, temples too appointed dancemasters to impart training to the girls. Inscriptions register grants of land to *Nāṭyāchārya* or *Naṭṭuva* the dance masters of the temples. An epigraph from Simhachalam temple registers some grants in support of a dance master referred to as *Abhinava Bharatāchārya*.[14] The Chēbṛōlu record of Jāyapa Senāni mentions the appointment of a dance master to impart training in various forms of dance to the three hundred temple girls donated to the temple at the age of eight years.[15] Sometimes, they were invited from neighbouring countries like *Kashmīradēśa, Draviḍadēśa, Kaṛnāṭa, Lāṭa, Ahichhatra*, and *Gauḍa*. The Malkāpuram grant of the period of Rudramadevi registers grants to the dance master and singers brought from Kashmīradeśa.[16]

The programmes of dance are always accompanied by music and instrument playing to the tunes of which performance of dances are held. Performers of the three, viz. dancers, singers and instrument players together constitute a single troop of the temple or the court. Records from different temples register grants to the dancing troop referred to as *Bhōgamuvāru* (those who provide amusement / enjoyment to God). Though both men and women comprise the unit, most of the times women alone form the entire group of dancers, drummers and singers. The temple sculptures provide ample references to this. A sculpture from Pālaṁpet shows a female dancer accompanied by two drummers both being women. **(Plate IX a)**. Two more sculptures from the same place project a female dancer in a specific pose of dance **(Plate IV b)** and a drummer with the instrument in her hands **(Plate V b).**

Similar to the dance forms, vocal music too in its classical and native styles developed in Āndhra during the period. The popularity of the classical style is reflected in the grants to the brahmans employed to recite *Sāmavēdā* in the temples. Literary evidences indicate various native styles of music. Somanātha mentions different tunes of music popular in Āndhra during his times in *Paṅḍitārādhyacharitra* while describing the greatness of the Saivite shrine, Srisailam.[17] He states that the devotees sang the episodes of *Dakshādhvaramu, Rudramahima, Sivatatvasāramu* with *Abhinayamu* in native style. Nannechoda describes certain native tunes of music as *Ēla, Sāhuṛi, Āṅdōli, Bhairavi*.[18]

Variety of musical instruments are used during these dance and music performances, the names of which can be gathered from the contemporary literary works and epigraphs. Nannaya quotes women singing and dancing according to the tunes of instruments like *Vēṇu, Kāhala, Patāha*, etc. on the occasion of *Raivataka* festival.[19] Tikkana gives a description of instruments of war music, *Saṅkha, Bhēṛi, Mṛidaṅga, Duṅdubhi, Niśāna*.[20] Gona Buddhareddy in his *Raṅganātha Rāmāyaṇamu*, mentions *Vīna, Mṛidaṅga* as the instruments played by women and according to the tunes of which few women sang in *Sudha mārga* (classical music) while some others danced in various local styles as *Kolāta, Chiṅdu, Chāriṇi,* and other dēśi traditions.[21] Vardhamanapura grant of Malyala Guṁda contains names of certain instruments as *Vīśa, Vēṇu, Tāla, Kāhala, Tuṇuva, Vanapa, Mṛdaṅga, Patāha*, etc.[22]

While it is clear that these programmes of entertainment served as great relievers from the pressures of life, it is also significant that through these, an attempt is made to bring religion within the reach of common sections of the society. The *bhakti* sects, more prominently Saivism, in its different forms made a sincere effort to spread the idea of devotion to Lord Śiva among the common people through the medium of performing arts. The five acts of Lord Śiva are represented in the form of dance to the accompaniment of music, both instrumental and vocal.[23] The doctrines of the sect, path of salvation offered by the sect, the greatness of the Lord, stories of devotees are all propagated through song and dance sequences in the temples, monastaries and on festive occasions in the fairs arranged near the temples. Some of these were performed only by women, while a few like *Pēraṇi* were performed by men exclusively. Besides, Virasaivism advocated for new mode of expression of *bhakti* by jumping into the fire, destroying body parts like limbs, hands, etc. Contemporary poets describe the activities of such devotees who were called *Mailārabhaṭulu*. *Kṛīḍābhirāmamu* contains a description of *Mailārabhaṭulu* expressing their devotion to Lord Śiva in the streets of Ōṛugallu.[24] Somana in his *Paṅḍitārādhyacharitra* too mentions the different devotees offering their body parts to Lord Śiva probably in fulfillment of their vows.[25]

Above these, another significant feature of performing arts is the political character assumed by them particularly the programmes of dance and music held in the courts. *Palnāṭi Vīracharitra,* contains an exhaustive description of the court dance.[26]

Court dances are described in other literary works of the period too, like *Raṅganātha Rāmāyaṇamu*.[27] Courtesans were dressed in golden coloured beautiful sarees and played *Kolāṭamu* and also performed dance in both *mārga* and *dēśi* styles while the ladies played in their accompanyments. Koṛavi Goparaju in his *Siṁhāsanadvātṛṁsika* gives a vivid description of the court dance.[28]

The themes of court dances generally relate to the greatness of the Lord over his subordinate deities. This can possibly be viewed in terms of ritualising the institution of kingship. Emphasis was more on the protective power of the God. The king was portrayed as a glorious and conquering warrior. Burton Stein interprets the court dances as an attempt to express the ritual power of the king in terms of his homology with God and emphasising the protective power of both.[29] An assimilation of the various local (native) and classical traditions was also made possible as the programme of dance, music and instrument playing reflect a perfect blending of both the *mārga* and *dēśi* styles, thus symbolising the attempts of the state to bring in incorporation of the elite and folk. Besides this, there was a perfect display of the royal riches through the decoration of the court, selective garments and ornaments of the king, queens and other maids of harem.[30]

Thus, performing arts can understood as contributing to the polity of the state by acting as integrative and incorporative elements. Women as participants had a greater contribution in this development. Besides epigraphs and literary evidences, temple sculptures too reflect this. The pillars of *Raṅgamaṅṭapa*, inner walls of the Ramappa temple contain numerous sculptures of women in dancing postures accompanied by instrument players.

In addition to these other art forms like *Vīdhināṭakamulu* (street-plays), puppet-shows were arranged in the streets of cities on festive occasions or in the vicinity of temples during fairs and festivals. The stories of devotees, episodes from the Purāṇas, Epics, constitute the themes for these programmes. They were sung in native styles and with the corresponding instrument playing were either enacted or shown through puppet-shows. Palkuriki Somana in his *Paṅditārādhyacharitra* describes these various art forms in great detail.[31]

On the occasion of *Sivarātri* celebrations at Srisailam, variety of programmes were held by the devotees. These include, streets-plays with themes like the story of Siriyāḷa, a great devotee of Siva, or enactment of *Basavapurāṇamu*, etc. A type of street-play called *Veḍḍaṅgamu* was played. Puppet-shows and collective dance programmes were also arranged enlightening the crowd about miracles performed by the devotees of Śiva. In addition, programmes like *Siḍi, Chiṅdu, Pēraṇi, Koḍaṅgāta, Veḍayāta, Gaḍalāta, Mṛōkulāta* (performing certain feats on pillar posts and wooden columns), etc. were also held on the occasion. There were singers who sang songs on the stories of devotees, philosophy of Śaivism and dancers who danced according to the tunes of music.

Krīḍābhirāmamu too has a complete depiction of the various recreatory programmes arranged in the streets of the capital city of Ōṛugallu. While *Jaṅgamas* sang songs on Lord Siva, contemporary heroic incidents like the war of Palnad were enacted.[32] Men and women of the caste of *Bavanilu* sang songs on village Goddesses like Ēkavira, Rēṇuka, etc.[33] Women of the lower castes too sang songs as Ēkavīra.[34] Street-plays were also arranged. One such play displayed the greatness of Macaldevi, the concubine of Prataparudra II, the Kakatiya emperor.[35]

Forest dwelling communities and those belonging to the lower classes of the society like *Jaṅgama, Sātāni, Jakkulu, Bavanīlu, Vīramushṭi, Pichchukuṅṭlu*, etc. are the main performers in these programmes.[36] They move from one place to another exhibiting their arts in the fairs regularly held near village centers or temples, sometimes in the capital cities on festive occasions. Their programmes are always accompanied by song, dance and instrumental music. These have a great significance in the sense that they bring religion to the doors of common sections of the society. They provide them a knowledge of Epics, Purāṇas in an easy understandable manner besides preserving the traditional forms of cultural expression like puppet-shows and street-plays.[37] Sometimes their programmes contain episodes from contemporary issues and thus create political awareness among the people. Religious movements of medieval period patronised these art forms greatly in their effort to popularise philosophy of devotion in the society. These arts enjoyed great patronage from the rulers too, by way of instituting fairs, festivals, or giving grants of *Aṅgaraṅgabhōga* services in the temples, as they facilitated the process of cultural integration of the elite and folk traditions. This measure is of great importance in a state with feudal polity, as it enables incorporation of forest dwelling communities, their deities along with their cultural forms into the traditional styles.

Cock-fights, animal-fights, wrestling, snake-shows are the other popular collective recreations in Āndhradeśa during the period as gleaned from the contemporary literary works.[38] While these were community entertainments, certain games and sports are individual in nature and are determined by various factors like age, gender, etc. Yet as noticed in the following pages, they represent regionalisation of culture as well.

Recreations

Basically recreations provide entertainment and are meant for spending the leisure hours.[39] According to Srinatha, people of Āndhra are engaged in various pastime activities during their free hours.[40] However, there are two more aspects which can not be overlooked. The recreational activities relieve one's mind from the physical and psychological stress and strain caused due to the nature of work, professional engagements or domestic responsibilities. While few others have a socio-political significance, such as hunting which can be regarded as a sport for royal members and at the same time acts as an exercise of authority.

Based on the persons' interests or the time during which the games are played, recreational activities can either be out-door or in-door games. Regional factors like environment, nature of social life, customs, beliefs and personal factors like age and gender differences too, at times influence the type of activities in which people are engaged. The contemporary literary evidences contain abundant references to the recreational activities of the people of Āndhra country. Attempts are made by many scholars towards classification of these according to age and gender differences.[41] While one attempts to classify the pastime activities of women, based on the socio-economic status, it appears that certain recreations are specific for the elite women. These include *Jalakrīḍalu* (water-games), *Vasantōtsavamu* (Holi), engaging in philosophical discussions, etc.[42] Hunting is an important sport even for women of royal families as observed from the temple sculptures. A sculpture from Srisailam depicts women in hunting process (**Plate I a**). Tikkana, in *Āndhra Mahābhāratamu*, mentions that women of ruling class used to drink to relieve their minds of psychological tensions.[43] Nannechoda, in his *Kumārasaṁbhavamu*, quotes that on the occasion of the marriage of Parvati with Lord Siva, there were various programmes of entertainment. Women were in a state of drunkenness and celebrated *Vasantōtsavamu* (sprinkling coloured water on each other).[44] He also describes the competitive attitude of young women while they played in water. The game was referred to as *Jalakrīda* or *Olālāta*. Competitions and discussions on various subjects were generally taken up in the houses of *Vēśyas*.[45] During the festival of *Kaumudi jāgaraṇa, Vēśyas* were engaged in various literary competitions throughout the night.[46] Their recreational activities are usually related to the interests of the men with whom they come into contact with reference to their profession.

The games of the children of middle class families are mostly simple and include playing with dolls, hide and seek and toys. Interestingly these games are common even for the children of higher classes. Godaguci, a small girl used to play with *Bommapottikalu* (clothes for dolls), *Guṛugulu* (a small cup), *Sonnārulu* (small toys), etc. When Lord Śiva was not drinking the glass of milk which she gave Him, in order to coax Him to drink milk, she offered all her toys to Him. She further says that she will take Him to the *Jātara* (fair) of Virabhadra held in the town.[47] Nannechoda, in his *Kumārasaṁbhavamu*, describes the playful activities of Parvati.[48] Parvati, like Godaguci in her childhood played with dolls and colourful toys. She cooked *Gujjanagūḷlu* (imaginery of food cooked in small mud-pots) for the toys. She performed marriages for the toys and constructed *Bommarillu* (a doll house) for keeping her dolls.[49]

Not only these, many other games like swinging, playing *Vāmanaguṇṭalu* (a tablet with fourteen holes for playing a kind of game with tamarind seeds), *Kandukakrīda* (playing with ball) also appear to be common for girls of both the common and higher classes of the society.[50]

There seem to be no gender preferences among the games played by children. Variety of pastime activities find mention in the contemporary literary works. They are meant for increasing the observation power of children.[51]

As children grew big, there is a tendency to separate boys and girls and this is clearly reflected in the games and choice of plays. While boys prefer more out-door games as hide and seek, *Sirisiṅgaṇāvatti* (a certain game played by boys), etc., girls prefer playing with toys and dolls.[52] Their activities such as cooking for the toys, serving, worshipping and performing marriages for toys indicate the nature of duties accepted by them as part of the tradition which had come to them through their mothers.

Games of young women are characterised by their complicated nature.[53] They tend to increase the intelligence power of the participants. At the same time, their out-door activities were designed to give them physical exercise. Literary references point to such games as *Kaṅdukakṛīda, Jalakṛīda, Ōlalāṭa*, etc. played by young women.[54] Some games contained rewards too.

Availability of time determines the nature of pastime activities for married women. Their leisure hours are generally in the afternoons, when they played more mature games which involve certain strategical thinking.[55] Further they spend their time in attending to religious discourses held in the temples and *maṭhas* in the evening hours.[56] Besides religion, even contemporary socio-political issues constitute part of these discussions, thus making possible for creation of an awareness in the minds of people assembled specially women.

Further, their relief from domestic chores comes from the songs. The contemporary literature throws a plethora of information on the different native tunes of music popular in Āndhradeśa. *Bṛha dēśi* of Mātaṅga lists a number of *dēśi* songs. Poets like Nannechoda, Palkuriki Somanatha, Gona Buddha Reddy mention marriage songs, songs meant for singing at the time of religious observances, domestic works like pounding and grinding rice or songs sung *Raṅganātha Rāmāyaṇamu* has a reference to marriage songs.[57] Songs in a specific form of literary composition called *Taṛuvōja* were sung at the time of pounding rice during functions like marriage.[58] *Krīdābhirāmamu* contains a reference to *Kamēśvaripāṭa*, a song sung on the occasion of the observance of *Kamēśvarinōmu*.[59] Nannechoda quotes devotional songs like *Gaudagītamulu* sung by women belonging to forest dwelling groups such as *Sabara*.[60] He also states that Parvati sang *Aṅkamālikalu* in praise of Lord Śiva.[61] Several songs popular in Āndhradeśa during the life time of Palkuriti Somana found their way into his works.[62] Of them, *Prabhāta Padamulu* (the songs of the dawn), *Tummedapadamulu* (songs with a specific rhyme), *Saṅsāramāyāstavamulu* (songs with a philosophical mood) bear a religious undertone.[63]

Thus, modes of recreation and performing arts which involved women in different ways served not only as pastime activities, but create an awareness in their minds about the contemporary socio-religio-political issues. Regionalisation of culture can be witnessed in the art forms as well as amusements. While women performers contributed to the blending of *mārga, dēśi* traditions, their games and sports appear to be common for both higher and lower sections of the society. Further, visiting fairs, participating in *Tirunāḷḷu* or *Jātaṛa* gave them an opportunity to integrate and interact with different people, bringing them closer and bridging the economic differences.

REFERENCES

1. By clearing the forests and establishing villages, the forest dwelling communities were brought under political control. The villages were generally granted to brahmans, monastic establishments or religious preceptors thus making possible the Sanskritisation process. By Brahmanisation, their deities were incorporated into the Vedic and Puranic pantheon. This is best reflected in the worship of village Goddesses as incarnations of Durga or Śakti.
2. Most of the literary compositions of this period in Āndhra correspond to translatory works of Sanskrit into Telugu like *Mahābhāratamu, Rāmāyaṇamu, Kumārasaṁbhavamu, Viddhasālabhañjika, Vijñaneśvaramu*, etc. Moreover poets like Nannechoda, Palkuriki Somanatha claimed that *Dēśi* form of writing is more sweeter and simpler to *Mārga* style.
3. The abundant epigraphical and literary evidences regarding court programmes, provision of *vṛittis* to the temple dancing girls speak a lot about the widespread patronage of these arts. The kings are described in the grants often as entertaining themselves with the programme of music, dance and instrument playing.
4. *HAS*, Vol. XIII, Part I, p. 33. Pillalamarṛi, Dharmasagar and Buthpur inscriptions too speak of this.
5. *Saṁgrahāndhra Vijñanakōsamu*, Vol. I, p. 638.
6. Veturi Prabhakara Sastry, 'Dēsi Sāhiti Soṁpu' in G. Subrahmanyam, (ed.), *Sāraswatha Vyāsamulu*, Vol. IV, (Hyderabad, 1981), pp. 1-6.
7. P.S. Kanakadurga, *Kākatīyulanāṭi Sāmājika Jīvanamu*, (Vijayawada, 1992), p. 183.
8. *Ibid.*, p. 182.
9. P.S.Kanakadurga, *Op. cit.*, 1992, p. 187.
10. Dr. Natraja Ramakrishna, Āndhra Nāṭyam in *Abhinaṅdana,* (Hyderabad, 1987), pp. 13-21.
11. Mallampalli Somasekhara Sarma, *Andhradesa Charitra-Samgrahamu*, (Vijayawada, 1991), p. 45.
12. *Basavapurāṇamu*, Ist canto, p. 19.

13. Vaidehi Krishnamoorthy, *Socio-Economic Conditions in Eastern Deccan*, (A.D. 1000-A.D. 1250), (Hyderabad, 1970), p. 253.
14. *SII*, Vol. VI, No. 1091.
15. V. Yasodadevi, 'A History of Andhra Country', in *JAHRS*, Vol. XXV, pp. 52-152.
16. *SII*, Vol. X, No. 305.
17. *Paṅḍitārādhyacharitra,* Parvata prakaraṇamu, pp. 258-263.
18. P.S. Kanakadurga, *Op. cit.*, 1992, p. 186.
19. *Āndhra Mahābhāratamu*, Ādi parvamu, 8th Āsvasamu, verse 174.
20. *Ibid.*, Udyogaparvamu, 4th Asvasamu, verses 116, 117.
21. *Raṅganātha Rāmāyaṇamu*, p. 29.
22. P.V. Parabrahma Sastry, *Kakatiya Sasana Sahityamu*, (Hyderabad, 1981), pp. 118-119.
23. K. Satyanarayana, *A Study of the History and Culture of Andhras,* Vol. II, (Delhi 1983), p. 88.
24. *Kridābhirāmamu*, verses 141 to 147.
25. *Paṅḍitārādhyacharitra*, Parvata prakaraṇamu, pp. 249-250.
26. *Palanāṭi Vīracharitra*, pp. 269-271. The court of Nalagāma was beautifully decorated with colourful paintings depicting stories from Purāṇas and Epics. It was attended by the king, ministers, feudatory chiefs, scholars, poets, officers of the king besides members of the royal family. Instrument players were ready with their instruments tuned to play the classical as well as native tunes. Singers and dancers were also settled in their places waiting for the orders of the king.

    As the king gave permission to begin the programme, the dancing girl named Kaṅjalōchana began her performance by bowing to the God, to the master, the king and to the associate deities. She then danced to the tunes of songs sung by songtresses. She expressed greatness of Lord Chennakēśava, the presiding deity of Māchenla in various local as well as classical forms of dance such as *Pēraṇi, Dēśini, Prēṅkhaṇamu, Suddha, Daṅḍika, Kuṅḍali, Bharataśāstra*, etc. enlivening the minds of all those who attended the court. The songs were composed both in Sanskrit and *Āndhrabhāsha* (Telugu).
27. *Raṅganātha Rāmāyaṇamu*, *Balakaṅḍamu*, p. 29.
28. *Siṁhāsanadvātṛṁsika*, Ist canto, verses 128-134.
29. Burton Stein, *Peasant State and Society in Medieval South India,* (Delhi, 1980), pp. 386-391.
30. *Palanati Viracharitra*, pp.267-268. The court was decorated with variety of floral designs and there were colourful paintings from the scenes of epics hanging on to the walls. full size mirrors were kept on all sides of the court. The floor was decorated with a beautiful, thick carpet. The throne meant for the king was adorned with precious jewels and was made of gold.

31. *Paṅditārādhyacharitra*, Parvata prakaraṇamu, pp.255-256.
32. *Krīḍābhirāmamu*, verses 116 to 125.
33. *Ibid.*, verses 127-130.
34. *Ibid.*, verse 131.
35. *Ibid.*, verse 177.
36. Arudra, 'Telugu Prajala Kaḷāṛūpālu', in *Praja Sāhiti,* Vol. VIII, No. 11, June, 1985, pp. 17-26.
37. *Ibid.*
38. *Saṁgrahāndhra Vijñana Kōśamu*, Vol. IV, p. 196.
39. *Ibid.*, p. 194.
40. Srinatha, *Bhēemeśvara Purāṇamu* (5-15), quoted in *Saṁgrahāndhra Vijñana Kośamu*, Vol. IV, p. 195.
41. For example works like Suravaram Pratapa Reddy, *Āndhrula Saṁghika Charitra,* Vadla Subrahmanya Sastry, *Telugu Sāhityamlō Krīdavinodālu*, Masana Chennappa, *Prāchina Kāvyālu - Grāmiṇa Jana Jīvana Chitraṇa*, etc.
42. *Siṁhāsanadvāṭṛṁsika*, 3rd canto, verses 178-183 describe the sports of royal women.
43. *Āndhra Mahābhāratamu*, 2nd canto, verses 88-89.
44. *Kumārasaṁbhavamu*, 9th canto, verses 51, 52.
45. B.N. Sastri, *Āndhradeśa Charitra-Saṁskṛiti,* Vol. I, (Hyderabad, 1992), pp. 118-119.
46. *Ibid.*
47. *Basavapurāṇamu*, 3rd canto, Godaguci Katha, pp. 61-62.
48. *Kumārasaṁbhavamu*, 3rd canto, verses 35-38.
49. *Ibid.*
50. Vadla Subrahmanya Sastry, *Op. cit.*, 1987, p. 81.
51. Games such as *Dāguḍumōothalu*, *Allonēraḷḷu Aṛugāṭalu, Vuyyāla, Gālipāṭalu, Gummaḍikāyalu, Kummaṛisārelu*, etc.
52. Such as *bommaṛillu, Bommalapeḷḷiḷḷu, Vennelakuppalu, Gavvalāṭalu, Vuyyāla, Ashṭāchemma, Attā Kōḍali yāta*, etc.
53. Such as *Sogaṭālāṭa, Vāmanaguntalu, Roṅḍli*, *Kōlaṭam, Nālugustaṁbālāṭa, Kuppalāṭa*, etc.
54. Nannaya and Ketana refer to *Kandukakṛiḍa* (playing with ball). Nannechoda describes *Jalakṛīdalu* (water sports).
55. Games like *Vikunthapāḷi, Chadaraṅgam, Vāmanaguṅṭalu, Siḍisogaṭālu*, etc.
56. P.S. Kanakadurga, *Op. cit.*, 1992, pp. 166-167.
57. *Raṅganātha Rāmāyanamu,* p. 73.
58. Arudra, *Samagrāṅdhra Sāhityam*, Vol. I, (Madras,1977), p. 77.

59. *Kṛīdābhirāmamu*, verses 136-138.
60. *Kumārasaṁbhavamu*, 6th canto, verse 48.
61. *Ibid.*, 3rd canto, verse 37.
62. *Paṅḍitārādhyacharitra*, Vāda prakaraṇamu, p. 118.
63. *Ibid.*

CHAPTER 9

Conclusions

The study aims at bringing women to the centre of historical process and attempts at studying the socio-political history of Āndhradeśa with a woman's perspective. Earlier studies on the society of medieval Āndhra concerned mainly on of social life in general and included a description of women among these, thus marginalising their contribution. The role of women in state formation, their participation in different professions have not been given much emphasis. Further, the classification of women into *Kulastrēe, Bhōgastrēe* and *Vēśya* does not include all categories of women.

Keeping these aspects in view, a division is made among women based on economic factor into two broad groups, the elite and the folk. The study concentrates on the attempts of the rulers to bring out an integration of the two sections on the one hand and maintaining the *Varṇa* order on the other. This study is taken up with contextual reading of the sources and reorientation of the theories to suit the hypotheses worked out.

The region of research confines to Āndhradeśa comprising the area extending from Mahendragiri in the north to Kalahasti in the south with Bay of Bengal and Srisailam forming the east and west boundaries respectively. The period from eleventh to thirteenth centuries marks a transition phase in the history of Āndhradeśa between the early and late medieval periods. Feudal elements were strengthening their hold on polity. Kakatiyas brought political unification of Āndhra which led to economic prosperity and great cultural progress. Another significant feature of the period includes the *Mārga-Dēśi* synthesis achieved by the rulers in every aspect of polity, society and religion.

The geo-ecological features of the region contributed to the formation of three cultural zones, the west zone of the coastal tract with a feudal polity, the dry zone of Telaṅgāṇa necessitating a peasant-warrior culture and the semi-arid forest zone involving dharmic, ideological control or ritual extension of sovereignty. Prior to Kakatiyas Āndhra region comprised peripheral part of the empires whose bases were outside Āndhradeśa. They exercised control on these areas through feudatory chiefs thus constituting a *Maṅḍalika* era. Internecine wars and frequent shifting of political boundaries are the important features of this period. By A.D. 1158, Kakatiyas rose to imperial status with their centre of political activity to Telaṅgāṇa and annexed the coastal and neighbouring regions. The kingship was more or less ritual, with a dual sovereignty, coercive in the core zone and ritual in the frontier regions. Control on forest zones was manipulated by inducting dharmic ideologies and policies of land reclamation. It was these attempts by the rulers of maintaining ritual relationship between the various power-loci of the state that necessitated women's involvement.

In line with the space provided by Dharmasastras towards the political rights of women in certain circumstances, women responded to the contextual demands in two ways, active and passive participation.

Rudramadevi, the Kakatiya empress proved herself to be the ablest successor of her father, Ganapatideva as suggested through her title, *Dāya-gaja-kēsari*. She not only exemplified the qualities of a great military general but also idealised herself as an efficient administrator. She instituted *Nāyaṁkara* system of revenue administration. *Nāyakuṛālu* Nagama was a minister of expertise knowledge in political diplomacy. Despite the ridicules of the society and contempt of the tradition towards women's political role, they successfully overcame the oppressions. Besides these two, there were other women who became political successors to their husbands' areas of control and assumed titles like *Mahāmaṅḍaleśvara*. In their capacity as wives of *Maṅḍalika chiefs,* women exercised ritual sovereignty over the areas of their control through gift giving, land reclamation policies, *Saptasaṅtāna* deeds, etc. Even women belonging to forest dwelling communities like Eṛuka, took up certain jobs in the military administration.

In extension to their personal and direct involvement in the state affairs women like Prōlama, Chānama, Sīlama, Māṅchāla determined the course of wars through their acts of counselling. Undoubtedly a royal princess acts as a binding medium in bringing together two warring states through marriage. During the period, in Āndhradeśa, most of the ruling families both imperial and intermediary are connected to each other through marriage alliances. Moreover, the relationship between husband-wife, deity-devotee and lord-servant are linked with political relations inseparably. The abundant epigraphical references substantiate this argument. Thus women's role in state formation appears to be manifold in this period, a point which needs much focus.

The Indian tradition fixes the gender roles of men and women to be public and private respectively and Dharmasastras emphasised a complementarity between the two. Thus, these divisions appear to be less rigid and certain amount of interchangeability is always noticed. Besides providing political rights of succession, law-givers created ample space for women to enter into valid contracts in business and allow them rights on property. This largely explains the economic participation of women in medieval times. Though women of elite did not take up any economic activity, those of weak economic sections of the society undertook variety of professions to supplement the family income. Some of them might not be paid such as those of artisan women but contributed to the economic activity of the family. A great political significance is attached to the institutions of courtesans and concubines. The state framed laws in accordance with the ancient traditions providing maintenance allowance for the concubines. While it protected the prostitutes from the exploitation by customers and the society on the one hand, it also prevented these girls from adopting to treacherous/dubious behaviour thereby protecting the customers.

The temple is another area where women in great numbers took employment. The various socio-political changes of the period culminated by the rise of devotional sects created a parallel world of authority on the spiritual plane. Attempts were made to authenticate and legitimise the new feudal polity through a homology between the god and the king. It is in this connection both the god and the king had to follow elaborate Aṅgabhōga and Raṅgabhōga rituals which needed a diverse body of functionaries among whom women play a dominant role. The services of women in the temple of whatsoever capacity were made hereditary and a share in the temple property is allotted to them. The rapid expansion in temple building activity, recruitment of temple girls in large numbers together with their constant increase in the service requirements necessitated an organisational pattern for the temple girls. The guild is named according to the regional variations. Thus, temple girls through their professional associations, became a part and parcel of the institution of the temple.

The wages, most of the times were in kind and thereby become part of the family property over which both husband and wife become joint owners. Therefore, women's involvement in professions does not speak of their economic independence. However, women enjoyed liberal property rights during the period, thanks to the liberation of rules and extension of the domain of *Strīdhana* by Vijñaneśvara, the author of *Mitākshara* which was closely followed in Āndhradeśa during the period.

Questioning Manu's theory of dependence of women at every stage of her life, Vijñaneśvara insists that it should not restrict her economic freedom. The extent of economic independence of women is reflected in their grants to temples and various charitable institutions.

The system of learning in Indian tradition is modeled to preserve the family system and kinship relations. A woman has to carry the legality and prestige of the family created by man to the future generations in her role as a mother. Thus, generally formal education was provided for men and non-formal, mostly traditional education for women. However, the contextual demands necessitated women atleast of the families of ruling elite, courtesans and girls in temple service to undergo formal educational training, the syllabi of which varied according to the need. The aspects of non-formal education which revolve round the preservation of family system were confined to women of middle classes. Despite these variations based on caste and class, religious education is provided to all irrespective of caste or gender difference through the bhakti cults arranging discourses in Vedas, Purāṇas in the temples or monasteries. These discourses held in the form of religious assemblies also paved way for women of middle and low classes of the society to develop an awareness towards contemporary socio-political changes.

As a consequence to this development, the rise of religious literature stressed the need for performing rituals for family welfare and continuity of tradition. Various religious and social observances are performed in lieu of this changing trend. As their objectives concern with family welfare and religious merit, women's participation becomes more conspicuous. *Vṛatas* were observed for progeny, prosperity and religious merit and these are accompanied by the gift-giving, i.e. *dāna* and *dakshiṇa*. Women of both elite and folk sections of the society contributed to this development more or less in a similar way, the only discriminating factor being the mode of observance and the nature of gift which is largely determined by the socio-economic status. Certain amount of political significance is also attached to these religious and social observances when viewed in terms of the ritual sovereignty exercised by the rulers of the period. Thus, elite, folk, sacred and secular motives run through every observance whether religious or social. However, the line of demarcation is very thin. For example, every festival or observance is sacred and common to every member of the society, yet it has a secular purpose and differs in its mode of practising from elite to folk.

These differences and similarities are carried out also in the dressing and ornamentation patterns of the period. Adornment is a medium of distinction by which people and their hierarchies are recognised by mere sight. Despite variations according to class and socio-economic status, adornment with its three components, i.e. dress, ornaments, and cosmetics becomes functional and contextual. This is indicated by the titles assumed by victorious kings claiming to have snatched away the ornaments of women of defeated kings. Similarly, harlots cannot gain anything without adornment. Special occasions like celebration of festivals, marriage need contextual wearing for both the categories of the society. Yet they differ in the nature of cloth, metal used for ornaments and in the product of cosmetics applied to the skin.

However, a perfect culmination of the sacred and secular aspects of social life could be seen in the performing arts and amusements prevalent during the period in Āndhradeśa. The courtesans and the temple girls performed with great amount of excellence, both *mārga* and *dēśi* styles of dance. Literature too gave importance to both classical (Sanskrit) and native (indigenous-Telugu) languages. The songs sung by women during various work processes indicate the different native styles of music developed during the period which paved their way into classical tradition similar to the dance forms. Religious movements took recourse to these art forms and amusements such as dance, music, street-plays, ballads, puppet shows to popularise their faith among common masses. Purāṇic stories of devotees, contemporary socio-political incidents are enacted in different ways enabling common people to understand the concept of dharma in an easy and understandable manner and at the sametime develop an awareness in the contemporary political matters. The same trend of integration of Sanskritic and local traditions is also noticed in the recreations of the period such as hunting. While hunting serves the purpose of pastime as well as an act of exercising ritual control for women of royal families, the same is a means of livelihood for women of forest-dwelling comminutes. The temple sculptures reflect this idea in different ways. In addition, most of the games and sports of small girls, maiden or elderly women of the lower strata of the society seem to be common even for the women of higher strata of the society. Thus regionalisation of culture is observed in the cultural development of Āndhradeśa. The space of women as performers in this process is clearly visible in literary and epigraphical references.

To conclude, it can be argued that the Indian tradition, family system and kinship relations suggest complementarity between the two genders male and female though a demarcation is drawn between their space to be public and private respectively. It is this aspect which is symbolised in the *Mārga-dēśi* synthesis of the Kakatiya rule in Āndhradeśa. Unless the study of history is taken up with a wholistic perspective bringing women to the centre of historical process, it becomes very difficult to understand the phenomenon.

Thus an attempt at the reconstruction of socio-cultural picture of medieval Āndhra from a woman's perspective and making woman as the central point of argument, helps us in a better understanding of the different socio-political and economic changes of Āndhra region during eleventh to thirteenth centuries, for civilisation has been jointly created by both men and women and traditional historiographies only highlight the contribution of men.

APPENDIX - A

CHART - VIIA

GRANTS BY WOMEN – LAND

Sl. No.	Donor	Status	Donee Temple	Particulars of land grant	Service Instituted	Date of inscription	Source
1	2	3	4	5	6	7	8
1.	Gaṅgaṁba	Queen	Drākshārāmam temple	Some measure of land		31st year of K. Choḷa	S II, Vol. IV 1022
2.	Suramadevi	Queen	--do--	Village	Gaurivṛata Sankubhimapuram free of taxes	A.D. 1252	1043
3.	Aitasāni	D/o of Temple sāni and W/o Upendradeva of Rāpaṛti	--do--	Village Viśwanāthapaṭnam	For Aṅgaraṅgabhōgas and offerings to the deity	A.D. 1263	1245
4.	Gunḍamadevi	Queen	Mulasthāneśvara temple, Nadinḍla	Gunḍasamudramu (a lake)	For offerings to the deity.	–	684
5.	Jāyama	Servant of K. Choḍadeva	Drākshārāmam temple	30 puṭtis of field in Suṅkaṭūru of Pṛolinādu, free of all its taxes	For the choultry instituted by her in Drāksharāmam. She also provided arrangements of rice, cereals, and money for salary to the employees of the choultry. For the daily offerings to the deity, she provided arrangement of 80 leaves and 40 nuts (betel and areca). In addition, she kept	A.D. 1084	1015

1	2	3	4	5	6	7	8
					300 bullocks with the temple bōyas for supply of ghee.		
6.	Pinnamajiyyar	Queen	Kodaṅḍa Rāma temple, Kāza	Lands for various services in the temple : 1) 3 kh of land. 2) Wet land of 4 marṭuṛus behind Eṛṛamcheṛuvu and 2 kh land and 12 kh land	Daily offerings For Aṅgaraṅgabhōga	A.D. 1164	704
7.	Ganapamadevi	Queen	Gopinātha temple	Garden land in Nijagaragapāḍu village and an oil pressing unit in the same village	For a lamp	–	939
8.	Queen's name not very clear (Padmavati)	Queen	Drākshārāmam	Khunḍenapalli	For daily worship services	–	1286
9.	Akkamadevi	Wife of a chief and D/o a Seṭṭi	--do--	Village Maṛuvāḍi in Drākshārāmam	For performing Ḍōlōtsava (swinging) on Davanapunnami festival at the temple	A.D. 1287	1368
10.	Maṇikama	Templesāni	Gopāla temple, Padakākāni	Several lands in Koṭikaṅḍi (Pedakākāni)	She installed the iḍol, constructed the maṅṭapa and provided arrangements for worship service.	A.D. 1264	700
11.	Vallema, W/o Paḍalu Chuṅḍa	–	Mukhalingam temple	8 Puṭṭis of garden land in Choḍanāḍu	For burning two lamps in the temple, grant was	–	1014 S I I, Vol.V

1	2	3	4	5	6	7	8
	Bhima				made by both husband and wife.		
12.	Ballama	Templesāni	--do--	Lost…		A.D. 1111	1025
13.	Lakshmidevi	Queen	Siddheśvara temple, Roṇaṅki	2 Puṭṭis of land	For offerings to the deity	A.D. 1093	1347
14.	--do--	--do--	--do--	--do--	--do--	–	1348
15.	Pina Oḍaya Mahādevi	Queen	Ksheerārāmes vara temple, Pālakolanu	A total of 3 kh of land at different places in Vipaṛuta village	Given to the bōyas of the temple for supplying ghee to burn the lamp	A.D. 1306	124
16.	--do--	--do--	--do--	10 puṭṭis of land 5 puṭṭis of land The land is situated to the north of Uppucheṛuvu and all its boundaries are specified	To the brahmans (1000) For offerings containing rice, ghee, curries of 3 varieties curd, betel leaves, nuts of specific quantities. The grant also states that Divaḷi and Sivarātṛi festivals are to be celebrated by lighting 1000 lamps in the temple by the brahmans	A.D. 1306	125
17.	Gaṅgādevi	Wife of a chief	Simhachalam	4 Puṭṭis of land in in Kāvoramu of Pṛakkināḍu with its boundaries marked with religious symbols	For offerings of betel leaves, nuts, sugarcane, spices etc. to the deity on the occasion of Sukla Ekādasi	A.D. 1226 S I I, Vol. VI	1203
18.	Bhimadevi	--do--	--do--	Garden land bought by her for the the purpose	For 5 garlands of flowers to the deity. She also put 18 māḍas in the temple treasury for 2	A.D.1348	979

1	2	3	4	5	6	7	8
					kuṅchas of prasādamu as vṛitti to the person who works in the garden.		
19.	Sriyādevi	Queen	Keśavadevi temple, Koṇidena	Land in Soṅgharevula (details lost)	For various worship services to the God.	A.D. 1153	634
20.	Laxmidevi W/o Rapaṛti Maṅgirāju	–	Simhachalam	Village Manapamu in Ahaṛu Pākanāḍu	For offerings to the deity	A.D. 1216	692
21.	Sriyādevi	Wife of a chief	Simhachalam	Garden land	For Tiṛumāla (garland) It appears that she bought the land and appointed, one Siṁhanāyaka to supply Tiṛumāla from the land. His salary is a share in the daily offerings made to the deity.	A.D. 1346	989
22.	Valyapa	Brahman	Vallabheśvara temple, Jonnalagaḍḍa	6kh of land and 10 Na of land in Jonnalagaḍḍa	To the priests of the temple of Vallabheśvara constructed by her and for offerings to the deity.	A.D. 1173	188 S II, Vol. X
23.	Ārama, Ketama	Concubines of Koṭa Keta	Sitārāmasvami temple, Eṛrabalem	Certain measure of land in the north of Kāmalakoṭi	For offerings to the deity. They also caused for installation of Utsava idols (Alongwith their father)	A.D. 1213	260
24.	Kommāsāni	Nāyaka	Someśvara temple, Juttiga	Certain measure of land kept under Sānimunnūṛu	Also a lamp. The grant was made along with her sons for the merit of her husband.	A.D. 1259	364

1	2	3	4	5	6	7	8
25.	Nāgava	Sānikāpu woman	Nilakaṅṭeśvara temple, Nārāyaṇapuram	A piece of wet land near Peddacheṛuvu		A.D. 1102	654
26.	Queen of Vallabharāja	Queen	Gopālakrishna Svami temple, Mālepāḍu	A piece of land yielding certain quantity of rice	To the 108 servants of the temple.	–	29
27.	Gōkasāni	W/o a general	Choḍeśvara temple	2 different lands one of 7 kh and the other 1 kh Na 10.	For offerings to the deity and to a priest	A.D. 1170	172
28.	Janḍubai	Relative of a chief	Venkateśvara temple, Duṛgi	Dry land 1 m behind lake, dryland of 1 kh, another piece of land of 1 m and 1 kh near Tāḍlapalli	For offerings to the deity and for Aṅgaraṅgabhōga services	A.D. 1251	334
29.	Rudramadevi	Queen	Viśveśvara śiva, the preceptor of Kakatiyas and head of Goḷaki Śaiva maṭha	Mandara village in Velanāḍu and Velaṅgapunḍi village	For establishing a maṭha (monastery), educational institutions, hospitals and other institutions on behalf of Goḷakimaṭha. Also for a maternity hospital.	A.D. 1261	395
30.	Nāgaladevi		Tripurāṅtakam temple	Some unit of land	To God Tripurāṅtakeśvara	–	87 Tripurāṅ takam temple Inscription
31.	Eṛakamma	Princess	Mukhalingam temple	Gift of wet land measuring 20 janakolas yielding 3 puṭṭis in Dantavuṛamu		–	37 T I A P
32.	Sahaja Vedāṅgi	Queen of Western	Pulipoḍāṛu Jain Monastery	Gift of blackland of 50 maṛtuṛus and	To Jaina basadi at the request of jain teachers	A.D. 1105	169 A.P. Govt.

1	2	3	4	5	6	7	8
	Somaladevi	Chalukya Jayasimha		some amout for a lamp and flower garden	and grant was made with the consent of the ministers	Report on Epigraphy : 1965	
33.	Wives of Kolavadiya Bāḍiyōja and Wives of Kirthivarma		Mosaṁgi (maski)	Grant of land 13 maṭṭars and 70 maṭṭars in Peṛiya Mosaṁgi village	To a brahmin, Keśava Paṇḍita with the consent of the king.	A.D. 1030	135 A.P. Govt. Report on Epigraphy : 1966
34.	Somaladevi along with Muttayya		Gaṅgeśvara temple installed by Bhimarasa and Gaṅgādevi at Koḍūṛu	Certain amount of land	To God with the permission of the king who was camping at Kollipāka region.	A.D. 1116	138
35.	Rudramadevi (Rudradeva Maharaja)	Queen	A priest, Yelesvaradeva	Grant of a village Ambalipally	–	A.D. 1246	14 A Monograph on Yeleśwaram Escavations
36.	--do--	--do--	--do--	Grant of villages Kṛoṭṭalūṛu, Gummalam, Ipūṛu		–	--do-- No. 30
37	Kamalabai	W/o Gaṅgaya Sāhiṇi, a Kāyastha chief	Isānya Gurudevara, a priest of Pushpagiri temple	Grant of village Gaṅgāpuram in Mulikināḍu	For worship services in the temple.	A.D. 1257	No.6 B.N. Sastri: Kayastha Rajulu
38.	Prolama		Lokeśvaradeva	20 Maṛṭaṛs of land	--do--	–	No. 126 Inscriptions of A.P. Warangal Dt.
39.	1. Valyasāni	Sister of Recherla chief, Nāmireḍḍi	Pillalamaṛṛi temple	2 maṛṭars of land to the east of Ravipadu	For offerings to the deity	A.D. 1202	No. 3 B.N. Sastri : Recherla

1	2	3	4	5	6	7	8
	2. Itasāni	W/o Nāmireḍḍi	--do--	2 martars of land at Iṛugāṛubaṅda	-do- Viśvanāthadeva		Reddy Vamsacha ritra, Sasanamulu :
	3. Itasāni	W/o Nāmireḍḍi	--do--	3 martars of land in the same village	-do- Aiteśvaradeva		
40.	Eṛakasāni	W/o Recherla Chief Betireḍḍy	--do--	(1) 4 marṭars of land near lake Eṛakasamudramu, 46 m of field at land near lake Laxmisamudramu. All these are in the village Eṛakapuram founded by her. She also constructed a tank, Eṛaka Samudramu and a temple Eṛakeśvara	For daily worship services, to the priests, for maintenance of the temple and to different temple servants.	A.D. 1208	No. 6
				(2) 2 m dry land in Eṛakapuram and 2 m wet land and 1 m land	For the Goddess Tripurāridevi installed by her and for her offerings.		
				(3) 10 m dry land, 1 m land in the same village and 1 m wet land near Laxmisamu-dramu, 1m near canal and also 10 m dry land.	For the worship services in two temples constructed in the name of her father and mother.		
				(4) 1 m wetland, 5 m dryland in Mōtukūṛu	For worship services to the temple constructed in the name of her brother at Mōtukūṛu.		

1	2	3	4	5	6	7	8
41.	Eṛakasāni	W/o Recherla Chief Betireḍḍy	Pillalamaṟṟi	(1) Remaining dry land of Eṛakapuramu, two gardens free of all taxes (2) 2 m wet land and 1/2 m land near the same tank (3) 2 m land and 1 m near canal 4) 1 m near another tank and 2 m near the same tank.	To the temple priests and for the worship services to the temple Eṛakesvara (in her name) For other temples of Śiva constructed by her. To the temple constructed by a Saivite priest and pointiff. For another temple of Siva	A.D. 1215	No. 6
42.	Eṛakasāni	W/o Recherla Chief Betireḍḍy	Pillalamaṟṟi	5 1/2 m of land near tank Eṛakasamudramu.	To a choultry constructed by her and for a Chaliveṅdra, 4 m for meals to students 1 m to cooks 1/2m for water men of Chaliveṅdra	–	No. 7
43.	Sitādevi	W/o a chief	Nonaṁbeśvara temple, Anaṅtapur	Grant of land	For feeding 90 individuals in the choultry attached to the temple	A.D. 1168 Inscriptions of Āndhra deśa Vol. II, Pt. 1	No. 299
44.	Mayiṅḍamma		Jain temple Anantapur	--do--	To a jain monastery for feeding the monks	–	No. 310
45.	Jayāṁbika	M/o Velanāḍu king (Queen	Kuntimādhava temple,	Grant of village Navakhaṅḍavāḍa in	She also built the Prākārās, Gopurās and	A.D. 1186	No. 113

1	2	3	4	5	6	7	8
		mother)	Piṭhāpuram	Prolunāḍu	installed deities. The grant is for the worship services in the temple.		
46.	Queen mother (name not clear)		To one Aggiśarma of Chāmalūru	50 m of land		–	No. 128
47.	W/o a king	–	Kosinepalle temple	30 m of land	As Pannasa (hereditary land grant)	–	No. 163
48.	Cholamahādevi	Queen	Chilamakūru temple	Grant of land		–	No. 269
49.	Cholamadevi also called Vasantipori	Queen	Vasaṁtiśvara temple	300 units of land and 2 gardens	For worship services and as hereditary grant, made with the consent of local chiefs	–	No. 375
50.	Ganapamba D/o Ganapati deva	Kota Queen	A brahman, Rudra Peḍḍiṁgāru in the presence Kakatiya emperor, Ganapatideva	Village Mogaluṭla, with all its revenue as a full grant	Grant is for the expenses connected with the performance of Srāddha ceremonies at Gaya for her deceased husband Beṭarāja.	A.D. 1219	Epigraphia Andhrica, Vol. IV, No. 11
51.	Paṁdaṁbika	Queen	Temple at Tāḍikoṇḍa Constructed by her in the name of her husband	(1) 1 kh dry land, 1 m wet land (2) 1 kh dry land, 1 m wet land (3) 30 m wet land (4) 2 kh dry land 30 m wet land (5) 1 kh dry land.	For offerings to Kāmiśvara For betel leaves and nuts For Bhōgaṁuvāru (dancing girls) For Bhōgaṁuvāru also for a lamp For a bōya who keeps 25 sheep	A.D. 1266	--do-- No. 13

1	2	3	4	5	6	7	8
					(For the merit of her husband who predeceased her.		
52.	Mailaladevi	Queen	Ānjaneya temple, Rāmakrishna puram	1 m land to the north of lake in Rekaṁpalle	For worship services	–	H A S Vol. XIX Km-17
53.	Dhennamahā devi	Queen (Kanduri Choḍas)	Rāmeśvara temple, Tummēṭi	Land grant and monetary grants as specified in the record. Also certain amounts received towards tax.	To the lamps, worship services and offerings. It was said that she made the grant on her own will.	–	--do-- Mn. 10
54.	Mallasāni and Gaṅgasāni	Wives of the Treasurer of Queen Rudramadevi	To 5 temples constructed by them.	Various lands with boundaries specified were given. A monastery was also built.	For different worship services like lamps, offerings, betel-leaves priests and monastery maintenance.	A.D. 1280	--do-- Mn. 41
55.	Mailāṁbika	Queen	Bhimanārāyaṇa temple, Pānugallu.	Grant of village, Piṭṭaṁpalli	One half of the village should be to the brahmans and the other half of to the temple services.	–	--do-- Ng. 7
56.	Mailāṁba	Queen	Pachhala Somēśvara temple, Panugal to 108 brahmans of the temple (priests)	(1) Grants of an agrahāra (2) 10 units of land (3) 1 unit (4) Remaining land	108 brahmans God's personal enjoyment. Priests of the temple. Vocal music, instrumental music, dancing, incense, garlands, etc.	A.D. 1124	--do-- Vol. XIII No. 36

1	2	3	4	5	6	7	8
57.	Chākama	D/o Talāri, a royal servant	Mādhavadeva temple, Alaṁppuram	Land grants	Renovation.	A.D. 1091	Telangana Inscriptions: Vol. II
58.	Mannādevi	Queen	Brahmeśvara temple, Alaṁpuram	Grant of a village	For renovation of the temple and for daily worship services	A.D. 1101-02	B.N. Sastri: Mahabubn agara Jilla Sarvasvamu: No. 35
59.	--do--	--do--	--do--	--do--	--do--	--do--	--do-- No. 36
60.	--do--	--do--	--do--	(1) Land in Aiyaja 300 vishyaa (2) Houses	Worship services in the temple For priests and brahmans	A.D. 1107-08	--do-- No. 42
61.	--do--	--do--	To a brahman Vemāchārya	Bellera village	As agrahāra	–	--do-- No. 43
62.	--do--	--do--	Alaṁpuram Sthanapati (Temple head priest)	Grant of village Dāmagaṭla in Kannenāḍu	For his services in the temple.	A.D. 1108-09	--do-- No. 45
63.	Mallahaṇi devi	--do--	Gift particulars not given	--do--	Probably the village Gaṅgāpuram is the gift to the temple.	–	--do-- No. 63
64.	Mailala Mahādevi	--do--	Kūḍali Saṅgameśvara temple	Gift of land and some money	To fishermen for making the devotees cross the river.	–	--do-- No. 126
65.	Dhennamahā devi	Queen	Nṛisiṁhadeva temple, Māmiḷḷapalli	Land below the lake of Tummēṭi and wet land near a well.	To the temple for offerings to the deity	–	--do--
67.	Suramatidevi		Drākshārāmam	15 tūmus of land near Palevaram	For daily offerings and burning a lamp. Given to the temple bōyas.	A.D. 1137	Drākshārāma Inscriptions: No. 25

1	2	3	4	5	6	7	8
68.	Pedapōtamasāni W/o Vallūṛi Potanā Charya		Drākshārāmam	1 kh of land.	For maintenance of lamp	A.D. 1292	--do-- No.193
69.	Dēvakabbe	Wet nurse	To a temple of of Śiva set up by her in her name	Lands in Choppadandi village. Also some monetary gift.	For the worship services to the deity.	A.D. 1008	I A P : KD No. 11

CHART - VIIB

GRANTS BY WOMEN – LIVE STOCK

Sl. No.	Donor	Status	Donee Temple	Details of Live Stock					Remarks	Date of Inscription	Source
				Cows	Goat	Sheep	Bullocks	She-buffaloes			
1	2	3	4	5	6	7	8	9	10	11	12
1.	Padmāvati	Wife of a minister	Drākshārāmam temple				50		Also one gold coin for Nitya Paḍi (offerings)	A.D. 1081	1006 S I I Vol. IV
2.	Solava		--do--				50			A.D. 1092	1009
3.	Kupama	D/o a minister	--do--				50			A.D. 1055	1010
4.	Rekama	W/o a royal officer	--do--				50			A.D. 1073	1011
5.	Choḍamahā devi	Queen	--do--				50			A.D. 1166	1052
6.	Rājasāni	D/o Satyāsāni	--do--	50						–	1062
7.	Guṇḍama	W/o minister	--do--				50		Also gave some land.	–	1089
8.	Gaurasāni	Reddi	--do--				50		For the merit of her husband	A.D. 1197	1092
9.	Dannamadevi	Queen	--do--				50			–	1095
10.	Komaṛi	D/o temple sani	--do--				50			A.D. 1121	1251
11.	Guḍisāni	Temple girl	--do--				50			A.D. 1249	1300
12.	Gauramadevi	W/o a chief	--do--					50		A.D. 1186	1313
13.	Yalayamahā devi	Queen	Drākshārāmam temple					50		46th yr of K. Choḷa deva	1319
14.	Bijjavaśankari	Temple sani	--do--					50		48th --do--	1326

1	2	3	4	5	6	7	8	9	10	11	12
15.	Sejjama	W/o a chief	--do--	50						–	1327
16.	Kāmasāni	W/o a palace servant	--do--					50	For the merit of her parents	A.D. 1180	1335
17.	Kommāsāṇi	D/o a bōya	--do--			55				–	687
18.	Paṁḍamadevi	Queen	--do--					55	For maintaining this service, 1 māna to Tribhuvana Nāyaka	A.D. 1163	1113
19.	Lavanyavati devi	Queen	--do--					50		–	1184
20.	Sabbama	--do--	Govardhanaśvami temple, Nādiṅḍla			55				A.D. 1133	804
21.	Vennama	D/o Paḍālu Kāṭaya	--do--			55				A.D. 1150	806
22.	Aṅtyama	D/o Surapareḍḍi	--do--			55				A.D. 1148	807
23.	Nuṁkama	Sāni of the temple	Choḍanārāyaṇa temple, Tsandavole			55				A.D. 1125	945
24.	Choḍāṁba	D/o Gaṅgamāṛāya	--do--			55				A.D. 1147	946
25.	Pochaladevi	Queen	Srikākuḷam temple	25						–	976
26.	Surasāni	D/o Temple sāni	Drakshārāmam					5 (0)		A.D. 1079	1261
27.	Rājaka	--do--	--do--					50		A.D. 1123	1357
28.	Gokamaha devi	Queen	--do--					50		A.D. 1180	1365
29.	Kommapa	D/o a royal servant	Mulasthanadeva temple, Nādiṅḍla			55				A.D. 1150	674

1	2	3	4	5	6	7	8	9	10	11	12
30.	Paṁdamāṁba	Queen	Draksharamam					25		–	1041
31.	Vennama		Nādiṅḍla temple			55				A.D. 1169	666
32.	Gadiyamadevi	Queen	--do--			55				–	672
33.	Tenṭasāni	Sister of the king	Someśvara temple, Kolanu					55	Also made a land grant of certain measure in Vāsanḍūṛu to the boyas who were incharge of the she-buffaloes and who supply ghee.	A.D. 1200	167 S I I Vol. V
34.	Eṛakamahā devi	Queen	--do--					50	Also made certain measure of land north of lake to the bōyas for their maintenance.	A.D. 1194	172
35.	Kaṭṭama		Madhukiśvara temple, Mukhalingam			50			For the merit of her mother Paṁpakamma	A.D. 1078	1115
36.	Nallavaṁgṛa nḍḍlu	Queen	Bhavanarayana temple Sarpavaram					100		–	23
37.	Kommasāni	Nāyaka	Nārāyaṇaśvami temple Bhimavaram					25		A.D. 1183	67
38.	Kusamana	Seṭṭi	--do--			50				–	77
39.	Pina Oḍayamahā devi	Queen	Ksheerārāme śvara temple, Pālakolanu	50						A.D. 1266	121

1	2	3	4	5	6	7	8	9	10	11	12
40.	Pina Oḍaya mahādevi	Queen	--do--	50					For the merit of her son. Indicates the death of her son, husband of Rudramadevi.	–	122
41.	Nāgama		--do--					50	To the bōya who is incharge of these livestock, a land grant is given as vṛitti. A land of 30 puṭṭis at Palakuṁbaḍi to the north of Oḍḍipaṛthi is allotted for him. He has to supply ghee to burn the lamp.	–	140
42.	Pina Oḍaya Mahādevi	Queen	--do--	50					3 kh. of land is given to the bōyas as vṛitti. For the merit of her husband	–	123
43.	Choḍava Mahādevi	Queen	--do--					50	Wife of Viraperṃāḍidevara	–	15
43a.	Mānavamma Mahādevi	--do--	Bhāvanārāyaṇa temple, Sarpavaram					50	Wife of Viraperṃāḍi devara	–	12
44.	Aṇḍār	--do--	--do--					50	--do--	–	15
45.	Viṛaja Mahādevi	--do--	--do--					50	--do--	–	18

1	2	3	4	5	6	7	8	9	10	11	12
46.	W/o Proluja Raṭṭaḍi	Raṭṭaḍi (Reḍḍi)	Rājanārāyaṇa temple, Bhimavaram			50				–	72
47.	Kāpāsāni	Nāyaka	--do--					50		–	89
48.	Pina Oḍaya Mahādevi	Queen	Ksheerā rāmeśvara temple, Pālakolanu	50					She also made a grant of 3 kh. of land in two units (each of 1 kh. 10 Na.) to the bōyas for supply of ghee.	–	127
49.	Suramareḍḍi	Reḍḍy	--do--	50					The grant is made for the merit of her husband, in-laws and parents	A.D. 1294	153
50.	Names lost 2 donors	D/o Temple sāni	Rājanārāyana temple				50			A.D. 1210	85
51.	Lokateproli Eṛṛi		Malleśvara temple	25						A.D. 1241	83 S I I Vol. VI
52.	Sriyādevi	Queen	Śankaraśvami temple, Koṭyadona	1	50				For the lamp 3 kh of land in Rāyūṛu	A.D. 1263	609
53.	Anantalaxmi Komidevi	Queen	Simhachalam	50					For the merit of her daughter	A.D. 1342	983
54.	Five wives, four concubines, one daughter of Koṭa Keta along with two other		Amareśvara temple, Amarāvathi					715	Each of them gave about 55 she-buffaloes to the God for burning a lamp. However, the daughter gave 110 for two lamps	A.D. 1197	228

1	2	3	4	5	6	7	8	9	10	11	12
	women, a total of 12 ladies names of all are given in the grant								to different bōya persons for supply of ghee.		
55.	Vaṅṭala Kamasani	Palace attendant	--do--			55			Husband is also a servant of the king.	–	240
56.	Laxmidevi	W/o a chief		51					Also a lamp stand	A.D. 1319	714
57.	Sumitrādevi	M/o a chief		50					For the merit of her son. She also made a land grant of one puṭṭi and some money for the service of burning a lamp.	A.D. 1335	715
58.	Chimmādevi	W/o of a chief of Oḍḍāḍi	Simhachalam	50						A.D. 1342	942
59.	Umadevināya kāṇi	W/o a military general	--do--	25					Her husband made a land grant on this occasion.	A.D. 1314	938
60.	Pārvatināya kāṇi	W/o a military general	Simhachalam	25					Also a lampstand, her husband too made a lamp grant of same nature. Total 5 cows were given.	A.D. 1297	935
61.	Choḍamadevi	W/o a chief	--do--	50					Her son too made a grant of same nature. Total 100 cows are given.	A.D. 1283	934

1	2	3	4	5	6	7	8	9	10	11	12
62.	Somāṇḍiya mma	Queen	Bhāvanara-yana temple, Bāpaṭla	25					For a lamp	A.D. 1144	135
63.	Kāmidevi	--do--	Keśavadeva temple, Koṇidena				55		--do--	A.D. 1148	647
64.	Laxmidevi W/o Rāpaṛti Maṅgirāju		Simhahalam	50					For two lamps for the merit of her son. Also a lamp stand	A.D. 1266	692
65.	Maṁkama Nāyakuṛālu & her husband	W/o an officer of Gaṅgas	--do--			100			For two lamps	A.D. 1291	928
66.	Uyyanna Pandyani W/o Srirāma Paṇḍita	Brahman	--do--	25					Also a lampstand. It appears that she bought them by paying suitable price.	A.D. 1304	967
67.	Sriraṅgalaxmi	M/o a chief	Simhchalam temple	52					Also a lamp stand and a garden for flowers (details lost)	A.D. 1308	992
68.	Goṇḍava, D/o Janniya Bhaṭṭa		Svayaṁbhūde va temple, Valiveṛu			50				A.D. 1061	8 S I I Vol. X
69.	Mudigoṇdama devi	D/o a vṛitti sāni	Vāsukiṛāvi Someśvara temple, Juttiga						50	—	13
70.	Prolipāva	a dancing girl	--do--					50		A.D. 1141	110

1	2	3	4	5	6	7	8	9	10	11	12
71.	Aitama, W/o a royal servant	Reḍḍi	Gokarṇeśvara temple, Dāvulūru			55				A.D. 1143	112
72.	Kuṅḍa....	W/o a chief	Mulasthenes vara temple Nāḍiṅḍla			–			Unspecified no. of sheep for a lamp.	A.D. 1150	124
73.	Kaṅṭama	Mother-in-law of royal officer	Malleśvara temple, Bezawaḍa					55		A.D. 1153	133
74.	Prolama	Bōya	Rāmalingeśvara temple Sātulūru			55				A.D. 115	163
75.	Prolama	Sāni	Trikōteśvara temple, Sattenapally			55				A.D. 1169	169
76.	Prolisāni D/o Mallenāyaka		Rāmalingeśvara temple, Velpūru			55				A.D. 1176	195
77.	Sūramadevi	Concubine	--do--					55		A.D. 1209	249
78.	Aitasāni	D/o Concubine servant of Ganapatideva	--do--	25					Along with her husband, for the merit of the king	A.D. 1239	290
79.	Muppaladevi	Queen	Tripurāṅtakam temple	25						A.D. 1242	296
80.	Prolasāni	Bōya	--do--	50					In the name of her husband	A.D. 1246	311
81.	Jāyāsāni	Bōya	--do--		50				--do--	A.D. 1249	327
82.	Lakumābai		--do--	10					Another 10 cows by her husband	A.D. 1250	331

1	2	3	4	5	6	7	8	9	10	11	12
83.	Nāgu		--do--	30						A.D. 1155	347
84.	Eṛikāsāni	Reḍḍi	--do--	25					Along with her husband Sura Reḍḍi	A.D. 1267	368
85.	Māṛama Bṛeka	Brahman	Prasanna Keśava temple, Kolavennu	12						A.D. 1256	353
86.	Ghanṭasāla Kāmaka	Veśya	Agastyeśvara temple, Imani			50			Also certain land of 4 Na. to the bōyas for runing the lamp. For the merit of her mother.	A.D. 1125	84
87.	Gokasāni	W/o a general	Chodesvara temple, Mopaṛṛu			55				A.D. 1170	172
88.	Prolama		Rāmeśvara temple, Velupūru			55				A.D. 1172	178
89.	Guṇḍadevi	Concubine of Koṭa Keta	--do--					55	For her mother's merit	A.D. 1209	252
90.	Guṇḍamanā yaki	W/o a military general	Mukhalingam			50			For a lamp	– T I A P Vol. I	7
91.	Muppalamahā devi	W/o a chief	Malliśvara temple, Bezwada						--do--, no. of cows not specified	A.D. 1246	66
92.	Puḍōlimādovi yar	Tamil brahman	Kālahasti	32						31st yr. of Kulottunga chola	659
93.	Ponnavasāni	W/o Tantṛapāla	--do--		96 & 1ram					14th yr. --do--	662

1	2	3	4	5	6	7	8	9	10	11	12
94.	Puḍōlasāni		--do--			72				15th yr.	665
95.	Gaṅgādeviyār		--do--		1ram	96				--do--	667
96.	Nuṅgamadevi	W/o a chief	--do--		96					19th yr.	671
97.	a woman		--do--				50			20th yr.	672
98.	--do--		--do--				–		Alo a lamp stand no. of animals not specified	31st yr.	674
99.	Gaṇḍaraditta W/o Aṅgarāja		--do--				96		--do--	33rd yr.	691
100.	Caḷukkikula Meḍaviyan	W/o a chief	--do--			19 s.g., 2 rams				10th yr	728
101.	Solavūṛiyār D/o Narasiṅgade var		Ṭeki temple				96			10th yr. of Rajendra choḷa	746
102.	Abbama	W/o brahman Minister	Keśavadeva temple, Ollāḷa			50			For a lamp	A.D. 1097	8 Epigraphia Andhrica Vol. IV
103.	Nāgaladevi		Tripurāṅtakam temple			25				–	12
104.	Mābāvi	Merchant class	--do--	15					For the merit of her son.	A.D.1225	94
105.	Bhimāsāni		Drākshāramam	25					Also some land grant	A.D. 1166	1000
106.	Bhadraladevi		--do--					400	For 18 lamps	–	1275
107	Laxmidevi	W/o a chief	--do--					50	Also a lamp stand	A.D. 1157	27

1	2	3	4	5	6	7	8	9	10	11	12
108	Gaṅgādevi	--do--	--do--					50	Also a lamp stand	A.D. 1135	32
109.	Lingādevi	Bōya	--do--		30 rams						50
110.	Anantavarma devi	Queen	--do--					50		A.D. 1128	70
111.	Mārāyadevi	--do--	--do--					50		--do--	135
112.	Lōlayadevi	--do--	--do--					50		--do--	138
113.	Mallamāṁba W/o Goṅka		--do--					50		A.D. 1096	142
114.	Kommāsāni a relative of Goṅka		--do--					50		A.D. 1153	78
115.	Maulamadevi D/o Villayarranā yaka		--do--					50	Also about 17 Kulōttuṅga māḍas	–	62
116.	Yādavadevi	Queen						50		A.D. 1163	218
117.	Vallema		Mukhalingam temple			100			For 2 lamps	A.D. 1081	13

CHART - VIIC

GRANTS BY WOMEN – MONEY AND ORNAMENTS

Sl. No.	Donor	Status	Donee	Nature of Grant		Service Instituted Article/ Ornament	Date of Inscription	Source
				Temple	Monetary			
1	2	3	4	5	6	7	8	9
1.	Somaladevi	Princess	Drākshārāmam temple		Diamond Studded Bracelet		–	1007 SII, Vol. IV
2.	Bimmaladevi	Queen	--do--		A mirror		–	1145
3.	Sabbama	W/o a chief	--do--	93 Neṛagadyānas	Golden Bracelet and a lamp stand	Burning a lamp. Also appointed 4 bōyas with a salary of 1 m. each for supply of ghee	A.D. 1221	1224
4.	Peṛiyaṅḍi	A palace attendant	--do--		One metal lamp stand	For burning a lamp	–	1249
5.	Komaṛi	D/o Temple sāni	--do--	30 Neṛagadyānas		For chowrie bearing	A.D. 1132	1253
6.	Muppama	M/o A chief of Kōnakaṅḍravādi	Bezawada	10 māḍas		For burning a lamp	A.D. 1140	722
7.	Kommama D/o Muttināyaka	D/o Servant of the king belonging to Śudra class	Choḍanārāyaṇadeva temple Tsandavole	16 biṛudugadyas		For a lamp	A.D. 1154	943
8.	Kommama	D/o	--do-- Gaṅgamārāya	--do--		For a lamp	A.D. 1138	944
9.	Śaṅkarama	D/o Temple	Drākshārāmam sāni	25 Neṛa	Golden gadyāṅas	For a lamp chowrie	A.D. 1229	1372

1	2	3	4	5	6	7	8	9
10.	Pemmāṅdi D/o Choṭēṅdi	Probably of Tamil origin	Mukhalingam	5 māḍas		For a lamp	–	1039 SII Vol. V
11.	Betama Nāyakurālu	Nāyaka	--do--	--do--		For a lamp	A.D. 1098	1044
12.	Gaurama W/o Guṭaṅḍi Nāyaka	Nāyaka	--do--	10 māḍas		For a lamp Mentions the grand mother and mother's names	A.D. 1123	1091
13.	Vennama	Nāyaka	--do--	5 māḍas		For a lamp	A.D. 1121	1105
14.	Piṛatyaṁbika	Brahmin	Srikuram	5 māḍas		For a lamp	A.D. 1283	1179
15.	Aḍunāchi	Tamil	--do--	5 māḍas		For a lamp	A.D. 1170	1331
16.	Sobiṛamma	Nāyaka	--do--	5 māḍas		For a lamp	A.D. 1137	1339
17.	Patimanāyakur ālu	Nāyaka	--do--	5 māḍas		For a lamp	A.D. 1142	1281
18.	W/o Numkināyaka	Nāyaka	--do--	5 māḍas		For a lamp	A.D. 1142	1278
19.	Anaṅtalaxmi Komidevi	Queen	Simhachalam		1 golden flower garland, 1Tṛisaramu, a chain of pearls, 1 lampstand, 1 golden chain, (Biḷasaramu)	For the merit of her daughter Sitadevi	A.D. 1342	983 SII Vol. VI
20.	Surāṁba D/o Eṛiya	Jaṅgama and a palace attendant	Bhāvanārāyaṇ a temple, Bāpaṭla	12 Biṛudu māḍas		For a lamp	–	172
21.	Nāgāṁbika	Queen	--do--	12 --do--		For a lamp	–	137
22.	Ponnamadevi	Queen	--do--	6 Chāmaramādas		For a lamp	A.D.1135	170

1	2	3	4	5	6	7	8	9
23.	Bṛammāsāni	Nāyaka Probably W/o a chief	--do--	12 Biṛudugadyas		For a lamp	–	171
24.	Pṛolama	D/o a female palace attendant Surama	--do--	Biṛudu māḍas		For a lamp	A.D. 1151	178
25.	Kolamma	W/o Taṁbināyaka	Simhachalam	12 Gaṅḍamādas & 5 chinnas		For a lamp and for her son's merit	A.D. 1288	885
26.	Gaṅgādevi W/o Raṅganātha Bhaṭṭopādhyāya	Brahman	--do--	12 gaṅdamādas and 5 chinnas		For a lamp and for her husband's merit	A.D. 1289	886
27.	1) Lakumadevi W/o Pātra Pōtarājajiyyana 2) Bayyamadevi sister of Pātra Pōtarāja	--do--	--do--	20 Gaṅḍamāḍas		For her teacher's merit	A.D. 1344	900
28.	Gaṅgādevi	Queen	--do--	4 Mallamāḍas		Lamp grant	–	1207
29.	Akkamma	Nāyaka, W/o Kaḷiṅga Pariksha, an officer of Gaṅgas	Simhachalam	5 Padmanidhi gaṅḍamāḍas		Given to one Naṛuva Nachapa donated by the king to the temple as salary She has to perform the services of holding mirror, keeping Raṅgōli (floral designs on (floor)	–	1099

1	2	3	4	5	6	7	8	9
30.	Queen of Ballanarēndra	Queen	Nagēśvara temple, Pedda Kallepalli	5 Kulottuṅga māḍas		Given to bōyas for a lamp	A.D. 1154	87
31.	Somaladevi W/o Ballādhinātha	--do--	--do--	--do--		For a lamp	A.D. 1154	88
32.	Mēḍasāni W/o Bhimināyaka		Bhāvanārāyaṇa temple Bapatla	17 Biṛudu māḍas		For a lamp	A.D. 1145	129
33.	Kāmasani	Brahman (W/o minister)	--do--	12 --do--		--do--	A.D. 1155	150
34.	Eṛrakāṁba	Seṭṭi	--do--	12 --do--		--do--	A.D. 1151	176
35.	Suraṁba	W/o A chief Choḍaya	--do--	6 Chāmara māḍas		--do--	A.D. 1130	193
36.	Tāḷḷa Vuyyama	Nāyaka	Simhachalam	12 Gaṇḍamāḍas		--do-- For the merit of her father	A.D. 1340	917
37.	Rēkamadevi	A female attendant (Paramour?)	Channakeśava temple, Kamūṛu	6 Uttamagaṇḍa māḍas		For a lamp	A.D. 1129 SII, Vol. X	88
38.	Queen (Name missing)	–	Nilakaṇṭeśvara temple, Nārāyaṇapuram	8 māḍas		Also she constructed a temple	A.D. 1145	699
39.	Name lost		--do--	5 māḍas		For a lamp	A.D. 1137	689
40.	Suraparāja		--do--	5 māḍas		--do--	A.D. 1127	668
41.	Surama D/o Damama		Nādiṇḍla Mulasthāneśvara temple	12 Biṛudu gadyas		--do--	A.D. 1153	128
42.	–	Temple dancing girl	Anaṁtabhōgeśvara temple, Kolluru	5 Rājanārāyaṇa gadyas		--do--	A.D. 1137	101
43.	Damamba	–	--do--	--do--		--do--	A.D. 1137	100

1	2	3	4	5	6	7	8	9
44.	Pedudama D/o	--do--	--do--	--do--		--do--	A.D. 1140	108 TIAP, Vol. I
45.	Gōpama		Vāsudevapaṭnam	80 māḍas		--do--	A.D. 1131	421
46.	Kāmakōṭi		--do--	10 māḍas		--do--	–	422
47.	Aytama W/o Peṛmāḍi	Tamil probably	Nileśwara temple, Niḍuṅjeṛuvu	5māḍas		--do--	A.D. 1117	150
48.	Aḍapa D/o Rājamānika seṭṭi	Merchant class	--do--	--do--		--do-- for the success of arms of Choḍa gaṅga, the king	A.D. 1124	166
49.	Aytamasāni	Bōya	--do--	--do--		--do--	A.D. 1127	167
50.	Viṁjama	D/o Leṅka Gōkanāyaka an officer of Gaṅgās	--do--	--do--		--do-- For the success of arms of Choḍa gaṅga. The grant was made along with her father	A.D. 1131	173
51.	Eṛakama and her husband	D/o Temple sāni	--do--	--do--		--do--	–	177
52.	Māmiḍamma D/o Prolamāṁba		--do--	--do--		For celebration of Amavāsya Uṭsava	–	263
53.	Surama		--do--	--do--		For a lamp	–	188
54.	Bhumaṅḍi and her father Tyagi	Dancer	Mukhalingam temple	10 māḍas		--do--	–	25
55.	Somalamaha devi	Queen	--do--	5 māḍas		--do--	–	30
56.	Kupama	Concubine of general Potaya	--do--	--do--		--do--	A.D. 1123	48

1	2	3	4	5	6	7	8	9
57.	Komarama D/o Mallema Nāyakurālu	Temple sāni	--do--	--do--		--do--	A.D. 1124	49
58.	Chennama Nāyakurālu	Sister of Head sāni of Nakarapuvāḍa	--do--	--do--		--do--	--do--	50
59.	Naṁgama W/o Pasāyita kommi	Temple sāni	--do--	--do--		--do--	–	57
60.	Eṛakamma	D/o --do--	--do--	--do--		--do--	–	58
61.	Guṅḍama D/o Meḍana	Temple sāni	--do--	--do--		--do--	A.D. 1129	63
62.	Mrigavati D/o an officer Lemka		--do--	--do--		--do--	--do--	64
63.	Kanduma	W/o an officer	--do--	--do--		--do--	A.D. 1138	97
64.	Padlama		--do--	--do--		--do--	A.D. 1142	110
65.	Numkama	W/o Minister	Mukhalingam	5 māḍas		For a lamp	A.D. 1143	116
66.	Somama	W/o a chief	--do--	--do--		--do--	A.D. 1148	122
67.	Betama	W/o an officer	--do--	--do--		--do--	A.D. 1148	123
68.	Mosamadevi	Queen	--do--	--do--		--do--	–	125
69.	Surama	Brahman	--do--	--do--		--do-- for her sister's merit	A.D. 1148	126
70.	Maṁkama	Mudiseli (merchant)	--do--	30 --do--		Gift of 6 lamps	A.D. 1156	129
71.	Eṛṛakama	Brahman	--do--	5 --do--		Gift of lamp. For running this, a land of one putti was granted to a priest.	A.D. 1179	133

1	2	3	4	5	6	7	8	9
72.	Duggama	Merchant	--do--	5 Surabhi māḍas		Gift of a lamp for the merit of her husband and son. Kept in the custody of two Nāyakas.	A.D. 1185	134
73.	Paḍruma nāyakurālu		Srikuram	--do--		Gift of a lamp	A.D. 1142	209
74.	Suṭṭaṁdi	Temple sāni	--do--	--do--		--do-- For the merit of her mother	--do--	210
75.	Eṛrakama nāyakurālu		--do--	--do--		--do--	A.D. 1152	220
76.	Kāpama nāyakurālu		--do--	--do--		--do--	--do--	221
77.	Prōlama nāyakurālu	Temple sāni	--do--	--do--		--do--	--do--	222
78.	Bejjama nāyakurālu		--do--	--do--		--do--	A.D. 1157	223
79.	Bonnama nāyakurālu	Temple sāni	Srikuram	5 Surabhi māḍas		--do-- For the merit of her mother	--do--	224
80.	Pṛithvi mahādevi	Queen	--do--	10 māḍas		--do--	A.D. 1174	230
81.	Maṅkama nāyakurālu		--do--	5 māḍas		--do--	A.D. 1182	231
82.	Bhimāvati		--do--	--do--		--do--	A.D. 1217	242
83.	Māmiḍiamma D/o Pṛōlama		--do--	--do--		For Amavasya Utsava every month	A.D. 1246	263
84.	Jayammadevi		--do--	5 Mallamāḍas and 4 māḍas		For a lamp. In addition 4 māḍas for flower garden for the merit of grand daughter	A.D. 1257	270

1	2	3	4	5	6	7	8	9
85.	Pirāṭṭi Somidevamma	Brahman	--do--	5 Gaṅdamāḍas and 15 chinnas		For a lamp	A.D. 1283	287
86.	Tāllamāṁba	--do--	--do--		Two gold necklaces and silver vessel	To the deity	–	369
87.	Muppama	M/o a chief	Malliśvara temple	10 Māḍas		For a lamp	A.D. 1140	15 Durga Malleśvara Temple Inscriptions
88.	Anyama		Pōlavaram temple	5 Gold māḍas		For a lamp	A.D. 1255	122 Inscriptions of Āndhradesa
89.	Valyasāni		Someśvara temple, Rajahmundry	Not specified		2 lamps	A.D. 1211	142
90.	Pudolikilāvi	Tamil brahman	Kālahasti	5 Gold Kāsus		Evening lamp	10th year of Rājarāja Chola	726
91.	Maduvaṭṭi	--do--	--do--	1½ Māḍa of gold		--do--	11th yr. of Rājarāja Chola	638
92.	Saṅkaramma	D/o a sāni of the temple	Drākshārāmam temple	25 Gadyas	1 gold chowrie	Chāmara kolupu	A.D. 1129 Drākshārāma inscriptions	85
93.	Lakumādevi	Queen of Prataparudra	Rāmanātha temple, Yeḷgēdu	Grant of local taxes like pannu,		For the merit of her father. For various worship	A.D. 1301 IAD : KD	37

1	2	3	4	5	6	7	8	9
				Kaṇika, Pullaṛi (grazing) etc.)		services to the deity		
94.	Machapa Nāyakurālu	W/o an officer of Gangas	Mukhalingam temple	5 Māḍas		For a lamp	A.D. 1123 Mukhaling am Temple inscriptions	47
95.	Nāraṇadevi & her daughter		--do--	--do--		--do--	A.D. 1131	72
96.	Maṅkamahā devi	Queen	--do--	--do--		--do--	A.D. 1134	85
97.	Kommanāya kurālu	Kayastha	--do--	--do--		--do--	A.D. 1138	99
98.	Maṁkama		--do--	--do--		--do--	A.D. 1140	105
99.	Kosamamahā devi	Queen	--do--	--do--		--do--	A.D. 1140	106

CHART - VIID
GRANTS BY WOMEN — OTHERS

Sl. No.	Donor	Status	Donee Temple	Nature of Grant	Remarks	Date of Inscription	Source
1	2	3	4	5	6	7	8
1.	Jakkamāṁba	W/o royal servant	Drākshārāmam temple	Gift of lamp		A.D. 1253	1034 S I I Vol. IV
2.	Lakkumadevi	–	--do--	--do--	For the merit of her parents	–	1060
3.	Parākamma	W/o an officer	--do--	--do--		–	1096
4.	Rājadevi	Queen	--do--	--do--		A.D. 1135	1156
5.	Meḍaṁbika	–	--do--	--do--		–	1157
6.	Meḍasāni	Sister of Kolani Chief	--do--	--do--	For the merit of her parents	–	1158
7.	Viṁjaṁbika	W/o an officer	--do--	--do--		–	1159
8.	Laxmidevi	D/o Kona chief	--do--	--do--		–	1161
9.	Rājaladevi	Queen of Anaṁtavarma	--do--	--do--	For protection of the throne	A.D. 1128	1191
10.	Padmaladevi	--do--	--do--	--do--	--do--	--do--	1192
11.	Choḍitidevi	--do--	--do--	--do--	--do--	--do--	1194
12.	Sriyadevi	--do--	--do--	--do--	--do--	--do--	1195
13	Lilavatidevi	--do--	--do--	--do--	--do--	--do--	1196
14.	Laxmidevi	M/o Lilavatidevi	--do--	--do--	--do--	--do--	1197
15.	Kaḷyāṇadevi	Queen of Anantavarma	--do--	--do--	--do--	--do--	1198
16.	Mahādevi	W/o Daṇḍanāyaka	--do--	--do--	--do--	--do--	1211

1	2	3	4	5	6	7	8
17.	–	W/o Eṛuva Toṅḍayarāja	Drākshārāmam temple	Gift of lamp		A.D. 1121	1216
18.	Valyama	Queen of Veṅgi Goṅka	--do--	--do--		–	1218
19.	Muttanamma	W/o of brahmin	--do--	--do--		–	1219
20.	Kommidevi	W/o a chief	--do--	--do--		A.D. 1132	1220
21.	Kājadāsi Māyaṅḍiamma		--do--	Gift not specified	For the merit of her husband Kadidasi Bhimandara	A.D. 1194	1234
22.	Komarāsāni	D/o a temple sani	--do--	Gift of a lamp	For her parents	–	1247
23.	Prolama	D/o Surama, a servant of Kulottunga Choḍa Goṅka	--do--	Gift of 5 lamps		A.D. 1151	1120
24.	Suraṁbika	D/o Chelvisetti, a Jaṅgama by caste	--do--	Gift of lamp		–	1121
25.	Guṅḍamadevi	Queen	--do--	Gift of 4 lamps		–	1137
26.	Guṅḍamaṁbika	Queen	--do--	Gift of 2 lamps		A.D. 1132	974
27.	Kallavaśaṅkari	D/o Temple sani	Drākshārāmam	Gift of a lamp		–	1305
28.	Nagaśaṅkari	Temple sani	--do--	--do--		–	1356
29.	Gokamahadevi	Queen	--do--	--do--		A.D. 1180	1365
30.	Guṁdaṁbika	Queen	Mulasthāna temple Nādinḍla			A.D. 1171	680
31.	Nachamaṁba	Wife of a minister	Kolanu Someśvara temple	Gift of evening lamp		– Vol. V 169	S.I.I.,

1	2	3	4	5	6	7	8
32.	Vāsama	Seṭṭi	Somanātha temple	Gift of a lamp		–	183
33.	Vāsama	--do--	--do--	--do--		–	185
34.	Laxmi	--do--	Bhimeśvara temple, Bhimavaram	Construction of a Naṁdipillar and installation of Naṁdi idol on it. The stone for making the idol was brought from Koṭilingāla, Rajahmundry.	She caused for the installation of the idol on an auspicious day and probably committed self immolation. The idol was stated to have been destroyed earlier by thieves.	–	95
35.	Aitamaṁba		Gokarṇa temple, Guḍipūḍi	Construction of a maṇṭapa and gift of a lamp to be burnt in the twilight		–	192
36.	--do--		--do--	Gift of an evening lamp		–	193
37.	Guṁdaṁbika	Queen	Ksheerārāmeśv ara temple, Pālakolanu	Gift of a lamp	Contains prasasti of the queen	–	161
38.	Trolama	Veśya	Ksheerārāmeśv ara temple, Palakolanu	Gift of a lamp	To protect her Sānivṛitti She is the concubine of Rāyapanāyaka	–	164
39.	Tāllamaṁba W/o Rāmapātra	Brahman	–	Gift of a lamp		–	452
40.	Guṁdaṁbika	Queen	Bhāvanārāyaṇa temple, Bāpaṭla	--do--		–	S I I, Vol. VI, 142
41.	Bayyamadevi sister of pātra Potarājajiyyana	Brahman	Simhachalam	Gift of a Chāmara (chowrie)	She appointed a lady on salary of 10 Gaṁdamāḍas for this service of holding chowrie. Also for a garland, she made	A.D. 1375	901

1	2	3	4	5	6	7	8
					arrangement of a flower garden through Valaleṛu brahman of the temple.		
42.	Mumṛanamma	Merchant class	Malleśvara temple, Vippaṛla	Construction of the temple, lake at Vippaṛti, and also a choultry to feed 1000 members		A.D. 1073	586
43.	Gaṅgama	W/o Tantrapala a royal servant	Simhachalam	Instituted Alāvaṭam (fan) kolupu in the the temple.	For this one Siṅgana was appointed on a salary of 5 ṭankas.	–	826
44.	Lokama, grand daughter Govinda poṛeṛi		Bhairava temple Udaigiri	Erected a pillar	–	–	SII, Vol. X, 56
45.	Kommama	W/o a chief	Malleśvara temple,	Built a temple of Mādhavadeva at Peṛṛavali	Her son made grants of land to the same.	A.D. 1156	138
46.	Kāpasāni		Narendreśvara temple, Vippaṛṛu	Got the manṭapa of the plastered	For the merit of her parents	A.D. 1198	207
47.	Namuṅḍūri Kunasāni	Reḍḍy	Bhimeśvara temple Mogallu	Erected a pillar	For the merit of her in-laws, husband and son	A.D. 1315	512
48.	--do--	--do--	--do--	Stone pillar in the Naṅdimanḍapa	For the merit of her parents, grand parents	A.D. 1315	515
49.	Gokaṁbika	W/o a chief	Choḍeśvara temple, Mopaṛṛu	Gift of 2 lamps		A.D. 1170	171
50.	Melaṁbika	Queen	Tripurāṅtakam temple	Consecration of Mailaṁbikeśvara in the temple, and grant of Dittālu village	For Aṅgaraṅga services to the deity.	A.D. 1209	254
51.	Potaṁba	W/o a chief	Tripurāṅtakam temple	Golden dhavaja in the temple was installed by her.		A.D. 1342	550

1	2	3	4	5	6	7	8
52.	Rekama W/o Kālapanāyaka		Mukhalingam temple	5 puṭṭis of land	For a lamp	A.D. 1058	Temple Inscriptions of A.P. : Vol.I, 1
53.	Pālapa	W/o a soldier	Madhukeśvara temple, Mukhalingam	Gift of a lamp	For the merit of her husband when he was staying in army camp.	A.D. 1074	9
54.	Chennamanāy akuṛalu	Sister of head sāni of the temple	--do--	--do--		A.D. 1124	50
55.	Lokaṁbika D/o Somaṁbika		--do--	--do--	For the boyas, a land measuring 3 puṭṭis was donated in Dantavūru. The land was given to Teliki Kāpus for cultivation. The grant is for the victory to Chaḍagaṅga, the king.	A.D. 1105	29
56.	Lakshmi	Queen of Choḍagaṅga	--do--	--do--		A.D. 1110	36
57.	Surapa		Nileśvara temple, Niduṅjeṛuvu	--do--		–	149
58.	Viṁjama	D/o an officer	Nileśvara temple Niduṅjeṛuvu	Gift of a lamp	For the success of the king.	A.D. 1131	174
59.	Tiruvaṁḍi	Tamil	Mukhalingam temple	--do--		–	21
60.	Vāsama	Concubine of an officer of Rājendrachoḍa also Guḍisani	--do--	--do--		–	31

1	2	3	4	5	6	7	8
61.	Prithvimahā devi	Queen	--do--	--do--		A.D. 1191	38
62.	Tallapaṇi	W/o a chief	Srikurmam	Chāmara service		A.D. 1266	274
63.	A lady (name lost)		Purushottama Puram	Gift of a lamp		A.D. 1133	A.R. 1947-48, 146
64.	Jallamahādevi	Queen	Tekkali	Construction of the temple, consecration of a deity and gift of a lamp		A.D. 1131	A.R. 1953-54
65.	Revādevi	Sāni		Construction of a temple		A.D. 1070	A.R. 1967
66.	Mailaṁbika	Princess/Queen	Nāmālapādu, Khammam	Construction of a Siva temple in the name of her brother and another temple for Rāmanātha. Gift of a town and tank.		–	198
67.	Gaureśvarabai	W/o a Chief	Akkalareḍḍipalli, Mallikārjuna temple	Construction of a Siva temple.	For the merit of Tripurārideva, the chief.	A.D. 1283	B.N. Sastry : Kayastha Rajulu, 16
68.	Paḍumābai	D/o a chief	Paluvāyi village, Keleśvara temple	Renovation of the temple and grants of lands	For worship services. For the merit of father and husband.	A.D. 1255	P. 6
69.	Hachalāṁba	D/o Allugi, a chief	Pushpagiri temple	Construction of a temple and installation of idols in their names	Also grants were made for worship services	A.D. 1254	4
70.	Devakabbe	Wet Nurse		Construction of a tank called Achhabbe Samudra and grants of money 70 ḍrammas and lands (wet lands)	The tank is named after Achhabe, her master's daughter.	A.D. 992	Inscriptions of A.P.Kar imnagar Dt: 8
71.	Mailama	Natavāḍi Queen, Sister	Inugurti temples of Siva and	Construction of the temple and grants of clothes,	She had a title Dharmakirthi for her	A.D. 1221 of A.P.:War	Inscripitions

1	2	3	4	5	6	7	8
		of Ganapatideva	Gopāla Krishna	jewels, cows, land and flower gardens	meritorious services.		angal Dt. 59
72.	Muppamambika	W/o Natavāḍi Chief, Dugga	Niḍigoṇḍa temple	Construction of a temple in her name and grant of lowlands along with her husband.	For the daily worship services to the God.	A.D. 1104	17
73.	Mailama	W/o Beta, A minister of Prola, Kakatiya king.	Hanamkoṇḍa Jain temple	Installation of the image of God Jalandhareśvara in a cave.		A.D. 1117	22
74.	Mailamadevi	Kakatiya family	Bhairava temple, Inugurti	Installation of the image of God Jalandhareśvara in a cave		–	60
75.	Kundamaṁba	Natavāḍi Queen, sister of Ganapatideva	Siva temple, Niḍigoṇḍa	Construction of temple, consecration of images in her husband's name, father's name, brother's name and gave a part of the village Kundavaram to the temples. The remaining part to the brahmans as an Agrahāra	The grant says that the donor constructed temples at Kaleśvaram, Srisailam and Mantrakūṭa. She also gave Agrahāras to brahmans at various places.	A.D. 1219	57
76.	Kundamaṁba	Natavāḍi Queen, sister of Ganapatideva	Siva temple, Niḍigoṇḍa	Continuation of the above record. The village Kundavaram was earlier called Vemulatoṇṭa. She also constructed another village called Kundavaram in Chennur Taluq, Adilabad on the banks of river Godavari.	The grant too is a list of meritorious activities of the donor	A.D. 1219	58
77.	Mallanadevi	Relative of the the governor of Addaṅki	Temple of Gopiśvaradeva Tammaluru	Construction of temple, erection of pinnacles, grant of one paṭṭi dry field, two	Daily worship, all recreations to the deity and to the dancing girls	A.D. 1272 -1273	Nellore District Inscriptions:

1	2	3	4	5	6	7	8
				paddy fields and a flower garden.	of the temple.		72
78.	Vimal Aṇḍāḷ	Resident of Nellore region	Kālahasti temple	Gift of evening lamp		14th year of K.Choḷa	Āndhradeśa : Inscriptions : Vol. II, pt.I 663
79.	Elanacoḷa Mahadevi	Queen of Telugu Choḍa Renāḍu	Chilamakūṛu temple	Gift of a lamp		–	132
80.	Lokama	W/o Malaya Chief	Ishta Kamesvara of Velpur	--do--		A.D. 1240	105
81.	Dancing girl (name not specified)	Someśvara temple, Juttiga, temple girl	Someśvara temple, Juttiga	Gift of lamp		A.D. 1141	128
82.	Mailama sister of Ganapatideva	Natavāḍi queen	–	Construction of three villages Bayyaram, Dharmapuram, and Mahadevapuram, construction of a huge tank at Bayyāram	She had a title Dharmakirti for her meritorious activities. She is said to have constructed several temples for Siva.	–	Epigraphia Āndhrica, Vol. I
83.	Mailama of Viriyāla	Queen	–	Construction of 3 temples and a tank at Kāṭukūru	In the name of herself and her parents.	A.D. 1205	Hyd. Arch. Series XIX : Km. 4
84.	Kuppāṁbika	Queen	–	Construction of a temple in the name of her husband. Gave away several wet lands as vṛittis (A total of 21 m. of land was given to this temple).	The record also has a long list of meritorious activities of the donor including providing grants to brahmans and sending them to pilgrimages, making gifts of clothes, money, gems, construction of tanks temples, etc.	A.D. 1276	B.N.Sastri : Mahabub-nagar Jila Sarvasamu

1	2	3	4	5	6	7	8
85.	Bāgaladevi	Singer from Siṁhaḷadeśa	–	Gift of a lamp		A.D. 1258	Temple Inscriptions of A.P., Vol. I, 269
86.	Adityaṁba	D/o Gunḍarāju	Mukhaliṅgam temple	Gift of a lamp	She gave 50 she-buffaloes for the purpose to bōyas.	A.D. 1069	B.N. Sastri: Mukhalin gam : No.4

APPENDIX - B

Types of Ornaments

The literary texts of Medieval Andhra are abound with description of the ornaments worn by women of the period. Even the temple inscriptions registering grants of ornaments contain description of ornamentation pattern. The classification given below is based on the position of ornaments.

Head Ornaments

Netti Biḷḷaḷu is the term commonly used for head ornaments. The ornaments are worn on the head, at the parting of the hair, on either side of it, on the hair and at the end of the hair. To quote few :

Bangārupūceru	:	Golden flowers to be decorated in the hair.
Chandravanka	:	Sart or Ravi, Gold elaborately set with precious stones and resembled crescent moon or sun. This was adorned on either side at the parting of hair.
Chērcukka or Pāpaṭa boṭṭu or Pāpiḍicēru	:	Gold studded with precious stones. It was generally kept at the centre of the forehead at the parting of hair.
Chūḍamaṇi	:	A small circular ornament connected with a long chain arranged at the centre of the forehead. **(Plate VI b)**.
Koppu pūvulu	:	Flowers made of pearls to be decorated in the hair.
Lalaṭikamu	:	Fore-head ornament of gold set with precious stones or pearls.
Mutyālajalli	:	Hair net of pearls.
Mutyāla kuchhulu	:	A tassel made of pearls usually tied as a knot at the root of the tress of hair.
Nāgaramu	:	An ornament of gold worn at the centre of the hair.

Ear Ornaments (Plates I a, IV a, b, V a, b, VI a)

Kammalu or Kuṅḍalamulu is the term used for denoting ear ornaments. Earlier leaves of palm tree were used for the purpose, hence the word *Taṭaṅkamulu*. Based on the variations in their designs they are classified into –

Bavire or Bavirelu	:	An ornament usually of gold worn from the tip of the ear.
Kammapūvulu	:	Ear-rings made of gold in the form of flowers.
Kunṭilu or *Makarakuṅḍalamulu*	:	Large ear-rings usually made of gold. **(Plate V a).**
Mutyāla Kammalu	:	Made of pearls.
Nīlapurālu	:	Ear-rings of blue coloured stones.
Taṭaṅkamulu	:	Ear-rings made of palm leaf.
Vṛittakuṅḍalamulu	:	Large circular shaped ear-rings made of gold. **(Plate Vb).**

Nose Ornaments (Plates VII a)

Mukkera or *Muṅgara* denotes nose ornaments. *Nattu* was perhaps a mandalika variation of the same, it was a common practice among women of medieval Andhra to adore the nose with small ornaments usually made of gold studded with stones on either side of the nose as well as below at the centre of the two nostrils. Based on their location and design they are termed variously.

Aḍḍabaśa or *Bulāki*	:	A nose jewel worn at the centre of the nose (below).
Mukkera or Muṅgara	:	A nose ring generally made of a white stone studded in gold. It is also made with emeralds, corals, diamonds or pearls in which case, referred with the respective names of the precious stones.
Reṇḍuguṅḍla muṅgaralu	:	A nose ring having two pieces.
Tagarapu mukkera	:	Nose ring made of lead.

Neck Ornaments (Plates I a, IV a, b, V a)

Kanṭikahāramulu or *Kanṭabharaṇamulu* is the name for necklaces or chains. *Nānuchuṭṭlu* could probably be another *mandalika* variation for the same. Varieties of necklaces are worn by women of all classes of the society. They ranged from tight neck bands called *Patteda* to long chains, sometimes hung down to naval portion. These necklaces are in addition to the compulsory ornaments and the chain of black beads. Variations are noticed sometimes based on the religious faith such as *Nandidaṇḍa, Rudrāksha pūsalu* or *Tomāla daṅḍa* etc. The following are the different types of neck ornaments mentioned in the contemporary literary and epigraphical sources.

Banḍi guṛigiṅja tāvaḍamu	:	Necklace of Gurvinda seeds.
Bannasaramu	:	A necklace.
Chandrahāramu	:	A chain of gold in two or many rows **(Plate V a)**.
Chennumeṛugutākulu	:	A kind of shining necklace of leaf pattern.
Gonṭapūsalu	:	Small nuts made into beads and arranged in the chain.
Guṅḍla pēru	:	A chain of gold beads.
Guṛija pērulu	:	Necklace of Gurvinda seeds generally worn by women of forest dwelling classes. **(Plate IV a)**.
Māṅgalyamu or *Pasupuṭāllu*	:	The marriage token. The application of haldi is indicative of its auspicious nature and importance of its presence.
Meḍanūlu / Gaṭṭinūlu	:	A gold chain made of small thin bands.
Miṇukulu	:	Twinkling chains of gold.
Mutyālahāramu	:	A chain of pearls.
Mutyāla paṭṭeda	:	A neck band of pearls.
Mutyālasarulu	:	Small chains of pearls.
Nallapūsalu	:	A chain of black beads worn by married women.
Naṅḍi daṅḍa	:	A chain used by devotees of Śiva.
Nānu-chuṭṭlu	:	A gold necklace of beads linked together.
Pachhapūsalu	:	A necklace of golden beads.
Penusanna golusulu	:	Small thin chains of gold.
Pikilipūladaṅḍalu	:	A chain made with the wings of small birds called *Pikilipittalu*.
Rudrāksha pụsalu	:	A chain of Rudrāksha seeds or Rudrāksha Saramulu.
Saṛipeṇalu	:	Gold or silver chains.
Taḷi boṭṭu	:	The marriage token. However, its name is suggestive of the earlier use of two palm leaves tied together to a thread indicating the union of two persons through marriage.
Tōmāla daṇḍa	:	A garland of Tulsi leaves.
Vēpāku chiguḷḷa daṅḍalu	:	A chain made with the tender leaves of Neem tree.
Veduṛu mutyamulu	:	A chain made of bamboo pearls.
Tṛisaramu	:	A gold chain of three lines.

Shoulder/Hand/Wrist Ornaments (Bracelets, Bangles)

The upper part of the elbow as well as its lower half upto the wrist is adorned with different types of ornaments. The former are called bracelets and the latter bangles. Precious metals like gold and silver together with pearls or costly stones are moulded into different shapes skilfully by the artisans. Their workmanship is clearly noticed in the bracelets. *Kaṇkaṇamu* or *Kaḍiyamu* is the popular name for the bracelets. The term *Chekaṭṭu* refers to hand ornament whereas the term *Daṅḍa-Kadiyamu* refers to the shoulder ornament. The following is the list of shoulder and hand ornaments mentioned in the contemporary literature and reflected in the sculptures of the period.

Shoulder Ornaments (Plates IV a, V, b, VI a, VII a)

Chāmāla kaḍiyālu : Golden bracelets.
Harikaṅkaṇamulu : Golden bracelets.
Ittaḍi kaḍiyālu : Bracelets of brass.
Kaṭṭe vaṁkīlu : Twisted cane rings.
Lakka tāyetulu : Amulets of false coral.
Moṛavaṅka kaḍiyamu : A shining curved golden bracelet.
Nāgabettamu : Bracelet of the shape of a snake.
Nāgavattulu : Bracelet of the shape of a snake.
Ottula kaḍiyālu : Golden bracelets.
Pasiḍi ṛava kaḍiyālu : Bracelets of gold studded with emeralds.
Sari-daṅḍa tayetulu : Talismans for upper arm.
Vaṁkīlu : Curved ornament worn round the upper arm.

Hand and Wrist Ornaments (Plates I a, III a, IV a, VI a)

Chēkaṭṭu paḷelu : Bracelets of gold or coral beads alternatively arranged.
Manjīra kaṅkaṇālu : A bracelet having bells.
Maṇipuramu : A wrist ornament.
Muṛugulu : Golden wire twisted in the form of bangle.
Mutyāla chēkaṭṭu : Bracelet of pearls.
Nalla muduka gājulu : Ordinary glass bangles, black in colour.
Pagaḍāla chēkaṭṭu : Bracelet of corals.
Ratna kaṅkaṇamulu : Bracelets of diamonds.

Waist Ornaments (Plates II b, IV a, IV b, V a, b, VII a)

Ornaments worn on the garments surrounding the waist come under this head. Commonly, these are made of gold and silver metals. Often pearls are studded in the middle. *Oḍḍāṇamu* is the general name for waist ornament.

Gajjela oḍḍāṇamu	:	Silver or gold waist ornament, having bells.
Kīljaḍa	:	A twisted ornament tied around the waist.
Molanūlu	:	Silver or gold waist ornament, occasionally has bells.
Oḍḍāṇamu	:	A cestus or belt of gold or silver waist ornament worn on the dress.
Ratnamēkhala	:	Waist ornaments made of precious gems **(Plate VI a).**

Anklets (Plate I b, IV a, b, V a, b)

The foot ornaments are commonly referred to as *Aṅdiyalu.* They are mostly made of silver metal and occasionally made of gold.

Gajjelu/Andiyalu/Muvvalu	:	Anklets having bells made of silver.
Kāncheēnūpuṛa kaṅkaṇamulu	:	Anklets having bells.

Finger Ornaments (Plate V a)

Anguḷīyakamu or *Uṅgaramu* is the term for denoting finger ornaments. Though the ring finger is used for the purpose of ornamentation, sometimes other fingers too are decorated with a variety of ornaments. Gold and precious stones are generally used in the making of finger ornaments.

Toe-Ornaments

Generally worn by married women. *Maṭṭiyalu* is a common term. Like the finger ornaments, these are also worn at all the toe-fingers. Following is their nomenclature.

Bobbilikāyalu	:	Toe-ornaments for the great toe.
Gilkumaṭṭelu	:	Toe-rings made of tin.
Kaṅchu meṭṭiyalu	:	Bell metal toe-rings for the fourth toe.
Liṅgapukaya maṭṭelu	:	Toe-rings of the shape of the Śivaliṅga.
Maṭṭiyalu	:	Toe-ornaments made of silver.
Piḷḷaṅḍlu	:	Silver toe-rings for the fourth toe.
Vīramaddiyalu	:	Silver toe-rings for the large toe, worn on the occasion of war.

APPENDIX - C

Bridal Decoration

The contemporary literary sources contain ample references to bridal decoration process. One can see a lot of similarity in the items of beautification used is the earlier period and the present day products. Most of the preparations were made at home using the herbs and herbal oils.

Given below is a description of the bride as mentioned in some of the literary texts of Medieval Andhra.

Kumārasaṁbhavamu

The poet, on the occasion of the narration of the marriage between Lord Śiva and Goddess Parvati gives a clear picture of the process of bridal decoration which was in practice in Āndhra during his life-times.

The bride (Parvathi) was given bath with scented water containing perfumes of good quality. Sandalwood paste was applied to the body. Collyrium was applied to the eyes in a manner which made them look dark and lustrous. *Vannu* was anointed to lips. Her long black hair was combed and decorated with flowers. Finally on the fore-head a brooch of scarlet colour made of *Sindhōoramu* was put in the shape of a swan. A beautiful sari was selected for the bride. Similarly, best variety of ornaments were chosen. The waist ornament was made of precious gems and called *Ratnamēkhala*. Gold chains were put on the breasts. Diamond studded ear-rings were put on the ears. This way the bride was made to look graceful.

Raṅganātha Rāmāyaṇamu

Sitā, the bride was given an oil bath with *Saṁpeṅga* oil. Yellow coloured pure quality of sandal wood, musk, Ox-gall, etc. were mixed to form a paste which was used to clean the body as well as hair. Perfumes were mixed in water to give it a fresh fragrance. Yellow and white coloured skirt and a top containing a variety of designs in beautiful colours were chosen as garments for the bride. The blouse was of silk and having flowers stitched with golden threads.

Variety of ornaments like necklaces of precious stones, pearls, rubies, emeralds are selected. They include *Bannasaramu, Hāramulu, Mukkera, Kammalu, Baviṛelu, Kaḍiyamulu, Molanūlu* made of red stone called *Padmarāgamu* (ruby made of red stone of the finest quality), bells of *Gomēdhikamu* (Topaz, agate), etc. Hair was adorned with flowers.

Palnāṭi Vīracharitra

Manchala was the bride whose beauty is sketched by the poet through the bridal decoration. The bride's hair was massaged with oil made of gold flower (Sampenga) and was washed with perfumed water. Once the hair was dried properly it was combed into a long *'veni'* and towards its end a tassel of pearls was tied. Hair was decorated with flowers made of gold all throughout its length. Other head ornaments adorned include the *Pāpata* made of gold with pearls and diamonds studded in it, *Ceṛcukka* (Sart and Ravi) on either side of the parting of the hair, and a golden *Nāgaramu* studded with stones.

The two eyebrows were linked with a saffron mark as brooch. Collyrium was applied to the eyes. Nose ornaments like pearl *muṅgara* were kept. In addition, different types of chains made of precious metals and valuable stones of all varieties were put on her body. Ear-rings were long and were made of gold. Neck band of pearls was kept in addition to the locketed chains. Diamond and precious stone bangles were adorned to the hands. Colourful glass bangles also were put on the hands of the bride. Bracelets were of emeralds. Finger ornaments were kept. The legs had anklets and bells. *Lattuka* was applied to the legs to make them look red and beautiful. The silk sari selected for the bride was looking quite gorgeous with golden *zari* all over. The blouse was also of silk and had flowers stitched on it with golden thread.

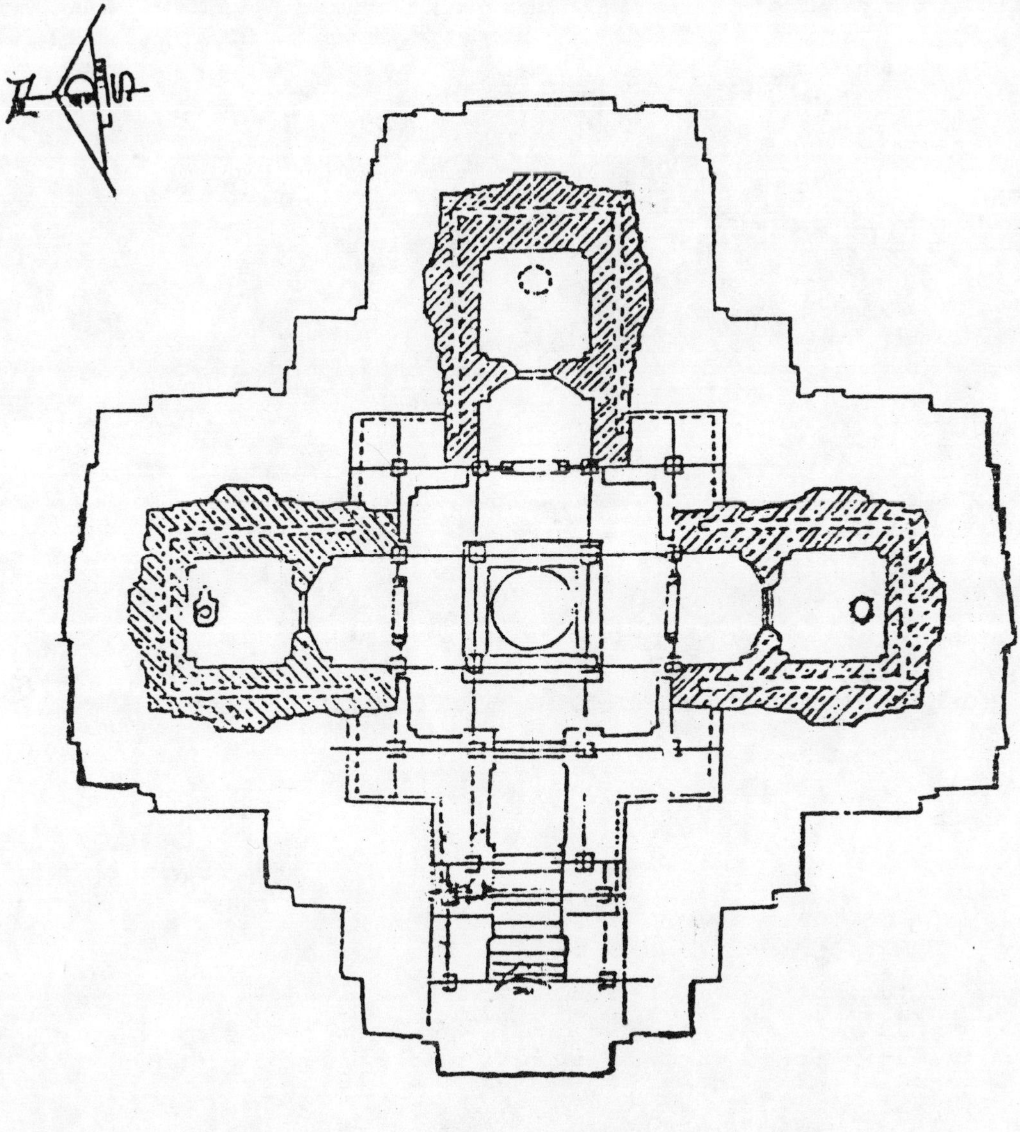

Figure 1 : Ground plan of Thousand Pillar Temple, Hanumakonda showing the *Rangamanḍapa* in the centre.

Bibliography

Inscriptions and Archival Material

Andhra Pradesh Government Reports on Epigraphy, (1965, 1966), Govt. of A.P., Hyderabad.

Annual Reports on South Indian Epigraphy, Director General, Archaeological Survey of India, New Delhi.

Archaeological Report on Indian Epigraphy, (1945-46), Department of Archaeology, Government of India Press, Calcutta, 1952.

A Collection of the Inscriptions on Copper-plate and Stones in the Nellore District, Parts I to III, (eds.), A. Butterworth and V. Venugopal Chetty, Asian Educational Series, New Delhi, 1990.

A Monograph on Yelesvaram Excavations, A.P., Government Archaeological Series, No. 14, Mohd. Addul Waheed Khan, Govt. of A.P., Hyderabad, 1963.

Epigraphia Andhrica, Vol. I, (ed.), Dr. N. Venkataramanayya, Govt. of A.P., Hyderabad, 1969.

---Vol. II, (eds.), Dr. N. Veknataramanayya and P.V. Prabrahma Sastry, Govt. of A.P., Hyderabad, 1974.

--- Vol. III, (eds.), Dr. N. Venkataramanayya and P.V. Prabrahma Sastry, Govt. of A.P., Hyderabad, 1974.

--- Vol. IV, (ed.), P.V. Prabrahma Sastry, Govt. of A.P., Hyderabad, 1975.

--- Vol. V, (ed.), N. Mukunda Row, Govt. of A.P. Hyderabad, 1988.

Hyderabad Archaeological Series, No. 13, (Corpus of Inscriptions in the Telangana Districts of H.E.H. The Nizam's Dominions), Part II, (ed.), P. Sreenivasachar, Calcutta, 1940.

Hyderabad Archaeological Series, No. 19, (ed.), P. Sreenivasachar, Govt. of A.P., Hyderabad, 1956.

Inscriptions of Andhradesa, Vols. I and II, (ed.), M. Rama Rao, Sri Venkateswara University, Tirupati, 1967, 1968.

Inscriptions of Andhra Pradesh, Cuddapah District, (ed.), P.V. Parabrahma Sastry, Govt. of A.P., Hyderabad, 1977.

Inscriptions of Andhra Pradesh : Karimnagar District, (ed.), P.V. Parabrahma Sastry, Govt. of A.P., Hyderabad, 1974.

Inscriptions of Andhra Pradesh : Warangal District, (ed.), N. Ramesan, Govt. of A.P., Hyderabad, 1974.

Inscriptions of Telangana, Vols. I and II, Lakshmanaraya Parisodhaka Mandali, Hyderabad, 1935.

Mackenzie Manuscripts, Vol. 26 - Hanamkonda Kaifiyat.

--- Vol. 48 - Prataparudra Charitra and Mogalthuru Kaifiyat.

--- Vol. 390 - Velugotivari Vamsavali.

South Indian Inscriptions, Vol. IV, (ed.), Rao Bahadur H. Krishna Sastry, Government Press, Madras, 1923, Reprint, Mysore, 1986.

--- Vol. VI, (ed.), K.V. Subrahmanya Aiyer, Government Press, Madras, 1925, Reprint, Delhi, 1986.

--- Vol. V, (ed.), Rao Bahadur H. Krishna Sastry, Government Press, Madras, 1928, Reprint, Delhi, 1986.

--- Vol. X, (ed.), J. Ramayya Pantulu, Government Press, Madras, 1948, Reprint, Mysore, 1986.

Temple Inscriptions of Andhra Pradesh, Vol. I, (Srikakulam District), (eds.), Dr. N. Ramesan and N. Mukunda Row, Govt. of A.P., Hyderabad, 1980.

Telugu Literary Works

Āndhra Mahābhāratamu, Adi, Sabha, Virata Parvamulu.

Annamayya, Yathavakkula, *Sarveśvara Satakamu,* Andhra Sahitya Parishatpatrika, Madras, 1919.

Buddha Reddy, Gona, Kacha and Vittala, *Raṅganātha Rāmāyaṇamu*, (ed.), Pingali Lakshmikantham, Telugu University, Hyderabad, 1989.

Ekāṁranātha, *Pratāparudra Charitra,* (ed.), Dr. C.V. Ramachandra Rao, A.P. Sahitya Academy, Hyderabad, 1984.

Goparaju, Koravi, *Siṃhasanadvātṛṁsika*, (ed.), Gadiyaram Ramakrishna Sarma, A.P. Sahitya Academy, Hyderabad, 1982.

Goparaju, Koravi, *Siṁhāsanadvātṛṁsika*, (ed.), Vemparala Suryanarayana Sastri, Part I, Andhra Sahitya Parishat, Kakinada, 1960.

Jayapa Senani, *Nṛittaratnākaramu*, (ed.), Rallapalli Ananta Krishna Sarma, Hyderabad, 1969.

Ketana, Mulaghatika, *Daśakumāracharitramu*, Vavilla, Chennapuri, 1925.

Ketana, Mulaghatika, *Vijñaneśvaramu*, (ed.), C.V. Ramachandra Rao, Manasa Publications, Nellore, 1977.

Manchana, *Kēyūrabāhucharitramu*, (ed.), Gadiyaram Ramakrishna Sarma, A.P. Sahitya Academy, Hyderabad, 1966.

Manchana, *Kēyūrabāhucharitramu*, (ed.), Timmavajjhula Kodandaramayya, Sarasvata Kutiramu, Madras, 1960.

Manchana, *Kēyūrabāhucharitramu*, (ed.), Vedam Venkataraya Sastri and Brothers, Madras, 1970.

Nannechoda, *Kumārasaṁbhavamu*, (ed.), Korada Mahadeva Sastri, Telugu University, Hyderabad, 1987.

Panditaradhya, Mallikarjuna, *Sivatattvasāramu*, Krishna Patrika Press, Hyderabad, 1968.

Sarvappa, Kase, *Sri Siddhēśvara Charitramu*, (Kakatiyarajula Charitra - Pratapacharitra), (ed.), Khandavalli Lakshmiranjanam, Andhra Writers Association, Hyderabad, 1960.

Singana, Madiki, *Sakalanītisammatamu*, (ed.), Manavalli Ramakrishnakavi, Madras, 1923.

Somanatha, Palkuriki, *Basavapurāṇamu*, (ed.), Nidadavolu Venkatarao, Andhragranthamala, Chennapuri, 1952.

Somanatha, Palkuriki, *Basavapurāṇamu*, (ed.), G.V. Subrahmanyam, A.P. Sahitya Academy, Hyderabad, 1968.

Somanatha, Palkuriki, *Sri Paṇḍitāradhya Charitra*, (ed.), Dr. Chilukuri Narayana Rao, Andhra Granthamala, Madras, 1939, (Reprint), 1974.

Somesvaradeva, *Rāja Mānasollāsa* (*Abhilashitardha Chintamani*), Mysore Vidyapith, Mysore. Translation of *Vaidyaka Vibhāgamu* by Sastrula Visvanatha Sarma, Indian Medical Texts and Monographs, Published by D.V. Subbareddy, Hyderabad, 1961.

Srinatha, *Palanāṭi Vīracharitra*, (ed.), Pingali Lakshmikantham, Visalandhra, Hyderabad, 1991.

Vallabharaya, Vinukonda, *Kṛīdābhirāmamu*, (ed.), Veturi Prabhakara Sastri, Manimanjari, Hyderabad, 1960.

Velugōtivāri Vaṁsāvali, (ed.), Dr. N. Venkataramanayya, Madras University Press, Madras, 1939.

Vidyanatha, *Pratāparudra Yasōbhushaṇamu*, Telugu Translation by Dr. Chalamacharla Rangacharyulu, Srinivasa Publications, Hyderabad, 1972.

Dictionaries

Apte, Vaman Shivaram, *The Student's Sanskrit English Dictionary*, Motilal Banarasidas, Delhi, 1993.

Brown, Charles Philip, *Telugu-English Dictionary*, Second Edition, (Revised), Asian Educational Series, Madras, 1992.

Isvaradutt, Kunduri, *Sasana Sabda Kosamu*, A.P. Sahitya Academy, Hyderabad, 1967.

Reddy, G.N., *Telugu Nighantuvu*, Telugu University, Hyderabad, 1989.

Subbarayudu, Mahakali, *Sabdartha Chandrika, Andhra Nighantuvu*, Vavilla Brothers, Madras, 1913.

Suryarayandhra Nighantuvu, 8 Volumes, Andhra Sahitya Parishat, Kakinada.

Vavilla Nighantuvu, Volumes, Vavilla Brothers, Madras, 1969.

Encyclopaedia

A Historical Atlas of South Asia, (ed.), Schwartzberg, E., Joseph, University of Chicago, Chicago, 1978.

Andhra Vijñana Sarvasvamu, Telugu Bhasha Samithi, Madras, 1916.

Encyclopaedia of Indian Women, Akashdeep Publishing House, Delhi, Reprint, 1990.

International Encyclopaedia of Social Sciences, (ed.), David, R. Sill, Macmillan Company, New York.

Samgrahandhra Vijnanakosamu, (ed.), Mamidipudi Venkatarangayya, Samgrahandhra Vijnanakosa Samiti, Hyderabad.

Telugu Vijñana Sarvasvamu, (Telugu Samskriti), Telugu Bhasha Samiti, Madras.

Modern Published Works : English

Altekar, A.S., *The Position of Women in Hindu Civilisation*, Motilal Banarasidas, Delhi, 1962.

Anderson, Perry, *Lineages of the Absolutist State,* Britain, 1974.

Appadorai, A., *Economic Conditions in Southern India, 1000-1500, A.D.*, Madras University Historical Series, No. 12, Madras, 1936.

Appadorai, D.A., *History and Conditions of Women in South East Asia*, Orient Longman, Bombay, 1954.

Appadurai, Arjun, *Worship and Conflict under Colonial Rule : A South Indian Case*, Orient Longman, Bombay, 1983.

Baig, Tara Ali, *Women of India*, Ministry of Information and Broadcasting, Government of India, Delhi, 1958.

Balendu Sekharam, K., *The Andhras Through Ages,* Sri Saraswati Book Depot, Hyderabad, 1973.

Beard, Mary, R., *Woman as a Force in History*, Macmillan Co., New York, 1946.

Bhandarkar, R.G., *Vaishnavism, Saivism and Minor Religious Systems,* Indological Book House, Varanasi, 1965.

Bhattacharya, N.N., *Medieval Bhakti Movements in India*, Sri Chaitanya Quincentenary Commemoration Volume, Munshiram Manoharlal, Delhi, 1989.

Boulding, Elise, (ed.), *Handbook of International data on Women,* John Wiley, New York, 1976.

Boulding, Elisc, *Women in the Twentieth Century World,* John Wiley, New York, 1979.

Bowles, Gloria and Klein Ranateduelli, (ed.), *Theories of Women's Studies.* Routledge and Kegenpaul, London, 1983.

Carroll, A. Berenice, *Liberating Women's History – Theoretical and Critical Essays,* University of Illinoise Press, Chicago, 1976.

Chattopadhyaya, B.D., *The Making of Early Medieval India*, Delhi, 1993.

Clarisse, Bader, Tr. Martin Mary E.R., *Women in Ancient India*, Chowkambha Sanskrit Series, Varanasi.

Classen, J, and Skalnik, P., (ed.), *The Early State : Theories and Hypothesis*, The Hague, 1981.

Chopra, P.N., Ravindran, T.K., and Subrahmanian, N., (ed.), *History of Medieval South India*, 3 Vols., Chand and Company Ltd., Delhi, 1979.

Das, R.M., *Women in Manu and His seven commentators,* Kanchana Publications, Bodhgaya, 1962.

Das, Sukla, *Crime and Punishment in Ancient India (A.D. 300-A.D. 1100)*, Abhinav Publications, New Delhi, 1977.

Davidson, Laurie and Loura Kramer Gorden, *The Sociology of Gender,* Rand Mac Nally College Publications, Chicago, 1979.

Deir Dre, Beddoe, *Discovering Women's History – A Practical Manual*, Pandora Press, 1983.

Desai, A.R., (ed.), *Rural Sociology in India*, Bombay, 1978.

Desai, Neera and Krishnaraj Maitreyi, *Women and Society in India*, Ajanta Publications, 1990.

Dubois Abbe, J.A., Beauchamp Henry, K., *Hindu Manners, Customs and Ceremonies,* Oxford University Press, Delhi, 1985.

Devahuti, (ed.), *Problems of Indian Historiography*, D.K. Publications, Delhi, 1979.

Devaki, Indra, *Status of Women in Ancient India – Survey of Social, Religious, Political and Legal Position in Ancient India*, Motilal Banarasidas, Banaras, 1955.

Dubey, S.M., (ed.), *Family, Marriage and Social Change on the Indian Fringe,* Cosmo Publications, New Delhi, 1980.

Elliot and Dowsons, *India as told by its own Historians*, Volumes, Allahabad, 1964.

Engels, Friedrich, *Origin of Family, Private property and the State*, Progress Publishers, Moscow, 1948, Reprint, 1983.

Errington, Frederick and Deborah Gewertz, *Cultural Alternatives and a Feminist Anthropology*, Cambridge University Press, London, 1987.

Eschmann, A., Kulke Hermann, Tripathi, S.C., *The Cult of Jagannatha and the Regional Tradition of Orissa*, New Delhi, 1978.

Fox, R.G., (ed.), *Realm and Region in Traditional India*, Vikas Publications, New Delhi, 1977.

Friedl, E., *Women and Men, An Anthropologist View,* New York, 1975.

Fuller, Marcus, *The Wrongs of Indian Womanhood,* Inter-India Publications, Delhi, Reprint, 1984.

Ghadially, Rehana, *Women in Indian Society – A reader*, Sage Publications, New Delhi, 1988.

Ghosh, S.K., *Indian Women Through Ages*, Ashish Publishing House, Delhi, 1989.

Glazer, Nona and Helen Youngelson Wachrer, (ed.), *Women in a Man Made World*, (A Socio-Economic Hand book), Chicago, 1977.

Greer, Germainne, *The Female Eunuch,* Toronto Bantom Books, 1972.

Guha, Ranajit, (ed.), *Subaltern Studies, Writings on South Asian History and Society,* Vols. I to V, Oxford University Press, Delhi, 1982-87.

Gulati, Saroj, *Women and Society in Northern India in 11th and 12th Centuries,* Chanakya Publications, Delhi, 1985.

Gupta, Kalpana Das, *Women on the Indian Scene,* Delhi, 1976.

Gupta, Kamala, *Social Status of Hindu Women in Northern India (1206-1707 A.D.),* Inter-India Publications, New Delhi, 1987.

Gupta, S.P., *Costumes, Textiles, and Cosmetics Coiffure in Ancient and Medieval India*, Motichandra Felicitation Volume, Oriental Publications, Delhi, 1973.

Gupta, Sankar Sen, *Folk Culture in India*, Indian Publications, Calcutta, 1969.

Gurevich, A.J., *Categories of Medieval Culture*, (Translation by G.L. Campbell), Routledge and Keganpaul, London, 1985.

Hanumantha Rao, B.S.L., *Religion in Andhra,* Tripura Sundari, Guntur, 1973.

Harvey, David, *The Condition of Postmodernity*, Blackwell Publications, Oxford, U.K., 1990, Reprint, 1992.

Hasan, Siraj-ul-Syed, *The Castes and Tribes of H.E.H. The Nizam's Dominions*, Asian Educational Series, New Delhi, 1989.

Hocart, A.M., *Kings and Councillors, An Essay in the Comparative Anatomy of Human Society,* University of Chicago, Chicago, 1970.

Holdernen, T.W., *Peoples and Problems of India*, Anupama Publications, Delhi, 1985.

Hopkins, T.J., *The Hindu Religious Traditions,* Dickenson Publishing Company, California, 1971.

Ide, Arthur Frederick, *Women Before History was Written*, Monument Press, Dallas, 1985.

Jain, Devaki, *Indian Women,* Director, Publications Division, Government of India, Delhi, 1975.

Jaiswal, Suvira, *Origin and Development of Vaishnavism*, Munshiram Manoharlal, Delhi, 1967.

Jha, D.N., *Feudal Social Formation in Early India*, Chanakya Publications, Delhi, 1987.

Jyotsna, K. Kamat, *Social Life in Medieval Karnataka,* Abhinav Publications, Delhi, 1980.

Kane, Panduranga Vaman, *History of Dharmasastras*, Vols. I to V, Bhandarkar Oriental Research Institute Series, No. 6, Poona, 1968-1974.

Kapadia, K.M., *Marriage and Family in India,* Oxford University Press, Calcutta, 1988.

Karashima, Noboru, *Southern Indian History and Society (A.D. 850-1800),* Oxford University Press, Delhi, 1984.

Kaushik, Susheela, *Women's Oppression, Patterns and Perspectives,* Shakti Books, New Delhi, 1985.

Kosambi, D.D., *An Introduction to the Study of Indian History,* Popular Book Depot, Bombay, 1956.

Kosambi, D.D., *On History and Society, Problems of Interpretation,* Department of History, University of Bombay, Bombay, 1985.

Kosambi, D.D., *Myth and Reality : Studies in Formation of Indian Culture*, Popular Prakashan, Bombay, 1962.

Krishna Kumari, M., *The Rule of Chalukya-Cholas in Andhradesa*, B.R. Publishing Corporation, Delhi, 1985.

Krishnaraj, Maitreyi, *Evolving New Methodologies in Research on Women's Studies,* Bombay, 1988.

Krishnaraj, Maitreyi, *Women's Studies in India-Some Perspectives*, Bombay, 1986.

Kupuswamy, B., *Social Change in India*, Vikas Publishing Corporation, Delhi, 1972.

Lalitha, K., *We were making History, Life Stories of Women in the Telangana People's Struggle,* Stree Sakti Sanghatana, Kali for Women, Delhi, 1989.

Leacock, Eleanor, Dube Leela and Shirley, Ardener, (ed.), *Visibility and Power, Essays on Women in Society and Development,* Oxford University Press, Delhi, 1986.

Leela Mulatti, *Bhakti Movement and the Status of Women – A Case Study of Veerasaivism,* Abhinav Publications, Delhi, 1989.

Lerner, *The Majority Finds it's Past,* Oxford University Press, New York, 1979.

Lerner Gerda, *The Creations of Patriarchy,* Oxford University Press, London, 1986.

Lucas, Angela, M., *Women in the Middle ages*, The Harvester Press, Great Britain, 1983.

Ludden, David, *Peasant History in South India,* Oxford University Press, Delhi, 1989.

Mabbet, Ian, *Patterns of Kingship and Authority in Traditional Asia,* Croom Helm, London, 1985.

Macnieal, Margaret, *Poems by Indian Women,* New York, 1923.

Madhavananda, Swami and Majumdar, R.C., *Great Women of India*, The Holy Mother Birth Centenary Memorial, Mayavati Press, 1982.

Manohar, K. Murali, *Socio-Economic Status of Indian Women*, Seema Publications, Delhi, 1983.

Manohar, K. Murali and Shobha, V., *The Status of Women in India - Some trends and Issues,* Kakatiya University, Warangal, 1981.

Mary, Frances, *Women in India – A Study of Medieval Period*, Amara Book Agency, Delhi, 1974.

Max Muller, F., *The Sacred Books of the East*, Vol. XXV, Buhler, G., *The Laws of Manu*, Motilal Banarasidas, New Delhi, 1975.

Mehta, Hansa, *Indian Women,* Butala and Company, Delhi, 1981.

Miles, Rosalind, *The Women's History of the World,* Paladin Grafton Books, London, 1989.

Misra, Rekha, *Women in Moghul India*, Munshiram Manoharlal, Delhi, 1967.

Mitchell, Juliet and Annoakley, (ed.)., *What is Feminism*, Basil Blackwell, Oxford, 1987.

Mohan, Lakshmikantha, *Telugu Fairs and Festivals*, International Telugu Centre, Telugu University, Hyderabad, 1988.

Moore, R.J., *Tradition and Politics in South Asia*, Vikas Publications, New Delhi, 1979.

Morewedge, Rosemarie Thee, *The Role of Women in Middle Ages*, Brighampton, 1975.

Morton, A.L., *People's History of England,* Lawrence and Wishant, London, 1948.

Mount, Hagen, *Women in Between Female Roles in a Male World,* New Guinea, London, 1972.

Murthy, Sri Rama, *Social and Cultural Life of Eastern Chalukyas of Vengi,* Moulana Abdul Kalam Azad Research Institute. Hyderabad.

Nandimath, S.C., *A Hand Book of Veerasaivism,* Dharwar, 1942.

Nandi, R.N., *Religious Institutions and Cult in Deccan (A.D. 600-1000),* Motilal Banarasidas, New Delhi, 1973.

Nandi, Ramendranath, *Social Roots of Religion in Ancient India*, K.P. Bagchi and Company, New Delhi, 1986.

Nand, Lokeshchandra, *Women in Delhi Sultanate*, Vohra Publications, Allahabad, 1989.

Narasimha Rao, R, *Corporate Life in Medieval Andhradesa*, Hyderabad, 1967.

Narayana Rao, Velcheru and Roghair H. Gene, *Siva's Warriors, the Basavapurana of Palkuriki Somanatha,* Princeton University Press, Princeton, New Jersey, 1990.

Nilakantha Sastry, K.A., *A History of South India*, Oxford University Press, London, 1958.

Nilakantha Sastry, K.A., *Foreign Notices of South India*, (From Megasthenes to Mahavro), University of Madras, Historical Series No. 14, Madras, 1939.

Nilakantha Sastry, K.A., *The Cholas,* University of Madras, Historical Series No. 19, Madras, 1955.

Parabrahma Sastry, P.V., *The Kakatiyas of Warangal,* Govt. of A.P. Hyderabad, 1978.

Parasher, Aloka, *Materialist Historiography and The Invisibility of Rural Women,* CWDS, Delhi, 1990.

Prabhu, P.N.H., *The Hindu Social Organisation*, Popular Prakashan, Bombay, 1961.

Pai, D.A., *Religious Sects of the Hindus,* Cosmo Publications, Delhi, 1983.

Prakash Singh, Indu, *Indian Women, The Captured Begins,* Intellectual Publishing House, Delhi, 1990.

Prasad, Avadh Kishore, *Devadasi System in Ancient India*, H.K. Publications, Delhi, 1991.

Radhakrishna Murthy, K., *The Economic Conditions of Medieval Andhradesa*, (A.D. 1000-1500), Venkateswara Publications, Tirupati, 1987.

Rajendraprasad, B., *Chalukyan Temples of Andhradesa*, Abhinav Publications, New Delhi, 1983.

Ramachandra Rao, C.V., *Administration and Society in Medieval Andhra (A.D. 1038-1538) Under the Later Eastern Gangas and Surya Vamsa Gajapathis*, Manasa Publications, Nellore, 1976.

Ramanaiah, J., *Chalukyan and Kakatiya Temples of Jagtial and Adjoining Areas,* Hyderabad, 1983.

Rama Rao, M., *Select Andhra Temples*, Govt. of A.P., Hyderabad, 1979.

Rama Rao, M., *Select Kakatiya Temples*, Sri Venkateswara University, Tirupati, 1966.

Rama Rao, M., *The Temples of Kalinga*, Sri Venkateswara University, Tirupati, 1965.

Ramaswamy, Vijaya, *Textiles and Weavers in Medieval South India,* Oxford University Press, New Delhi, 1985.

Ramesan, N., *Temples and Legends of Andhra Pradesh,* Bharatiya Vidya Bhavan, Bombay, 1988.

Reddy, G.N., *Selected Essays of C.P. Brown, (1798-1884) on Telugu Literature and Culture*, G.N. Reddy Felicitation Committee, Tirupati, 1988.

Robb, Peter, *Rural India, Land, Power and Society Under British Rule*, Curzon Press, London, 1983.

Rothfeld, Otto, *Women of India,* Bombay, 1928.

Rowbothem, Sheila, *Women's Consciousness – Man's World*, Penguin Books, Delhi, 1973.

Samuel Raphael, (ed.), *People's History and Socialistic Theory,* Routledge and Kegan Paul, London, 1981.

Sarma, Radhakrishna, M., *Temples in Telingana,* Munshiram Manoharlal, Delhi, 1972.

Satyanarayana, K., *A Study of History and Culture of Andhras,* Vols. I and II, Peoples Publishing House, New Delhi, 1975, 1983.

Sen,Geeti, (ed.), *Perceiving India : Insight and Enquiry*, Sage Publications, New Delhi, 1993.

Sharma, R.S., *Aspects of Political Ideas and Institutions in Ancient India*, Motilal Banarasidas, Delhi, 1991.

Sharma, R.S., *Indian Feudalism,* Delhi, 1980.

Sharma, R.S., and Vivekanand, Jha, *Indian Society – Historical Probings – Essays in Memory of D.D. Kosambi,* Peoples Publishing House, New Delhi, 1984.

Sharma, R.S., *Social Changes in Eary Medieval India (A.D. 500 - 1200)*, Delhi, 1969.

Shastri, Shakuntala Rao, *Women in the Sacred Laws,* Bhavan, Bombay, 1960.

Sherwani and Joshi, (cd.), *A History of Medieval Deccan, Vol. II (1295-1724)*, Govt. of A.P., Hyderabad, 1974.

Singh, R.L., *India : A Regional Geography*, National Geographical Society of India, Varanasi, 1989.

Sircar, D.C., *Studies in the Religious Life of Ancient and Medieval India*, Motilal Banarasidas, Delhi, 1971.

Soma Reddy, R., *History of Religious Institutions in Andhradesa (A.D. 1300 to A.D. 1600)*, New Era Publications, Madras, 1984.

Spate, O.H.K., A.T.A. Learmonth and B.H. Farmer, *India, Pakistan and Ceylon, The Regions*, Bombay, 1972.

Stein, Burton, (ed.), *All the King's Mana : Perspectives on Kingship in Medieval South India*, New Era Publications, Madras, 1984.

Stein, Burton, *Peasant State and Society in Medieval South India*, Oxford University Press, Delhi, 1980.

Stein, Burton (ed.), *South Indian Temples – An Analytical Reconsideration*, Vikas Publications, Delhi, 1978.

Stuard, Susan Mosher, *Women in Medieval Society*, University of Pennsylvania Press, Pennsylvania, 1976.

Subba Rao, B., *Personality of India, Pre and Proto Historic Foundation of India and Pakistan*, 2nd Edition, Baroda, 1958.

Sundaram, K., *Studies in the Economic and Social Conditions of Medieval Andhra (1000-1600 A.D.)*, Triveni Publishers, Machilipatnam, 1968.

Sundaram, K., *The Simhachalam Temple*, Simhachalam Devasthanam Publications, Visakhapatnam, 1984.

Suryakumari, A., *The Temple in Andhradesa*, Gian Publications, Delhi, 1988.

Suryanarayana, K., *History of Minor Chalukya Families in Medieval Andhradesa*, B.R. Publishing Corporation, Delhi, 1986.

Swamiji Shivacharya, Sivamurthy, Dr. T.J., *Virasaiva view of Man and Woman in Relation to God*, Sirigere, Karnataka, 1985.

Tikoo, Prithvinath, *Indian Women, (A Brief Socio-Cultural Survey)*, B.R. Publishing Corporation, Delhi, 1985.

Thapar, Romila, *Ancient Indian Social History, Some Interpretations*, Orient Longman, Hyderabad, 1978.

Thapar, Romila, *From Lineage to State*, Oxford University Press, Delhi, 1990.

Tharu, Susie, and K. Lalitha, (ed.), *Women Writing in India (600 B.C. to Present)*, Vol. I, The Feminist Press, New York, 1991.

Thomas, P., *Indian Women Through Ages*, Asia Publishing House, Bombay, 1964.

Thurston, Edgar and K. Rangachari, *Castes and Tribes of Southern India*, Madras, 1909.

Vaidehi, Krishna Moorthy, *Social and Economic Conditions in Eastern Deccan (1000-1250 A.D.),* Hyderabad, 1970.

Venkataramanayya, Nelaturi, *The Eastern Chalukyas of Vengi,* Madras Univeristy Press, Madras, 1950.

Vivekananda, Swamy, *Our Women,* Advaita Ashrama, Calcutta, 12th Reprint, 1992.

Weber, Max, *Religion of India,* Free Press, New York, 1967.

Yazdani, G., (ed.), *The Early History of Deccan*, Vol. II, Part VII - XI, Oriental Publications, Delhi, 1982.

Yule, H. and Cordier, H., (ed.), *Travels of Marcopolo*, Vols. I and II, London, 1903.

Yusuf, Hussain, *Glimpses of Medieval Indian Culture*, Bombay, 1959.

Telugu

Acharya, Dr. N.L.N., *Bejjanki Devalaya Sipa Viseshalu*, Gayatri Publications, Siddhipeta, 1993.

Arudra, *Samagrandhra Sahityam*, Volume I, *Purva Chalukyayugam*, Secunderabad, 1965.

Arudra, *Samagrandhra Sahityam*, Volume II, *Kakatiya Yugamu*, Prajasakti Press, Vijayawada, 1989.

Arudra, *Vyasapitham*, New Students book Depot, Vijayawada, 1985.

Chakrapani Rao, Vadavalli, *Andhra Mahabharatamu, Draupadi Aitihasika Visleshana*, World Teachers Trust, Visakhapatnam, 1990.

Chengalrayachetti, Dr. K., *Andhradesa Samghika Ardhika Charitra*, Sarada Printers, Tirupati, 1991.

Chennappa, Masana, *Prachina Kavyalu – Gramina Jivana Chitrana,* Gayatri Publications, Hyderabad, 1991.

Chittibabu, *Palnati Viracharitra*, Vahini Publishers, Vijayawada, 1980.

Dharmarao, Tapi, *Pelli Dani Puttupurvotharalu*, Visalandhra, Vijayawada, 1983.

Hanumantha Rao, B.S.L., *Andhrula Charitra*, Guntur, 1983.

Indiradevi, K.S., *Andhra Charitra*, Guntur, 1983.

Indiradevi,K.S., *Andhra Mahabharatamu, Draupadi Patra Chitranamu*, Kiran Publishers, Kalahasti, 1986.

Isvaradutt, Kunduri, *Prachinandhra Charitraka Bhugolamu*, Hyderabad, 1962.

Kanakadurga, *J., Koravi Goparaju Simhasanadvatrmsika, Mahila Janajivanam,* Kothagudem, Khammam, 1992.

Kanakadurga, P.S., *Kakatiyulanati Samajika Jivanamu*, Manasa, Vijayawada, 1992.

Kusumabai, Dr. K., *Madiki Singanakavi*, Telugu Parisodhana, Hyderabad, 1988.

Laxmikanthamma Utukuri, *Andhra Kavayitrulu*, Bapatla, 1980.

Laxmikantham, Pingali, *Andhrula Sahitya Charitra*, A.P. Sahitya Academy, Hyderabad, 1976.

Laxmiranjanam, Khandavalli, T. Balendusekharam, *Andhrula Charitra-Samskṛti*, Madras, 1985.

Laxmiranjanam, K., *Kakatiya Yugam,* A.P. Sahitya Academy, Hyderabad, 1975.

Malayasri, *Kakatiyulanati Samajika Jivitamu*, Hyderabad Book Trust, Hyderabad, 1990.

Markandeya Sarma, Nagabhatla, *Devalaya Vastusilpa Lakshanamulu,* Nagabhatla Publications, Hyderabad, 1990.

Mrutyunjaya Rao, Dr. Jonnalagadda, *Vyasa Bharatamu*, *Nannaya Parishkaramu*, Rajahmundry, 1979.

Nagayya, G., *Telugu Sahitya Samiksha,* Navya Parisodhana Prachurana, Tirupati, 1990.

Narasimha Sastry, Nori, *Rudramadevi*, Jayanti Publications, Vijayawada, 1986.

Narayana Rao, Chilukuri, *Prachina Vidyapithamulu*, Jatiya Saraswata Nilayamu, Rajahmundry, 1921.

Narayana Rao, Kallakuri, *Pratapa Rudramadevi*, Adarsha Grandhamandali, Vijayawada, 1961.

Nirmala, Tammareddi, *Nannechodadeva Kumarasambhava Parisilanamu*, Satyasurya Publications, Vijayawada, 1989.

Parabrahma Sastry, P.V., *Kakatiya Sasana Sahityamu*, A.P. Saraswatha Parishat, Hyderabad, 1981.

Parabrahma Sastry, P.V., *Telugu Sasanalu*, A.P. Sahitya Academy, Hyderabad, 1975.

Prabrahma Sastry, P.V. *Kakatiya Charitra*, Government of A.P. Hyderabad, 1977.

Prabhakara Sastry, Veturi, *Catu Padya Mani Manjari,* Manimanjari, Hyderabad, 1988.

Prabhakara Sastry, Veturi, *Telugu Merugulu, Vyasa Samputi*, Andhra Granthamala, Madras, 1948.

Prasadarao, Chalasani, *Kakatiya Silpam*, Visalandhra, Hyderabad, 1987.

Pratapa Reddy, Suravaram, *Andhrula Samghika Charitra,* Sahitya Vaijayanti, Hyderabad, 1982.

Pratapa Reddy, Suravaram, *Hinduvula Pandugalu,* Sahitya Vaijayanti, Hyderabad, 1987.

Premlatha, Dr. Ravi, *Telugu Strila Chitralipi,* Hyderabad, 1991.

Radhakrishna Budaraju, (ed.), *Prachinandhra Sasanamulu (Upto A.D. 1100)* A.P. Sahitya Academy, Hyderabad, 1971.

Ranganathacharyulu, K.K., *Telugu Sahityam Marochupu*, Andhra Saraswata Parishat, Hyderabad, 1981.

Ranganathacharyulu, K.K., *Telugulo Toli Samaja Kavulu*, Andhra Saraswata Parishat, Hyderabad, 1983.

Ratnamohini, Dr. V., *Telugu Sahityamu – Saivamata Prabhavamu,* Master Printers, Hyderabad, 1992.

Sarvottama Rao, K., *Prachinandhra Kavayitrula Stri Svabhava Chitrana,* Vidyarthi Mitra Prachurana, Kurnool, 1990.

Sastry, B.N., *Andhradesa Charitra-Samskrti,* Vol. I, Moosi Publications, Hyderabad, 1992.

Sastry, B.N., *Andhrula Samghika Charitra, (B.C. 400 to A.D. 1100),* Mosi Publications, Hyderabad, 1975.

Sastry, B.N., *Bejawada Durgamallisvaralaya Sasanamulu*, Moosi Publications, Hyderabad, 1985.

Sastry, B.N., *Cherakuvamsa Charitra-Sasanamulu,* Moosi Publications, Hyderabad, 1989.

Sastry, B.N., *Kayastha Rajulu,* Moosi Publications, Hyderabad, 1991.

Sastry, B.N., *Kunduri Chodula Sasanamulu-Charitra, Samskrti*, Moosi Publications, Hyderabad, 1984.

Sastry, B.N., *Mukhalinga Devalaya Charitra, Sasanamulu,* Kakati Publications, Hyderabad, 1985.

Sastry, B.N., *Recherla Reddivamsa Charitra-Sasanamulu,* Moosi Publications, Hyderabad, 1989.

Sastry, B.N., *Sasana Samputi*, Volumes I and II, Moosi Publications, Hyderabad, 1974, Reprint, 1989.

Sastry, B.N., *Tripurantaka Devalaya Sasanamulu*, Moosi Publications, Hyderabad, 1984.

Sastry, B.N., *Vemulavada Charitra-Sasanamulu*, Moosi Publications, Hyderabad, 1991.

Somasekhara Sarma, Mallampalli, *Amaravati Stupamu-Itara Vyasamulu*, Madras, 1932.

Somasekhara Sarma, Mallampalli, *Andhradesa Charitra Samgrahamu*, Deluxe Publications, Vijayawada, 1991.

Somasekhara Sarma, Mallampalli, *Andhra Samskrti-Tarangini*, Govt. of A.P., Hyderabad, 1976.

Sriramaraju, Nadupalli, *Sivakavula Rachanalu-Samajamu*, Visalandhra, Hyderabad, 1991.

Subrahmanyam, G.V., *Saraswata Vyasamulu,* Volumes I to IV, A.P. Sahitya Academy, 2nd Reprint, Hyderabad, 1981.

Subrahmanyam, Vadla, *Telugu Sahityamlo Krida Vinodalu*, Hyderabad, 1987.

Suryanarayana Sarma, Vedula, *Kakati Prolaraju*, Narendranatha Sahitya Mandali, Tanuku, 1962.

Vaidehi, Alladi, *Andhradesamu-Streelu*, A.P. Sahitya Academy, Hyderabad, 1975.

Vaidehi, Alladi, *Andhrula Samghika Ardhika Charitra,* Hyderabad, 1978.

Varalaxmi, J., *Yugayugallo Bharatiya Mahila,* Hyderabad, 1977.

Virabhadra Rao, Chilukuri, *Andhrula Charitramu*, Manorama Press, Rajahmundry, 1916.

Virabhadra Rao, Chilukuri, *Kakatiyandhra Rajayuga Charitramu,* Vijnana Chandrika Mandali, Rajahmundry, 1936.

Veerayya, Rekaligemathamm, *Virasaiva Mahila Sivasaranurandru,* Sivanubhava Samithi, Hyderabad, 1980.

Venkatavadhani, Divakarla, G.R. Sarma, P. Narayanacharyulu, *Chitanyalahari*, Yuvabharati, Secunderabad, 1972.

Venkata Krishna Rao, Bhavaraju, *Prachinandhradesamu, Videsayatrikulu,* Rajahmundry, 1934.

Venkata Rao, Nidadavolu, *Telugu Kavula Charitra*, University of Madras, Madras, 1956.

Venkata Rao, Nidadavolu, *Vachana Basavapuranamu*, Srisailam Devasthanam Publications, Srisailam, 1981.

Venkataraya Sastry, Vedam, *Andhra Dasakumara Charitramu*, Madras, 1971.

Venkata Satya Rama Rao, Nanduri, *Andhra Sahityamu, Samghika Jivana Pratiphalanamu, (A.D. 1022-A.D. 1856),* Vaishnava Press, Pentapadu, 1979.

Venkatasubbaiah, Appajodu, *Mahabharatamu – Manava Svabhava Chitrana,* Hyderabad, 1977.

Journals : English

Arts and Ideas, Tulika Print Communications Services, Delhi.

Economic and Political Weekly, Bombay.

Feminist Review, Cambridge University Press, Britain.

Feminist Studies, University of Maryland.

History Today, London.

History Workshop, London.

Itihas, State Archives, Govt. of A.P., Hyderabad.

Lepakshi, State Archives, Govt. of A.P, Hyderabad.

Manushi, Delhi.

Modern Asian Studies, Cambridge University Press, London.

Peasant Studies, London.

Proceedings of Indian History Congress.

Proceedings of A.P. History Congress.

Signs, University of Chicago Press, Chicago.

Social Scientist, Delhi.

The Indian Economic and Social History Review, Delhi.

Women's History, Indiana University Press, Bloomington, U.S.A.

Women's Studies Quarterly, (Women's Studies International), Feminist Press, New York.

Telugu

Abhinandana, Dr. Tumati Donappa Sixtieth Birthday Volume, Abhinandana Samiti, Hyderabad, 1987.

Andhra Sahitya Parishat Patrika, Vols. 1 to 57, Kakinada.

Bharati, Volumes, Andhra Patrika Press, Vijayawada.

Journal of Andhra Historical Research Society, (ed.), R. Subba Rao, Volumes, Rajahmundry.

Kakatiya Samchika, (ed.), Maremanda Venkata Rama Rao, Department of Archaeology and Museums, Govt. of A.P., Hyderabad, Reprint, 1991.

Prajasahiti, Special Issue on Folk Arts, Vol. 8, No.2, Vijayawada, June, 1985.

Rajarajanarendra Pattabhishekha Samchika, (ed.), Bhavaraju Vankata Krishna Rao, JAHRS, Rajahmundry, 1922.

Select Articles : English

Appadurai, Arjun, 'Kings, Sects and Temples in South India (1300-1700 A.D.),' in Burton Stein, (ed.), *South Indian Temples, Analytical Study, Reconstruction,* Delhi, 1978, pp. 47-74.

Aruna Kumari, K., *'Concept of Stridhana in Mitakshara,' in PAPHC*, (8th session), Kakinada, 1984, pp. 42-44.

Bhattacharji, Sukumari, 'The Economic Rights of Ancient Indian Women' in *EPW*, March 2-9, Bombay, 1991, pp. 507-512.

Spivak, Gayatri, 'Subaltern Studies : Deconstructing Historiography' in Ranajit Guha, (ed.), *Subaltern Studies*, Vol. IV, Delhi, 1987, pp. 330-363.

Champakalaxmi, R., 'The State in Medieval South India : Emerging Perspectives' Presidential Address, *PAPHC*, 13th Session, Srisailam, 1989.

Chattopadhyaya, B.D., 'Political Processes and Structure of Polity in Early Medieval India – Problems and Perspectives', Presidential Address, *PIHC,* 44th session, Burdwan, 1983.

Chaudhuri, R., 'The Position of Women in Medieval India' in *Modern Review,* Vol. 93, No. 6, June, 1953, pp. 457-460.

De Casparis, J.D., 'Inscriptions and South Asian Dynastic Tradition' in R.J. Moore, (ed.), *Politics of South Asia*, Vikas Publications, Delhi, 1979, pp. 103-127.

Desai, Neera, Leela Dube, Vina Majumdar and others, 'Women's Studies and the Social Sciences : A Report from India' in *Women's Studies International,* The Feminist Press, No.3, April, 1984, New York, pp. 2-6.

Desai, Devangana, 'Art Under Fedualism in India (C.A.D. 500-1300)' in D.N. Jha (ed.), *Feudal Social Formation in Early India*, Delhi, 1987, pp. 391-401.

Habib Irfan, 'Towards a People's History of India', in *PAPHC*, Nagaram, 11th session, 1987, pp. 1-6.

Herilhy, David, 'Land, Family and Women in Continental Europe, A.D. 701-1200' in Susan Mosher Stuard, (ed.), *Women in Medieval Society,* Pennsylvania, 1970, pp. 13-45.

Honeyman, Kartina and Jordan Goodman, 'Women's World, Gender Conflict and Labour Markets in Europe, 1500-1700', in *JEHR*, Vol. XLIV, No. 4, Oxford, November, 1991, pp. 608-628.

Hufton, Olwen and Mc Millan, F. James, 'What is Women's History', in *History Today*, Vol. 35, London, June, 1985, pp. 38-48.

Kamerkar, Mani, 'History, Where Are the Women', in Maithreyi Krishna Raj, (ed.), *Women's Studies : Some Perspectives in India,* Bombay, 1986, pp. 86-94.

Kanakadurga, P.S.K., and Y. Sudhakar Reddy, 'Kings, Temples and Legitimation of Autochthonous Communities' in *JESHO*, Vol. 35, 1992, pp. 145-146.

Karve, Iravati, 'The Indian Village', in A.R. Desai, (ed.), *Rural Sociology in India*, Bombay, 1984, pp. 206-217.

Kirke, Neville, 'History, Ideas and Post Modernism : A Materialist View' in *Journal of Social History*, Vol. 19, No.2, May, 1994, pp. 221-240.

Kulke, Hermann, 'Fragmentation and Segmentation Versus Integration? Reflections on the Concept of Indian Feudalism and the Segmentary State in Indian History', in *Studies in History,* Vol. 4, No.2, 1982, pp. 237-263.

Kumar, Dharma, 'Private Property in Asia? The Case of Medieval South India' in *CSSH*, Vol. 27, No.2, April 1985, pp. 340-366.

Kumaraswamy, Y., 'Traces of Feudalism during the Eastern Chalukyan Period' in *PAPHC*, Warangal, 7th Session, 1983, pp. 30-37.

Laxmi Ranjanam, Khandavalli, 'Some Unpublished Inscriptions of Telangana' in *JAHRS*, Vol. 21, Rajahmundry, 1950-52, pp.104-112.

Moosvi, Shireen, 'Women and Work in Pre-colonial India, in *Papers on Indian History*, Presented at 53rd Session, *PIHC*, Centre for Advanced Study, Aligarh Muslim University, Aligarh, 1992-93, pp. 102-130.

Mukhia, Herbans, 'Was there Feudalism in Indian History' in *Journal of Peasant Studies*, Vol. 8, No. 3, London, April 1981, pp. 273-310.

Murthy, M.L.K., 'Environment, Royal Policy and Social Formation in the Eastern Ghats, South India (A.D. 1000-1500)', Presidential Address, *PIHC*, 53rd Session, Warangal, February, 1993, pp. 614-631.

Nandi, R.N., 'Origin and Nature of Saivite Monasticism : The case of Kalamukhas' in R.S. Sharma, (ed.), *Indian Society, Historical Probings,* Delhi, 1984, pp. 190-201.

Nandi, R.N., 'Origin of Virasaivism' *IHR*, Vol. 2, No. 1, Delhi, July, 1975, pp. 32-46.

Nandi Santibhushan and D.S. Tyagi, 'Forms of Villages' in A.R. Desai, (ed.), *Rural Sociology in India*, Bombay, 1984, pp. 206-217.

Narayanan, M.G.S. and Veluthat Keshavan, 'Bhakti Movement in South India' in D.N. Jha, (ed.), *Feudal Social Formation in Early India*, Delhi, pp. 348-375.

Omvedt Gail, 'Devadasi Custom and the Fight Against it' in *Manushi*, Vol. 4, No.1, Delhi, Nov-Dec. 1983, pp. 16-19.

Pande, Rekha and Jandhyala Kamesvari, 'Why Women's History', in *PAPHC*, Nagaram, 11th session, 1987, pp. 172-175.

Pande, Rekha and A. Padma, 'Property Rights of Women in Early Medieval Andhra,' in C.M. Agarwal (Ed.), *Nari-Facets of Indian Womanhood*, Vol. II, Indian Publishers and Distributors, New Delhi, 2000.

Pande, Rekha, 'Bringing in the Invisible Women Back into History,' *Adhyayan*, Vol. IX, No. 1-2, 1999.

Pande, Rekha, 'The Bhakti Movement and the Status of Women in 14th and 15th Century,' in J.P. Mishra, (Ed.), *Aspects of Indian History*, New Delhi, 1991.

Pande, Rekha, 'Transition and the recreation of Patriarchal Ideology,' *Journal of Historical Research*, Vol. VII, Assam, 1998.

Panikkar, K.M. 'The Middle Period', in Tara Ali Baig, (ed.), *Women in India*, Delhi, 1958, pp. 9-14.

Parabrahma Sastry, P.V., 'Contribution of Women to the Growth of Ancient Indian Culture' in L.K. Tripathi, (ed.), *Position and Status of women in Ancient India*, Vol. I, Department of Ancient Indian History, Culture and Archaeology, Banaras Hindu University, Varanasi, 1988, pp. 119-129.

Parashar, Aloka and Usha Naik, 'Temple Dancing Girls of Medieval Karnataka' in *IESHR*, Vol. 23, No.1, Delhi, Jan-Mar. 1986, pp. 63-92.

Ramakrishna, K., 'Land and Landlord in Dry-Zone Geo-eco System, Some Interpretations' *PAPHC*, Srisailiam, 1989, pp.157-166.

Ramaswamy, Vijaya, 'Aspects of Women and Work in early South India', in *IESHR*, Vol. XVI, Delhi, Oct., 1989, pp. 81-99.

Roy, Kumkum, 'The Challenge of Women's History' Mimeographed version of a paper presented at the *Workshop on Women's Studies, Methodologies,* Mother Theresa University, Kodaikanal, pp. 1-21.

Ryan Johnson, Sheila, 'Herstory as History, A New Field or Another Fad' in Caroll, A. Berenice, *Liberating Women's History, Theoretical and Critical Essays*, Chicago, 1976, pp. 400-429.

Satyanarayana, A., 'Women Now and Then' *Andhra Pradesh*, Vol. 23, No.1, Hyderabad, Nov., 1978, pp. 49-51.

Sharma, R.S., 'How Feudal was Indian Feudalism' in D.N. Jha, *Feudal Social Formation in Early India*, Delhi, 1987, pp. 165-197.

Sharma, R.S., 'Material Milieu of Tantricism' in R.S. Sharma, (ed.), *Indian Society, Historical Probings,* Delhi, 1974, pp. 175-189.

Sharma, R.S. 'Problem of Transition from Ancient to Medieval Society' in *IHR*, Vol. I, No.1, Delhi, March, 1974, pp. 1-9.

Singh, Sarvadaman, 'The Early Development of Kingship in Pre-muslim India', in I.W. Mabbet, *Patterns of Kingship and Authority in Traditional India*, Washington, 1985, pp. 85-107.

Stein, Burton,'Idiom and Ideology in Early Nineteenth Century South Asia, in Peter Robb, (ed.), *Rural India, Land Power and Society under British Rule*, London, 1983, pp. 23-58.

Stein, Burton, 'State Formation and Economy Reconsidered' in *MAS*, Vol. 19, pt. III, Britain, July, 1985, pp. 387-413.

Stein, Burton, 'The Segmentary State in South Indian History' in Richard Fox, (ed.), *Realm and Region in Traditional India*, Delhi, 1977, pp. 3-51.

Sudhir, P. 'Reconstructing Women's History, Problems and Paradigms' Paper presented to the *Workshop on Women's Studies*. Mother Theresa Women's University, Kodaikanal, Sept., 1987.

Tajbakhsh, Kiran, 'Post-modernism, Post-marxism and the Question of Class', Review article, *Journal of Social Scientist,* Vol. 19, No. 3-4, Delhi, 1991, pp.79-90.

Talbot Cynthia, 'Political Intermediaries in Kakatiya Andhra, 1175-1325' in *IESHR*, Vol. 31, No. 3, Delhi, 1994, pp. 262-289.

Thapar, Romila, 'Looking Back in History' in Jain Devaki, (ed.) *Indian Women*, Delhi, 1975, pp. 5-15.

Usha, Bande, 'Indian Women and Folk Arts' in *Hindustan Times*, Feb., 1982, pp. 9: 7-8.

Yadava, B.N.S. 'Problem of Interaction Between Socio-Economic Classes in the Early Medieval Complex' in D.N. Jha, (ed.), *Feudal Social Formation in Early India*, Delhi, 1987, pp. 198-219.

Yasoda Devi, V. 'The History of Andhra Country, Subsidiary Dynasties (A.D. 1000-1500)', *JAHRS*, Vol. 18 to 27, Rajahmundry.

Telugu

Arudra, 'Putrika Elanti Kuturu' Arudra, *Vyasa Pitham,* Vijayawada, 1985, pp. 54-59.

Bharati, Ravi, '*Srinathudu-Samakalina Samajamu*', in K.K. Ranganathacharyulu, *Telugu Sahityam, Maro Chupu*, Hyderabad, pp. 89-93.

Prabhakara Sastri, Veturi, 'Desi Sahiti Sompu', in G.V. Subrahmanyam, (ed.), *Sarasvatha Vyasamulu*, Vol. 4, A.P. Sahitya Academy, Hyderabad, 1981, pp. 1-6.

Premalatha, R., 'Janapada Sahityam - Kanyasulkam - Varasulkam' in *Abhinandana*, pp. 334-341.

Ramachandra Rao, C.V. 'Andhrulu-Samudravyaparamu - Valasalu (B.C. 600-A.D. 1700)', *Abhinandana,* pp. 58-82.

Ramachandra, Acharya, V., 'Nataka Tattvamu Kridabhiramamu', *Abhinandana,* pp. 130-135.

Ramakrishna, Nataraja, Dr., 'Andhranatyam', *Abhinandana,* pp. 13-21.

Somayajulu, Vavilala, 'Geyarachanalu - Prachinulu ' in G.V. Subrahmanyam, (ed.), *Sarasvatha Vyasamulu*, Vol. 4, pp. 365-396.

Someswara Rao, Dendukuri, 'Sammakka-Saralaka Jatara' in *Orugallu*, Warangal, March 7, 1986 and April, 1986.

Subbaraya Chetti, Ambati, 'Kakatiyulanati Samghika Jivanamu' *Kakatiya Samchika*, Hyderabad, Reprint, 1991, pp. 141-149.

Venkataramanacharyulu, Medepalli, 'Kakatiya Vamsamu' in *Kakatiya Samchika*, pp. 189-197.

Glossary

Types of Lands

Velipolamu	:	Dry land (A high level field depending on rain water)
Cēnu	:	Cultivable field
Tōmṭa Bhūmi	:	Garden land
Ceruvu	:	Tank
Garavubhūmi	:	Upland
Kshētramu	:	A holding of a cultivable land
Merakanēla	:	Upland
Meṭṭabhūmi	:	Upland
Nīrunēla, Nīrnēla	:	Wet land
Pushpa Vatika	:	Flower garden
Sasya Kshētramu	:	Land under active cultivation
Savukabhūmi	:	Saline Soil

Units of Land

Khanḍika/Khanḍuga	:	Plot of land measuring 64,000 Sq.yds.
Kunṭa	:	A measure of land equivalent to 33 cents.
Marturu/Martar	:	Certain land measure of uncertain measure generally used as an equivalent to nivartana.
Muppaṁdumu	:	A land of 10 tumus
Nandi Tūmu	:	A measure of land which went by the name 'Nandi'.
Paṁdumu	:	A measure of ten times of a tumu.
Vrihi khanḍika	:	A fertile paddy field measuring a Khanḍuka.

Money

Birudumaḍa or Birudugadya	:	A coin with distinctive mark of a king's appellation or title.
Cinnalu	:	A unit having a weight of 4 grains, or 1/8 of a pagoḍa.
Gadya/Gadyaṇa	:	A gold coin, equal to about 88 grains in weight.
Jīvita maḍa	:	A denomination of some cash paid as salary.
Ganḍacinnalu	:	A coin issued probably in the name of the king.
Maḍa	:	A kind of a coin, gold or silver, equal in its weight to half pagoda. Inscriptions mention different māḍas, viz., Gamdamāḍa, Kulōttunga-māḍa, Chamaramāḍa, Birudu-māḍa, etc.
Padmanidhi	:	The coins deposited in the treasury called Padmanidhi.

Livestock

Goriyalu	:	Sheep.
Inpaeḍlu	:	She-buffaloes.
Janyamodavu	:	Grànt of a ram along with ewes for procreation of the species for continuous supply of ghee.
Meṁkalu	:	Goats.
Modavulu	:	Milch cows.

Measures of food offered to the deity

Aḍḍa	:	A measure of two manikas.
Kunchamu	:	A vessel or instrument to measure four manikas of grain or any liquid.
Manika	:	Standard unit of measure.

Items of food generally offered

Appam	:	A cake prepared with rice and jaggery.
Garya/Gare	:	A kind of round cake made by pounding black-gram.
Nēyi	:	Ghee

Poṅkalu	:	Arecanuts.
Viḍiyamu	:	A pan made of betel leaves, arecanut, lime and spices.

Services in the Temple

Akhanḍa vatti	:	A wick used in a lamp to be perpetually burnt before a deity.
Alāvatam kolupu/ Chāmarakolupu	:	A service in which weaving the deity with a fan is involved.
Aṁgabhōgamu	:	Decoration and illumination of a deity.
Āvajamu	:	Kettle drum.
Bhōgamu	:	Entertainment/enjoyment.
Diviya/Dīpamu	:	A lamp.
Dvādaśaseva vilasini	:	A girl who does twelve specific services to a deity.
Mangalagītamulu	:	Auspicious songs sung in praise of a deity at the time of waving the lamp.
Mṛggu/muggu	:	The service of decorating the floor of the temple with variety of designs/patterns using flour or lime powder after cleaning and sweeping the compound/temple yard.
Nāmasaṁkīrtana	:	Uttering innumerable appellations of a deity.
Naṭṭava/Naṭṭavōja	:	A dance master/mistress.
Nibandhamu	:	Expenses or arrangements of an endowment to a God for the conduct of affairs in a temple.
Nityapaḍi	:	A compulsory daily offering to God in a specific manner.
Nṛttāngana	:	A dancing girl.
Pātra	:	A dancing girl.
Pātrabhōgaṁvaru	:	Persons employed in a temple for performing dance and playing musical instruments.
Prasadamu	:	A portion or remnant of the offering of eatables presented to a deity.
Raṁgabhōgamu	:	Amusement arranged for a deity and land granted

		for it / enjoyment of splendour other than personal decoration.
Raṁgavallulu	:	Designs of the floor made with flour or lime powder and decorated with colours/flowers.
Sandhyadīpamu	:	The service of lighting an evening lamp.
Sāni	:	A woman [derivative of the Sanskrit word Svamini]. In the temple, a female employee. At times also termed as Devarasani or Gudisani (Temple girl).
Sānulu-Manulu	:	The association of both male and female employees of the temple.
Sāni Munnūru/Munnuti Sānulu	:	The strength of the governing body of temple dancing girls.
Sāni Saṁpradayamu	:	The dancing girls who serve the deity for successive generations.
Trisandhyala kolupu	:	The service of offering food to a deity thrice a day.
Ubhayadīpalu	:	The service of burning two lamps (morning and evening) in the temple.
Vīṇakolupu	:	The service of playing Veena before a deity.

Index

Plates

Plate I (a) : Women in hunting, panel sculpture, Srisailam, 14th Century A.D.

Plate I (b) : Women folk in fishing activity; Types of nets and dress of women are clearly visible, Sculpture on *kakshasana*, Thousand Pillar Temple, Hanamkonda, 12th Century A.D.

Plate II (a) : Daily routine of women, milching and churning of curds; A sculpture from *Pavitrōtsava manṭapa*, Tirupati, 15th Century A.D.

Plate II (b) : Women's decoration with ornaments and drapery, a sculpture on *Kakshasana*, Ramappa Temple, Palampet, 13th Century, A.D.

Plate III (a) : Head offering by a woman; Vīragal, State Museum, Hyderabad, 13th Century A.D.

Plate III (b) : Madanika wearing an embroidary cloth; profuse ornamen-tation and peculiar foot wear, Bracket figure, Ramappa temple, Palampet, 13th Century A.D.

Plate IV (a) : Bracket figure, Ramappa Temple, Palampet, Warangal.

Plate IV (b) : Sculpture from Warangal, Women dressing themselves holding mirror, Hyderabad Museum.

Plate V (a) : A woman with *Patrakuṇḍalas* (ear ornament) and *chandrahara* (neck ornament), Ramappa Temple, Palampet, 13th Century A.D.

Plate V (b) : A courtesan with *Vrittakunḍalas* (ear ornament) : Ramappa Temple, Palampet, 13th Century A.D.

Plate VI (a) : Hair style, Ornamentation pattern, Sculpture from Tirupati.

Plate VI (b) : Simple Ornamentation, Hair Style, Sculpture from Lepakshi.

Plate VII (a) : A woman in Toilet scene, wall sculpture, Pacchala Somesvara Temple, Panugal, 13th Century A.D.

Plate VII (b) : Women keeping Rangavalli, Sculpture from Srisailam.

Plate VIII (a) : Women tending an Elephant, Sculpture from Srisailam.

Plate VIII (b) : Rangamantapa Pillars, Ramappa Temple, Palampet, Warangal.

Plate IX (a) : Sculpture of Women Dancers and Instfument players on the Rangamantapa pillar, Ramappa Temple, Palampet, Warangal.